Contaminations

Contaminations

Beyond Dialectics in Modern Literature, Science and Film

Michael Mack

University Press

© Michael Mack, 2016

Edinburgh University Press Ltd
The Tun – Holyrood Road
12(2f) Jackson's Entry
Edinburgh EH8 8PJ
www.euppublishing.com

Typeset in 10.5/13 pt Sabon by
Servis Filmsetting Ltd, Stockport, Cheshire

A CIP record for this book is available from the British Library

ISBN 978 1 4744 1136 3 (hardback)
ISBN 978 1 4744 1137 0 (webready PDF)
ISBN 978 1 4744 1138 7 (epub)

The right of Michael Mack to be identified as the author of this work has been asserted in accordance with the Copyright, Designs and Patents Act 1988, and the Copyright and Related Rights Regulations 2003 (SI No. 2498).

Contents

Acknowledgements	vi
Introduction: Climate Change and the Contamination of the Anthropocene	1
1 Contaminating Psychology with Biology: Descartes, Spinoza, Freud and Žižek	23
2 Contaminating the Visible with the Invisible: From Einstein via H. G. Wells to Hannah Arendt, Luhmann and Derrida	50
3 Contamination of Nature with Society: The Collapse of Natural Order from Melville to Wells and Ellison	77
4 Contaminating Judgement with its Suspension: Guilt and Punishment in Walter Benjamin, Herman Melville and Henry James	107
5 Contaminating the Digital: Action and Perception in Henry James and Alfred Hitchcock	129
6 Contaminating the Sacred with the Profane: Pier Paolo Pasolini and Biopolitics	159
7 Contaminating Posthumanism	191
Bibliography	216
Index	225

Acknowledgements

Several institutions and individuals supported the conception and completion of this study and substantially influenced its content and form. First of all, I am most grateful to the Leverhulme Trust who awarded me a research fellowship in 2012/2013 for a project entitled 'Science and the Ethics of Literature'. This award encouraged me to start work on the project, while completing *Philosophy and Literature in Times of Crisis*. I am also most grateful to the Humanities Research Centre at the Australian National University for awarding me a visiting fellowship in the summer of 2014. Collette Gilmour of the HRC has been most generous in her support and hospitality. I would like to thank Durham University's Faculty of Humanities for allowing me a term of research leave in the autumn of 2014 which gave me time to revise the book manuscript of *Contaminations*.

I would like to thank Gillian Beer for her support and most helpful advice. I am most grateful to Paul Mendes-Flohr for his generous encouragement, his sincere support, and invaluable advice that enabled the completion of this study. Avital Ronell, Nancy Cartwright, Antonio Damasio, Bernard E. Harcourt, Joseph Tabbi, Nonica Datta, Anna Grundy, Michael N. Forster, Richard Velkley, Norelle Lickiss, Jeff Malpass, Geoffrey Scarre, David Jasper, Peter Boxall, and Dipesh Chakrabarty were most supportive with encouragement and advice.

I am very grateful to Jackie Jones of Edinburgh University Press for her great help, her understanding and her invaluable advice. It is a pleasure working with her and her colleagues Adela Rauchova and James Dale. I would like to thank the anonymous readers for Edinburgh University Press. Each helped improve the structure and content of this book. I am also grateful to the Press Committee of Edinburgh University Press for invaluable feedback on the film studies aspect of this book. Many thanks to the artist Elisabeth Mack-Usselmann for allowing me to use her 1997 painting 'Contamination' for the cover image of

Contaminations. I would also like to thank Richard Stopford for his photograph of Elisabeth Mack-Usselmann's painting.

Work on this study benefited from discussions about literature and science at the University of Bergen: I am most grateful to Margareth Hagen, Margery Vibe Skagen, George Rousseau and Jan Baars.

I would like to thank Durham University's English department and Nicoletta Asciuto and Miriah Reynolds for help with the copy-editing of a first draft of the book manuscript. I am also grateful for most helpful discussions with Mark Sandy, Michael O'Neill, David Herman, Peter Garratt, Patrick Gray, Sarah Wootton, Abbie Garrington, Dan Grausam, Simon James and Sam Thomas.

All material is presented under the fair dealing agreement. The author and the Press will be pleased to receive details of anything used in contravention of copyright, and will make changes accordingly in the preparation of future editions.

I dedicate this book to my mother and to the memory of my father

Introduction: Climate Change and the Contamination of the Anthropocene

'The disorder of nature is apparent'
                                                    Nancy Cartwright

This work is a study in theory, intellectual history, science, cinema and literature, comprising American and English literature from the mid-nineteenth century to the present. It is an original work of research which could at the same time be read as an advanced critical analysis of the theory of contamination. This monograph introduces the figure of contamination as an alternative to dialectics: whereas dialectics separates two entities and traverses from one to the other (finally negating negation), contamination allows for the simultaneous interdependence of what has previously been conceived of as separate or opposed. Whereas dialectics unfolds through the positing of oppositions, contamination operates on the biological model of symbiosis ('the world of life not only consists of independent species, but every individual of most species is actually a consortium of several species' (Mayr 2002: xiv)).

The motif of contamination is implicit in postmodern literature and theory. In this sense the book offers an exploration into the theory of contamination, a theory which has not been explicitly addressed in a monograph before. By contributing towards a novel view of the figure of contamination, this study also constitutes an original work of research. Derrida's notion of the trace implies some form of contamination, but it is a neutral term (it could be a trace of something positive or negative). The figure of contamination as developed in this book, however, offers a new perspective on negativity which questions the current influence of Hegelian dialectics in contemporary theory and philosophy (from Robert Pippin to Slavoj Žižek, and Catherine Malabou).

Dialectics has been implicitly questioned in Hannah Arendt's critique of modern science. This is why Chapter 2 focuses on Arendt's critique of a scientific loss of the word. As we will see there, her contaminating approach to the secularisation controversy anticipates that of Derrida's deconstruction. Like the Frankfurt School, she is addressing both Descartes's *cogito* and its later revisions in German idealist notions of autonomy (Kant) and dialectics (Hegel). In this way the book also offers an advanced critical introduction to the critique of dialectics, to which it at the same time contributes as an original piece of research. How does it combine the accessible element of an advanced critical introduction with that of an original piece of research? By bringing to the fore what has previously been unspoken in philosophical and theoretical accounts.

Robert Musil's notion of 'Essayismus' is closely related to the figure of contamination as developed in this book. Musil attempts to develop an ethics of literature while working through the legacies of a systematic, dialectical and scientific modernity. As Mark M. Freed has recently shown, Musil's 'Essayismus does not seek to supercede modern philosophy by dialectically working through the *aporias* of the Western philosophical tradition (its logocentrism, for example) in the manner of deconstruction' (Freed 2011: 109). Instead, his Essayismus allows for 'a minimal cognition free from determination of *a priori* moral concepts' (Freed 2011: 153). In doing so, Musil conceptualises literature as a space where we can operate outside the *a priori* framework of systematic and dialectical ways of thinking: 'By privileging possibility over Truth and even over Reality, Essayismus points beyond a critique of denotative discourse and beyond an alternative way of seeing the world to function as the discursive strategy that is ultimately productive of an alternative way of *being* in the world, what Musil terms the Other Condition' (Freed 2011: 10). The figure of contamination points to this Other Condition that is no longer subject to the *a priori* framework that governs philosophical and scientific modernity from Kant's notion of autonomy to Hegel's dialectics. Contamination instantiates the Other by dissolving various oppositions (such as the one between the positive and the negative) which are the foundations of dialectics. Deconstruction and other postmodern schools have highlighted the problems that accompany such oppositions. As Freed has shown, they nevertheless partake of the systems (such as dialectics and logocentrism) whose aporias they attempt to trace and illuminate.

Entanglements of literature and science

The last decade has seen a resurgence of interest in the relationship between science and literature. Although Lorraine Daston and Peter Galison have recently charted the cultural history of the modern notion of scientific objectivity (Daston and Galison 2007), there does not exist a monograph that analyses the ways in which literary works have questioned the construction of the 'purely objective' from its point of emergence roughly around the 1850s.

Against this background, the main part of the following introductory section enquires how a contamination of discourses may be required to come to terms with the full range of risks associated with environmental contamination. Does the idea of contamination paradoxically help to de-contaminate dichotomising and potentially destructive habits of mind that posit autonomous modes of representation? As Bruno Latour has shown, the natural and the social are not separate, but rather entangled entities. The mutual contamination of society and nature does not, however, mean that one can be reduced to the other. Karen Barad writes:

> What is needed is an analysis that enables us to theorise the social and the natural together, to read our best understandings of the social and natural phenomena through one another in a way that clarifies the relationship between them. To write matter and meaning into separate categories, to analyse them relative to separate disciplinary technologies, and to divide complex phenomena into one balkanised enclave or the other is to elide certain crucial aspects by design. On the other hand, considering them together does not mean forcing them together, collapsing important differences between them, or treating them in the same way, rather it means allowing any integral aspects to emerge (by not writing them out before we get started). (Barad 2007: 25)

Similar to Barad's notion of entanglement, the figure of contamination as developed in this book denotes the reciprocal interdependence and intra-action[1] of different entities: 'we need a method for theorizing the relationship between "the natural" and "the social" together without defining one against the other or holding either nature or culture as the fixed referent for understanding the other' (Barad 2007: 30). As Barad points out, the entanglement of difference in form of diffraction has implications for the inseparability of ethics and science: 'It is not possible to extricate oneself from ethical concerns and correctly discern what science tells us about the world' (Barad 2007: 37). *Contaminations: Beyond Dialectics in Modern Literature, Science and Film* complements Barad's discussion of science and philosophy by analysing how literary works confound stable and pure forms of categorisation.

By taking literature seriously for a better understanding of empirical issues, this book is premised on Barad's (and also David Herman's) 'new understanding of how discursive practices are related to the material world' (Barad 2007: 34).[2] In analysing literary discourses in order to reach a new perspective on pressing issues of the material world, this book follows Barad in establishing an innovative notion of realism that departs from the mimetic paradigm of representation: 'Realism, then, is not about representations of an independent reality but about real consequences, interventions, creative possibilities, responsibilities of intra-acting within and as part of the world' (Barad 2007: 37; see also Mack 2012: 72–152). This book examines literature's capacity to confound categories (such as those of purity, order and visibility).

As the semantic field of the word 'contamination' indicates, it complements Barad's term 'entanglement' by arguing for a new non-dialectical approach to what we have come to perceive and represent as 'negative'. In this context, this book introduces the figure of contamination as an alternative to dialectics. Dialectics separates two entities and traverses from one to the other (finally negating negation). The figure of contamination, however, allows for the simultaneous interdependence of what has previously been conceived of as separate or opposed.

Moreover, the figure of contamination relates to Barad's concept of entanglement, which also shows how apparently self-enclosed or separate entities 'lack an independent, self-contained existence' (Barad 2007: ix). In contrast to Barad's notion of 'entanglement', however, my term 'figure of contamination' is oxymoronic: in Steven Connor's words, '*figura* means both form and face' (Connor 2006: 30), whereas contamination donates the blurred character of life. This formlessness and facelessness of contamination evokes Connor's description of the impossible figure of the fly: 'The fly is always itself, but that self does not form a figure, nor yet exactly figure a form. More than anything else, the fly is a figure of this unfigurability. The significance of the fly is that it marks the insignificant, an ordinary but vexatious remission in the given-ness or apparentness of things' (Connor 2006: 32). The figureless figure of the fly may encapsulate the holding together of opposites which the term contamination performs in this book.

As Donna Haraway has argued, there is also a sense in which the word 'figure' denotes entanglement and contamination. In this reading the term 'figure' evokes the blurred vision of figurations, a semantic field that goes back to the eighteenth century, as Haraway has shown:

> Figures help me grapple inside the flesh of mortal world-making entanglements that I call contact zones. The *Oxford English Dictionary* records the meaning of 'chimerical vision' for 'figuration' in an eighteenth-century source, and that meaning is still implicit in my sense of *figure*. Figures collect the people through their invitation to inhabit the corporeal story told in their lineaments. Figures are not representations or didactic illustrations,

> but rather material–semiotic nodes or knots in which diverse bodies and meanings coshape one another. For me, figures have always been where the biological and literary or artistic come together with all of the force of lived reality. My body itself is just such a figure, literally. (Haraway 2008: 4)

Haraway understands the term 'figure' to embrace the material world of cohabitation and symbiosis. There is no such thing as a self-contained form.

Drawing on Lynn Margulis's and Dorion Sagan's biological account of symbiosis as the fabric of life in their 2002 study, *Acquiring Genomes: A Theory of the Origins of Species*, Haraway states that 'the basic story is simple: ever more complex life forms are the continual result of ever more intricate and multidirectional acts of association of and with other life forms' (Haraway 2008: 31). This means that scientific approaches which privilege forms and notions of purity are misguided. Our philosophical and scientific perspective has been shaped by such preoccupation with pure entities that supposedly constitute nature's order, and differentiate it from the unsightly chaos of 'unnatural' disorder and other forms of contaminations or perversions: 'Objects entangle one another in a crisscrossing mesh of spacetime fluctuations' (Morton 2013: 65). Modern physics, from Einstein's relativity to quantum theory (see Chapter 2), has radically challenged Newtonian scientific methodologies that are premised on the assumption of pure and solidly distinct entities.

Contaminations enquires into the problem of various oppositions between pure entities such as nature and society, body and mind, science and the arts, subjectivity and objectivity, action and contemplation, the sacred and the profane. It examines for the first time how works of literature and cinema have contaminated constructions of the pure and the immune with their purported opposite. The book contaminates binary oppositions between madness and reason, between health and illness, between action and perception, between the biological and the psychological, between science and literature.[3]

This study has two main aims. Firstly, on a theoretical level, it questions the dialectics of opposing two supposedly 'pure' entities (such as mind and body) and offers the figure of contamination as an alternative to a way of thinking that is still based on notions of purity and immunity. Secondly, it practises contaminations of often separated historical periods (such as nineteenth-century and modernist literature), of national literatures (such as American, British and Italian literature), of genres (tragedy and comedy), of media (cinema and literature) and philosophical/scientific and literary writings.

6 Contaminations

The figure of contamination: an alternative to dialectics

Modern dialectics has shaped the history of ideas from Herder and Hegel onwards. The starting point is a negative position which dialectics negates, transforming it into a superior force. As Roberto Esposito has recently shown in his *Immunitas: The Protection and Negation of Life* (2011), J. G. Herder introduced the dialectical notion of 'compensation' into comparisons between the human and the animal. Humanity compensates for its instinctual weakness through technical and intellectual skills which in the end negate its lack, promising a longer and healthier life than that of other animals: 'The human animal can live longer than all others *because* – not despite the fact – he is constitutionally sick' (Esposito 2011: 90). The dialectical paradigm of compensation has thus informed philosophical anthropology from Herder via A. Gehlen and H. Plessner to N. Luhmann and it still influences contemporary discussions of posthumanism.

Esposito analyses the destructive aspects accompanying dialectical moves from the negative to the positive, wherein negation ends up negated: 'If the immune dialectic always implies the incorporation of a negative, this is both confirmed and radicalized by the functioning of autoimmunity: the dissolution of the negative from any positive role and its destructive doubling up on itself, or in other words, the destruction, through self-destruction, of the entire body it is intended to defend' (Esposito 2011: 165). This destructive and also self-destructive aspect of the dialectical negation of the negative emerges from an opposition between two entities which are spread out as not only distinct but also as separate if not opposed. Esposito argues that 'the entire Western tradition has remained held in this antinomic turn: the stranger is conceivable only in terms of its preventive dissolution' and that 'not even the attempts carried out by the most radical ethnology to shift the point of observation from the self to the other has managed to escape it' (Esposito 2011: 172). Esposito offers his notion of *immunitas* as an alternative to this tradition.

Following Giorgio Agamben's bio-political paradigm wherein life becomes dialectically excluded by being included – i.e. the inclusion of negation which results as negated or excluded – Esposito's starting point is a dialectics of immunity that should protect life by absenting it. He then goes on to ask whether there is a way out of this exclusionary and destructive impasse of dialectics: 'is there a point at which the dialectical circuit between the protection and the negation of life can be interrupted, or at least problematized? Can life be preserved in some other form than that of its negative protection?' (Esposito 2011: 16).

Employing Alfred Tauber's innovative understanding of immunity as an opening towards rather than as a negation of the body's environment, Esposito argues that *immunitas* is indistinguishable from a *communitas*. Esposito maintains that from Tauber's perspective, 'far from being a unit closed within blocked, impassable borders, the body is posited as an ecosystem that has evolved over time into what the author [i.e. Tauber] unhesitatingly describes as a "social community"' (Esposito 2011: 166). Esposito's notion of *immunitas* is still premised on a dialectical opposition wherein what has been posited as negative becomes negated. Immunity through the dialectics of negation morphs into community:

> If anything, the immune system must be interpreted as an internal resonance chamber, like the diaphragm through which difference, as such, engages and traverses us. As we were saying: once its negative power has been removed, the immune is not the enemy of the common, but rather something more complex that implicates and stimulates the common. The full significance of this necessity, but also its possibility, still eludes us. (Esposito 2011: 18)

In keeping with the tradition of a dialectical paradigm, which he nevertheless sets out to question, Esposito thus bases his notion of *immunitas* on the removal or negation of what he calls 'negative power'.

Similarly to related contemporary discussions of diverse issues and topics such as posthumanism and climate change, Esposito's conception of the immune is still informed by the dialectical constellation where the negative is finally negated. *Contaminations* discusses what Esposito understands by immunity under the term 'purity'. Here immunity or purity does not undergo a dialectical itinerary, where it finally opposes or negates itself. Rather than opposing something, purity or immunity becomes exposed as a construct which does not exist in either negative or positive form. The 'pure' or immune is always already contaminated by the impure, the negative. In contrast to Esposito's notion of *immunitas*, the figure of contamination as developed in this book does not attack or absent or negate the negative. The term contamination signals the capitulation to, rather than the defence against, forces which have come to represent entities that should be attacked or fought, such as mental illness, or failure, or scandal.

Esposito appraises his notion of *immunitas* as 'true dialectical exchange between a good that comes from an evil and an evil that is transformed into good, in a sort of progressive indistinctiveness comparable to the structurally double-edged character of the Platonic *pharmakon* (but also of the Latin *medicamentum* or High-German and Anglo-Saxon *Gift*)' (Esposito 2011: 127). Immunity turns into community by way of its negation – in other words, its finitude: 'This is the condition common to all that is immune: the endless perception of its own finitude' (Esposito 2011: 174). As we have seen, Esposito's self-negation of immunity in terms of what Derrida has previously theorised as autoimmunity still has a dialectal, superseding linear movement oriented towards its own negation.

Instead of approaching immunity or purity dialectically, as Esposito does, this book introduces the concept and the practice of contamination as an alternative to traditional dialectics. In this context, it undermines notions of negation and affirmation.

There have, however, been recent attempts to avoid negation *tout court*. The most striking may be Rosi Braidotti's, according to which 'the posthuman turn' is 'an amazing opportunity to decide together what and who we are capable of becoming, and a unique opportunity for humanity to reinvent itself affirmatively, through creativity and encompassing ethical relations, and not only negatively, through vulnerability and fear' (Braidotti 2013: 195). Here the negative aspects too are, if not negated, then at least marginalised. The figure of contamination, while highlighting what we would normally tend to avoid, abstains from attacking what we have come to perceive as negative.

Indeed, the figure of contamination simultaneously connects – rather than opposes – the anxious and the gracious, the abject and the beautiful. These entities have, according to Esposito, been opposed with each other. Rather than use one to attack the other, the figure of contamination allows for a space of interdependence, or, in Barad's terms, entanglement. The notion of interdependence derives from Spinoza (Mack 2010: 11–47) – a thinker who is also crucial for Braidotti's understanding of posthumanism. Her interest in Spinoza, as well as Hasana Sharp's (Sharp 2011: 85–153), derives from the philosopher's divergence from a dialectical way of thinking, with which Hegel took issue as Braidotti explains:

> The absence of any reference to negativity and to violent dialectical oppositions caused intense criticism of Spinoza on the part of Hegel and the Marxist-Hegelians. Spinoza's monistic worldview was seen as politically ineffective and holistic at heart. The situation changed dramatically in the 1970s in France, when a new wave of scholars rehabilitated Spinozist monism precisely as an antidote to some of the contradictions of Marxism and as a way of clarifying Hegel's relationship to Marx. The main idea is to overcome dialectical oppositions, engendering a non-dialectical understanding of materialism itself (Braidotti 1991; Cheah 2008), as an alternative to the Hegelian scheme. (Braidotti 2013: 56)

Rather than absenting itself from the negative, *Contaminations* combines what Braidotti calls Spinoza's 'vitalist materialism'[4] with both

P. P. Pasolini's and W. Benjamin's re-evaluation of negation. Benjamin attempted to change our perception of the negative, following his friend Gershom Scholem's interpretation of a Kabbalistic 'redemption through sin' (the apostasies of the seventeenth-century would-be Messiah Shabbatai Zvi are emblematic in this respect). In this way, he argued that redemption consists in its apparent opposite: in the going under of loss, failure and disappointment.[5]

Similarly, Pasolini confronts us in his films and in his literary work with the simultaneity of what is apparently opposed: the anti-social, or in other words negative, position of outcasts (as most strikingly in his film *Accattone*) and a peculiar form of grace, beauty and peace. Abel Ferrara opens his new film on the last day of Pasolini's life (with Willem Dafoe as lead actor), highlighting Pasolini's notion of scandal with the following quotation: 'Scandalizzare è un diritto, essere scandalizzati è un piacere' (To scandalise is a duty, to be scandalised is a pleasure). In his famous film *The Gospel According to St Matthew*, Pasolini contaminates the traditionally opposed figures of Jesus and Judas, by rendering the dividing line between the two increasingly blurred. How does such contamination occur? In parallel scenes Pasolini's Jesus uses the term '*scandalo*', first to describe himself and then Judas.

Celebrating scandal thus, Pasolini attempts to transform our perception of what we have come to represent as negative or hostile. The negative does not so much oppose and then give way to the positive as dialectics claims. It is bound up with its other instead. Interdependence rather than opposition informs the workings of the figure of contamination. Contemporary social and environmental concerns such as climate change or demographic challenges have made us aware of our interdependent, contaminated rather than pure or autonomous position within our environment.

The figure of contamination as developed in this book thus emerges from Pasolini's as well as Benjamin's respective re-evaluations of what we would normally attack or fight under the nomenclature of the negative. Pasolini frequently referred to the notion of scandal (*scandalo*) as a way of highlighting his embrace of what societal representation marginalises or excludes as the negative. Absenting negativity does not actually 'overcome dialectical oppositions', as Braidotti claims. Braidotti writes: 'The posthuman recomposition of human interaction that I propose is not the same as the reactive bond of vulnerability, but is an affirmative bond that locates the subject in the flow of relations with multiple others' (Braidotti 2013: 50). How, however, can there be a bonding with others that excludes a sense of vulnerability?

The lives of humans and animals are exposed to negative forces of vulnerability, decay and death. Alasdair MacIntyre has drawn attention to the extent to which vulnerability has been a neglected topic in the history of ideas: 'From Plato to Moore and since there are usually, with some rare exceptions, only passing references to human vulnerability and affliction and to the connections between them and our dependence on others' (MacIntyre 1999: 1). Proof of rapidly advancing climate change has, however, reinforced a sense of our vulnerability and potential finality as a species. According to Dipesh Chakrabarty, global warming has increased rather than diminished 'contemporary moods of anxiety and concern about the finitude of humanity' (Chakrabarty 2009: 197). Global warming confronts us with the negativity of globalisation.

Environmental catastrophes and the figure of contamination

Chakrabarty argues that globalisation is not only negative but also encompasses beneficial elements, alleviating poverty in countries such as China and India. He discusses globalisation as a contaminated entity which gives rise to both the Anthropocene and to the democratisation of prosperity throughout the globe. How can we describe the notion of Anthropocene? The term Anthropocene describes humanity as a geological force capable of changing the environment to a point of no return. Libby Robin and Will Steffen have defined the Anthropocene in such terms:

> The Anthropocene defines the momentous and *historical* change in circumstances whereby the biophysical systems of the world are now no longer independent of the actions of people. It is the Epoch dominated by humans. People have officially and geologically changed the course of nature at a global scale. The idea of the Anthropocene demands an integration of biophysical and human history, and provides the over-arching reason why the history of people on Earth has become core business of this largely scientific group. (Robin and Steffen 2007: 1699)

Natural and human histories are no longer separate, but contaminated entities. The chemist Paul J. Crutzen, who introduced the term Anthropocene, stresses the significance of interdependence when he, together with the environmentalist Thomas E. Graedel, employs the sociological term 'system' for a better understanding of climate change:

> Systems of all types share a few common characteristics, the most basic of which is that each is a group of interacting, interrelated, or interdependent elements forming a collective entity. Another characteristic of systems is that they are dynamic, reacting constantly to driving forces and perturbations

> from within and without. A consequence of this dynamism is that the longevity of a system is not assured: some systems remain virtually unchanged for long periods, others alternate rapidly between growth and decline, some sicken and die. (Graedel and Crutzen 1997: 2)

The system of our climate reacts to both biophysical and social changes: Chapter 2 discusses Nikolas Luhmann's systems theory, delineating how apparently closed systems are paradoxically all the more exposed to and interacting with their environments. The term Anthropocene denotes the exposure of the biophysical system to the ever increasing force of human activities and their concomitant residues in the form of carbon emissions. These emissions have gradually changed our planet's atmosphere since the beginning of the industrial revolution, from the late eighteenth century onwards.[6] This process rapidly gains in speed and force: if we neglect the contaminating, the Anthropocene repercussion of our action-driven lifestyle, depending on the consumption of energy resources, we may risk reaching a tipping point where the climate has changed beyond repair.

Chakrabarty argues, however, as if this fatalist turn after the tipping point had already occurred, asking: 'Is the Anthropocene a critique of the narratives of freedom? Is the geological agency of humans the price we pay for the pursuit of freedom?' (Chakrabarty 2009: 210). On this view the apocalyptical prospect of an inevitable destruction of our environment (human-induced and yet beyond any human remedy) outdoes the global promise of democracy and freedom as inaugurated by industrialisation. Human-induced climate change (i.e. the Anthropocene) overturns notions of eternal and infinite time spans, which have previously governed approaches to human history that conceived of nature as a mere background for humanity's quasi-immortal achievements:

> In today's climatologists' terms, we could say that Stalin and Braudel and others who thought thus [i.e. of nature as a backdrop] did not have available to them the idea, now widespread on the literature on global warming, that the climate, and hence the overall environment, can sometimes reach a tipping point at which this slow and apparently timeless backdrop for human actions transforms itself with a speed that can only spell disaster for human beings. (Chakrabarty 2009: 205)

The question remains: have we already passed the tipping point? Had we done so, attempts to remedy the situation would be useless. We would have no choice but to await the inevitable end of both natural and human history. Human agency would prove to be futile.

Chakrabarty appears to allow for some form of agency when he evokes the concept of universalism, writing that 'species may indeed be the name of a placeholder for an emergent, new universal history of humans that flashes up in the moment of danger that is climate change' (Chakrabarty 2009: 221). This universal is, however, purely negative, lacking any form of agency and indeterminacy. Past universal schemes were premised on Hegelian dialectics in which the negative negates itself, thus making room for positive futures. Chakrabarty differentiates a new form of universalism from the Hegelian one by insisting on this pure negativity that refuses to be negated: 'It is more like a universal that arises from a shared sense of a catastrophe. It calls for a global approach to politics without the myth of global identity, for, unlike the Hegelian universal, it cannot subsume particularities. We may call it a "negative universal history"' (Chakrabarty 2009: 222). This purely negative universal history is as homogeneous (if not more so) as its traditional dialectical version where negativity becomes superseded by its pure opposite.

Challenging various concepts of purity, *Contaminations* enables us to recognise the simultaneity of catastrophe and hope, of anxiety and grace. The figure of contamination helps us discover a new perspective on our world where juxtaposed differences are not so much opposed but mutually entangled with each other. This presupposes the collapse of various notions of order (see Chapters 2 and 3). The idea of contamination as developed in this book grows out of various readings of literary and cinematic works, but it chimes with what the philosopher of science Nancy Cartwright has recently called 'the dappled world'. Critiquing traditional notions of scientific enquiry based on an all-encompassing sense of order and validity, she writes:

> Since at least the time of Mechanical Philosophy, physicists have been busy at work on a theory of everything. For its part, contemporary economics provides models not just for the price of the rights for offshore drilling, where the market meets very nice conditions, but also for the effects of liberal abortion policies on teenage pregnancies, for whom we marry and when we divorce and for the rationale of political lobbies. My belief in the dappled world is based in large part on the failures of these two disciplines to succeed in these aspirations. The disorder of nature is apparent. (Cartwright 1999: 1)

Awareness of the collapse of the natural order makes us realise the dappled constitution of our world. Cartwright's notion 'dappled' could also be another word denoting the blurring of traditional divisions. According to the *OED* 'dappled' describes objects 'marked with roundish spots, patches, or blotches of a different colour or shade; spotted, speckled'[7] – a contamination of sorts.

A dappled world allows for mutual interactions between the sciences and the arts and the humanities. Public opinion still associates the sciences with objectivity and the humanities with subjectivity. This book shows how both entities are not to be perceived as opposites but rather as bound up with each other. The simultaneity of divergent concepts as well as substances validates the prospect of agency counteracting human-induced global warming. There is no such thing as either a purely negative universal history or a purely positive one (which has dialectically negated negation). The absence of purity may preclude the establishment of utopian futures but it also questions apocalyptical prospects of the inevitable end of human and natural history.

Social expectations shape aspects of scientific enquiry. They motivate the prioritisation of public funding for scientific enquiries and they lead to the establishment of social policies. Clearly scientists do not do their work in a self-enclosed space, cut off from society and culture at large. For this reason, this book envisages culture via the way communities face scientific issues (such as cloning/genetic engineering as discussed in Chapter 7). Misunderstood bio-medical topics distort meanings of culture and communities. *Contaminations: Beyond Dialectics in Modern Literature, Science and Film* addresses this problem with new knowledge derived from discussions of literary and cinematic works.

Jonathan Franzen's *Freedom*: contaminating hermeneutics with empiricism

An example from contemporary literature helps to sketch how this book envisages a new dialogue between traditional hermeneutics and the empiricist core of the social sciences and climate sciences. Via analyses of literary texts (such as Jonathan Franzen's *Freedom*), *Contaminations* discovers a new form of literature's socio-cultural significance: ways of uncovering fictions that govern society at large. Through this method, it also opens up new scholarly horizons on how we may come to see literature as an activity that potentially changes our way of interacting with the fictitious core by which we deceive ourselves about substantial issues such as climate change. Reality often outdoes fiction in being or appearing incredible. Philip Roth has emphasised how literature cannot avoid a confrontation with the often fictitious core that governs actual events and happenings, writing that:

> the American writer in the middle of the twentieth century has his hands full in trying to understand, describe, and then make *credible* much of American reality. It stupefies, it sickens, it infuriates, and finally it is even a kind of embarrassment to one's own meagre imagination. The actuality is continually

outdoing our talents, and the culture tosses up figures almost daily that are the envy of any novelist. (Roth 1961: 167–8)

Satire highlights the ways in which our socio-political context is stranger, sicker, and more infuriating than fiction. It shows us how incredible our reality actually is.

This holds true of Franzen's new novel, *Freedom*. Walter Berglund, one of the main protagonists of the novel, advocates the removal of mountaintops in the Appalachian forests. This is of course supported by the biggest coal producer, Vin Haven. Together with Vin Haven, Walter Berglund founds the 'Cerulean Mountain Trust' (Franzen 2010: 209). The crucial point is that Walter and the coal monopolist emotionally shift the argument from environmental exploitation – which is substantially at stake here – to environmental preservation of an endangered bird species. Similarly to *The Corrections*, the novel depicts the way in which we deceive ourselves by banishing highly emotionally charged destructive and unhealthy issues (such as mental illness as in *The Corrections*, or climate change as a scientific issue that cannot be discussed without the context of community concerns as in *Freedom*) into the background. Here it is the deceptive obsession with the health of birds that disguises a disgust with and active denigration and expulsion of those communities who live in the Appalachian Mountains. Expulsion from their habitat of course takes these communities out of their established work environment. Sam Tannenhaus has described this situation succinctly as follows: 'Walter, "greener than Greenpeace," strangely colludes with a superrich Texan to despoil a West Virginian mountaintop, though it means uprooting 200 local families, "most of them very poor" – all to create a sanctuary for a species of warbler not even on the federal endangered species list' (Tanenhaus 2010). Here the negative turns into the affirmative. There would be new job prospects in new locations. Politicians and journalists do not countenance any negative representations either of climate change or of the Iraq War.

The negative negates itself and turns positive: 'As for job security, it was enough to point to the declarations, issued by various members of the Bush administration, that America would be defending itself in the Middle East for generations to come. There was no foreseeable end to the war on terror and, ergo, no end to the demand for body armour' (Franzen 2010: 301). Here we witness how society falls prey to delusions about what it takes to be beneficial but what is in fact seeped in violence and blood (the Iraq War). Politicians, with the assistance of various media outlets, spin the reality of suffering and violence into issues that are to be affirmed. In quasi-dialectical manner war turns into a boon for the job prospects of the communities in the Appalachian Mountains, providing them with work in factories spread throughout the US. Workers for such factories will be in heavy demand because, so the spin goes, the production of body armour will be desperately needed thanks to the prospect of an unending war on terror.

This is of course a satire but one that is real, that relates to real issues in a manner that Franzen admires in the work of the Austrian early twentieth-century satirist Karl Kraus. Franzen denies that Kraus's satires on the politics and journalism of the twenties and thirties of the last century are to be confined to history and thus separated from pressing contemporary issues. He writes:

> And Kraus *is* foreign, more so than his better-known contemporaries, because his work was so particularly tied to his own time and place – to long forgotten controversies, to rivals now obscure, to newspapers and literary works that only scholars read anymore. And yet, paradoxically, Kraus has more to say to us in our own media-saturated, technology-crazed, apocalypse-haunted historical moment than his more accessible contemporaries now do. (Franzen 2013: 5)

Despite the historical and geographic distance separating Kraus's Austria from Franzen's America, his satires still speak to a contemporary American audience because they concern real social issues which are still pertinent today. A crucial one is the power of the media to distort warfare (in Kraus's case World War I) and turn it into something attractive or appealing.

Following Kraus's approach, Franzen sets out to alert us to how 'our own media-saturated' society falls prey to fictions or delusions of what is represented as positive, good or worthy. Walter and the coal magnate use the preservation of a non-endangered bird species for a media spin that represents the removal of mountaintops for the mining of fossil fuels as good rather than damaging for the environment. When Walter's wife Patty confronts him with his implicit support of the coal industry ('You think we should be burning more coal. Making it easier to burn more coal. In spite of global warming' Franzen 2010: 323), he acknowledges the fatalism that incongruously governs his environmental activism: 'We're heading for a catastrophe, Patty. We're heading for total collapse' (Franzen 2010: 323). Walter, the well-intentioned and decent environmentalist, here expounds what Chakrabarty has recently theorised as the inevitable and irreversible link that binds globalisation to global warming. The enjoyment of freedom and prosperity in previously poor regions (such as India and China, which have become emergent markets) is ineluctably tied to global warming whose prevention would, according to Chakrabarty, come at great economic and social costs to countries such as India or China.

In contrast to Walter Berglund, however, Chakrabarty sets out to safeguard the prosperity of previously impoverished communities in India and China. Walter does not value the lives of the poor inhabitants of the Appalachian Mountains. The satirical irony of the novel operates on the level of incongruity: Walter's moralistic stance fighting the evil of the Anthropocene (humanity's 'overpopulation') clashes with the ruthlessness of his actions (actually colliding with the interests of the coal industry). Walter separates society from nature, playing off the latter against the former. Walter thus creates a notion of nature as pure entity which he opposes to the pollutions caused by humanity. The human-induced destruction of our planet dialectically ensures the triumph of the positive after ecological collapse:

> I meant that world population and energy consumption are going to have to fall drastically at some point. We're past sustainable even now. Once the collapse comes, there's going to be a window of opportunity for ecosystems to recover, but only if there's any nature left. So the big question is how much of the planet gets destroyed before the collapse. Do we completely use it up, and cut down every tree and sterilize every ocean, and then collapse? Or are there going to be any unwrecked strongholds that survive? (Franzen 2010: 323)

In dialectical manner 'collapse' morphs into 'a window of opportunity': it is this uncritical and unreflective environmental discourse which Timothy Morton has in mind in his provocative book, *Ecology without Nature*. Nature has all too often been hypostasised as a pure and innocent image or notion cut off from the defilement of society, culture and humanity: 'Since the Romantic period, nature has been used to support the capitalist theory of value and to undermine it; to point out what is intrinsically human, and to exclude the human; to inspire kindness and compassion, and to justify competition and cruelty' (Morton 2007: 19). In Walter's discourse, nature denotes salvation, signalling the dialectical swerving of the negative into the positive: 'Once the collapse comes, there's going to be a window of opportunity for ecosystems to recover, but only if there's any nature left.' The affirmative and distortive media campaign which Walter launches on the bidding of the coal magnate reflects the wish for the uncontaminated presence of what we can emotively espouse as good or worthwhile, which in the quote above goes under the name of 'unwrecked [i.e. uncontaminated] strongholds'.

In the face of inevitable catastrophe we have to work even harder at ensuring a redemptive space for the positive, albeit one that is an island of survival surrounded by apocalypse. Walter's environmental activism actually supports the destruction of the environment: he campaigns for the mining of coal, the burning of which further propels the advance of climate change.[8] In search of the positive we delude ourselves about what is truly harmful. Activism here emerges as deception and self-delusion:

> Each new thing he encountered in life impelled him in a direction that fully convinced him of its rightness, but the next thing loomed up and impelled him in the opposite direction, which also felt right. There was no controlling narrative: he seemed himself a purely reactive pinball in a game whose only objective was to stay alive for staying alive's sake. (Franzen 2010: 318)

Actions as reactions are passive.[9] Walter Berglund is political, he is an activist. However, his actions lack the problematising aspect of reflection and contemplation (see Chapter 6). One path of action dialectically turns into its opposite pathway and thus in dialectical manner outdoes itself. Here actions cancel themselves out because they are not contaminated by what would reflectively call them into question.

Like Chuck Lambert (who turns from an academic critic of free market capitalism to a leading fraudster selling the investment case for a completely privatised and corrupt country of the former Warsaw Pact) in *The Corrections*, Walter Berglund evaporates his own sense of freedom or fulfilment by spinning ecological collapse into opportunities for preservation. The self in quest for its own preservation here destroys itself, precisely by being preoccupied with its own moralistic ideals, which ironically do more damage than good to the community (of the Appalachian Mountains) and to the planet as whole (paving the way for more coal mining through mountaintop removal). The very title of Franzen's novel evokes the traditional structure of a quest for the attainment of ethical ideals (such as freedom) only to show the damage it might do to our world. As Camilla Nelson has recently put it: 'In *Freedom*, this structural problem rapidly transforms into a vision of the world in which all happiness exists at the cost of others' happiness, and all freedom exists at the cost of others' freedom' (Nelson 2013: 3). Walter seeks his own ethical sense of wellbeing by incongruously violating that of his environment.

Yet Franzen's *Freedom* does not portray Walter as an egoist. The novel refrains from judging him.[10] Crucially, the targets of the novel's satire are various moralistic discourses that refer to high ethical values (such as environmental preservation or freedom) in the defence of both increased coal mining and the Iraq War. Far from passing moral judgement on Walter Berglund, straight from its opening the narrative voice observes a certain strangeness, a certain paradox in his dialectical way of acting: 'it seemed strange that Walter, who was greener than Greenpeace and whose own roots were rural, should be in trouble now for conniving with the coal industry and mistreating people' (Franzen 2010: 323). With the best of intentions, a socially responsible environmental activist behaves unethically.[11] How can we explain this?

Paul Mendes-Flohr's interpretation of Martin Buber's critique of political activism may help us understand the pitfalls of this one-dimensional approach to action which is uncontaminated by reflection:

> An ethical *noblesse oblige* compels one, in the words of the Jewish philosopher Martin Buber, to become a *homo politicus*, to be attentive to the needs of others and to be actively committed to promoting the social good. But at the same time, Buber teaches, one is to become a *homo problematicus*. While one is politically and socially engaged, one is to fend off the threat of self-righteousness and political arrogance, through a self-reflective scrutiny of one's motives and an acknowledgment of the complexity of the social reality in which one seeks to intervene. As a *homo politicus* one is to be bold and decisive, while as a *homo problematicus* one is to demand of oneself to be humble and ever on guard against one's ideological vanities and ethical conceits. (Mendes-Flohr 2010: 13)

Walter's preoccupation with what appears to him to be ethical actually blinds him to the social reality in which he attempts to do noble or good deeds. He is obsessed with the power of the positive, and crucially he characterises himself as 'Mr Good' (Franzen 2010: 481). The good of course keeps changing from circumstance to circumstance, from situation to situation.

Being so concerned with doing good, Walter is incapable of recognising the contaminated reality of what appears to be positive. He cannot problematise the good as being entangled with its opposite. Franzen's novel shows us how affirmation of the positive might merely be the affirmation of a self who appears to be self-less. Franzen's novel does not judge or condemn the selfishness which motivates Walter's apparently noble political actions. It observes, however, the trajectory of these actions in a non-judgemental, satirical way. As satire the novel makes us realise the violence and damage that might result from 'ethical' commitments that ruthlessly perpetuate their goals with complete disregard to their actual environment. Walter's problem is not his unacknowledged concern for himself but his self-righteousness, his political arrogance. As Martin Buber has argued in his famous *I and Thou*, the issue here is not the self but the quasi-ethical affirmation of the self who presumably does good deeds:

> What has to be given up is not the I, as most mystics suppose: the I is indispensable for any relationship, including the highest, which always presupposes

an I and You. What has to be given up is not the I but that false drive for self-affirmation which impels man [i.e. the human; *den Menschen*] to flee from the unreliable, unsolid, unlasting, unpredictable, dangerous world of relation into the having of things. (Buber 1970: 126)[12]

Franzen's *Freedom* depicts the way a self that affirms itself and its high moral ground in actual fact damages what it ostensibly is trying to care for and protect. Walter's activism partakes of his self-affirmation, even though he proclaims to act in a selfless, 'good' way. Morton has recently critiqued this non-reflective preoccupation with actions within contemporary environmentalism, writing:

> Indeed, one could successfully argue that it's the *presentism* of contemporary environmentalisms that put them on the wrong side of history. Consider the rhetoric of immediacy common to what I have called *ecomimesis*: stop thinking, go out into Nature, turn off your irony. Presentism also manifests in the injunction to stop thinking and *do something*, the paradoxical form taken by the contemporary beautiful soul, a defining, overarching subject position of modernity that has been with us since the late eighteenth century. (Morton 2013: 92)

Franzen's satirical novel contaminates our contemporary concerns for the present, for action, and for affirmation, with the reflexivity inherent in the working of irony. Affirmation that goes without the contamination of reflective, problematic, so-called negative moments violates its environment. It does so by imposing its affirmative and certain schemes on a reality that is, in Buber's words, 'unreliable, unsolid, unlasting' – in short, anything else but solely positive.

Methodology of *Contaminations*

This book undermines unproblematic understandings of affirmation by engaging a methodology shaped by the figure of contamination, contaminating literary and scientific forms of enquiry. Here the first methodological procedure is dedicated to the act of hermeneutic uncovering, which is literary criticism's form of discovery. The second methodological procedure shows how these hermeneutic forms of discovery are the so far missing methodological requirement to solve scientific problems of timely concern to different communities. This second methodological strand thus establishes a critical dialogue between kinds of literary or artistic new knowledge and areas of scientific enquiry whose process of discovery requires an engagement with data derived from the diverse research findings of different hermeneutic enquiries.

The new knowledge explored in this book thus helps to advance interdisciplinary research at the interface between the empiricist core of science and the understanding of culture and communities. The crucial point here is that we cannot understand the empiricist core of science without understanding the ever changing cultural framework in which evidence-based research takes place. *Contaminations* attempts to show how literature is capable of changing both the substantial and the subjective aspects that comprise our lives. Literature and the arts have a two-pronged and radically divergent field of activity: one side is ethereal or non-substantial – what the term fiction may denote in this context – and the other transmogrifies the way we relate to issues of substance in the emotive and embodied sphere of society. Literature's independence from life paradoxically provides a new lease on life. The literary performs the crossover between substance and subjectivity which determines much of our health-related socio-political world. The interaction between subjectivity and substance (and vice versa) constitutes the intersubjective realm of politics (the topic of Franzen's *Freedom*) as well as economics, and accounts for their tendency to fall prey to various fictions that are taken to be real with often deleterious if not lethal effects. These fictions grow out of monolithic concepts which proscribe a 'one size fits all' approach to medical and socio-economic issues. The ethics of literature counters such homogeneous conception of our humanity and thus opens up new horizons for scholarship.

Brief overview of the book

Chapter 1 introduces the problem of a traditional divide between nature and society, between science and ethics, which is premised on Descartes's prioritisation of the mind over the body. It critically engages with Slavoj Žižek, who argues that our experience in the world is purely a mental one and that all corporeal experiences are nothing but illusions. It does so through a discussion of how some strands in contemporary neuroscience (A. Damasio) contaminate body and mind. They thus develop Spinoza's notion of a parallelism between the corporeal and the cerebral which also informs Freud's new science of psychoanalysis. Chapter 2 moves from the mind–body opposition to the division between nature and society as analysed in Bruno Latour's history of science. It discusses how oppositions between mind and body, nature and society, science and the arts have given rise to the modern as well as modernist concerns with invisibility. Chapter 3 analyses the critique of the notion of a natural order against the background of the French Revolution's reign of terror.

Through a close reading of Melville's *Moby Dick* (with references to Hawthorne's *The Scarlet Letter*) it shows how the presentation of the collapse of nature's order prepares for a modernist contamination of science with literature. Chapter 4 considers how a deferral of judgement informs a modernist preoccupation with the internal workings of the mind. A suspension of judgement preconditions literary as well as scientific explorations of stigmatised topics such as mental illness or aging. Chapter 5 analyses H. James's as well as A. Hitchcock's psychology of action. It shows for the first time how James and, in a cinematic way, Hitchcock discover perception to be a form of action. Chapter 6 theorises Pasolini's notion of scandal (*scandalo*) in terms of the figure of contamination, which allows for a blurring of traditional and dialectical distinctions between action and contemplation as discussed in the previous chapter. Chapter 7 delineates ways in which we can overcome humanist as well as posthumanist dialectics of inclusion and exclusion, also engaging with the persistence of positing pure forms and opposing them with each other in the contemporary context of posthumanism.

Notes

1. Barad writes: 'The notion of intra-action is a key element of my agential realist framework. The neologism "intra-action" *signifies the mutual constitution of entangled agencies*' (Barad 2007: 33).
2. As David Herman has put it: 'At issue here is the way that narratives cue interpreters to engage with discourse models or storyworlds as referential targets' (Herman 2013: 44).
3. As Mads Rosendahl Thomsen has recently put it: 'But literature has the capacity to present nuanced positions, because it does not have to convince and draw conclusions, but can operate through multiple perspectives and in different registers within the same work, ranging from seriousness to dark irony' (Thomsen 2013: 73).
4. 'This vitalist materialism rests solidly on a neo-Spinozist political ontology of monism and radical immanence, engendering a transversal relational ethics to counteract the inhuman(e) aspects of the posthuman predicament' (Braidotti 2013: 115).
5. For a detailed discussion of Benjamin's and Scholem's understanding of the term 'redemption through sin' see Vatter (2014: 171–2).
6. 'The precise date of onset of the Anthropocene is arguable, but Crutzen set it to coincide approximately with James Watt's invention of the steam engine in 1784, because of analyses of air trapped in polar ice that dated the rapid growth of carbon dioxide and methane concentrations to the late eighteenth century. The Anthropocene is not just a new way to look at the past; it strongly affects the future. Crutzen argued, for example, that anthropogenically induced carbon-dioxide emissions may affect global climate for the next 50,000 years' (Robin and Steffen 2007: 1699).

7. *The Oxford English Dictionary* online, www.oed.com [accessed 27 November 2014].
8. Morton mentions another uncritical form of calling upon the well-being of birds as 'evidence' against renewable energy: 'The reactionary response to wind farms in the United Kingdom, for instance, has tried to bog down environmentalists with the idea that birds will be caught in the blades of windmills' (Morton 2007: 6).
9. In this context Morton critiqued environmental activism as follows: '*Ecology without Nature* takes seriously the idea that truly theoretical reflection is possible only if thinking decelerates. This is not the same thing as becoming numb or stupid. It is finding anomalies, paradoxes, and conundrums in an otherwise smooth-looking stream of ideas' (Morton 2007: 12).
10. Stephen Burn has analysed the ways in which Franzen abstains from characterising anyone or anything in pure terms as either this or that. One could say that he practises literature as a form of contamination, or as Burn writes: 'Franzen's imagination characteristically works by fusing opposites on every level – formal, thematic, geographic – so his novels become a kind of synthesis of divergent forces' (Burn 2008: xi).
11. There are striking parallels between Walter Berglund and Franzen himself: Franzen has admitted to his own love of birds and to his anger about the destruction of the environment: 'I made a conscious decision not to worry about the environment. There was nothing meaningful I personally could do to save the planet, and I wanted to get on with devoting myself to things I loved. I still tried to keep my carbon footprint small, but that was as far as I could go without falling back into rage and despair. But then a funny thing happened to me. It's a long story, but basically I fell in love with birds' (Franzen 2012: 12).
12. 'Ein Aufgeben also nicht des Ich, aber jenes falschen Selbstbehauptungstriebs, der den Menschen vor der unzuverlässigen, undichten, dauerlosen, unübersehbaren, gefährlichen Welt der Beziehung in das Haben der Dinge flüchten lässt' (Buber 1979: 94).

Contaminating Psychology with Biology: Descartes, Spinoza, Freud and Žižek

Between Spinoza and Kant: Catherine Malabou, Freud, Damasio and Žižek

As we have seen in the Introduction, the current crisis of climate change calls into doubt traditional oppositions between natural history and human history. Our contemporary environmental predicament has made us cognisant of our being a physical force of nature, far from residing in a disembodied, intellectual/spiritual realm. Paul Crutzen and Eugene F. Stoermer's term 'Anthropocene' describes humanity's predominating presence in nature that derails homeostasis to the tipping point of planetary collapse.

Against this background, the following chapter introduces the problem of a traditional divide between nature and society, between science and ethics, which is premised on Descartes's prioritisation of the mind over the body. Our present condition of an Anthropocene planetary crisis in fact collapsed the still regnant philosophical proposition which assumes various divisions between the natural and the human, between nature and society, between natural and human history.

One striking proponent of the hold of this philosophical axiom which demotes the embodied world as inferior, if not delusory, is Slavoj Žižek, who argues that our experience in the world is purely a mental one and that all corporeal experiences are nothing but illusions. One target of Žižek's polemics against a Spinozan parallelism of mind and body is contemporary neuroscience. Žižek establishes his own Cartesian and Kantian position as progressive and labels Spinoza's notion of the mind as the idea of the body as regressive. Contemporary neuroscientific findings have backed up Spinoza's philosophical alternative to a Cartesian prioritisation of the cerebral over the corporeal, showing that the mind not so much controls as depends on bodily inputs.

Turning the tables on Žižek's self-proclaimed progressive stance, this chapter therefore analyses his dismissal of contemporary neuroscience as philosophical regression. What causes Žižek's unease with cognitive science is precisely a Spinozan conception of a parallelism of mind and body (rather than a controlling position of the former over the latter). In contrast to Catherine Malabou's recent account of the incompatibility of contemporary neuroscience and psychoanalysis, this chapter analyses the ways in which Freud's critique of both philosophical and theological prioritisations of the mind over the body anticipates neuroscientific findings of various contaminations between the cerebral and the corporeal. Freud locates the site of this interconnection between mind and body in the libido, the product of contamination. The libido is neither purely cerebral nor purely physical: it is both.

In contrast to Freud, Žižek argues that the libido is uncontaminated, that is, nothing but cerebral – a plague of phantasy (Žižek 2009). In reducing Freud's drives to states of pure disembodiment, Žižek presents us with a Cartesian version of psychoanalysis which dismisses the emotions of the brain. This is not Freud's understanding of psychoanalysis. As Eric R. Kandel has shown (and contra Malabou's Žižekian reading), Freud took neuroscientific investigation of the embodied mind seriously. This is his Spinozan, Darwinian and Nietzschean or anti-Cartesian heritage. Antonio Damasio famously established Spinoza's key role in developing a new conception of the mind's interdependence on the body, which has been foundational for contemporary neuroscience:

> What is Spinoza's insight then? That mind and body are parallel and mutually correlated processes, mimicking each other at every crossroad, as two faces of the same thing. That deep inside these parallel phenomena there is a mechanism for representing body events in the mind. That in spite of the equal footing of mind and body, as far as they are manifest to the percipient, there is an asymmetry in the mechanism underlying these phenomena. He suggested that the body shapes the mind's contents more so than the mind shapes the body's, although mind processes are mirrored in body processes to a considerable extent. On the other hand, the ideas in the mind can double up on each other, something that bodies cannot do. If my interpretation of Spinoza's statements is even faintly correct, his insight was revolutionary for its time but it had no impact on science. (Damasio 2003: 217)

With these sentences Damasio attempts to summarise the groundbreaking significance of the seventeenth-century philosopher Baruch Spinoza for twenty-first-century neuroscience. In the paragraph above Damasio focuses on Spinoza's thought about the mutual contamination of mind and body. Contrary to Descartes, who allocated a commanding or ruling function to the mind – which he physiologically tried to locate in the pineal gland – Spinoza argued that mental images originate in bodily perceptions and sensations. Spinoza famously argued that the mind is the idea of the body.

This implies a parallelism between mind and body. Damasio and other leading neurologists have discovered that body, brain and mind are intricately connected, and that bodily emotions are the foundation of mental feelings and a sense of consciousness: 'The inescapable and remarkable fact about these three phenomena – emotion, feeling, consciousness – is their body relatedness' (Damasio 2000: 284). As Damasio points out in the paragraph above, Spinoza's insight into the parallelism between mind and body, groundbreaking though it was, 'had no impact on science'. In *Spinoza and the Specters of Modernity* I have shown that his thought has had significant – albeit marginalised – repercussions in political, historical, cultural, biological and psychoanalytical theory. Freud in particular developed his notion of a 'new science' as part of Spinoza's shift from the Cartesian as well as Kantian idealist notion of the mind's (autonomy or) full control over merely bodily or contingent external events. This Freudian shift in the understanding of mind science will be discussed in the next section of this chapter.

Do we do justice to Freud when we characterise him as a covert Spinozist? As we shall see below, he was certainly highly critical of Kant's perception of the mind's autonomy from external or pathological exposures. Strikingly, contamination is a notion that derives from a medical context of pathology. Kant uses the term autonomy in the sense of purity from any form of infection or contamination. The body is prone to becoming infected; it is exposed to contaminating forces.

Kantian autonomy denotes a cerebral immunity from contamination. It is not surprising that Kant casts our embodied and natural environment into the medical language of pathology. As we shall see in the next chapter, both Kant and modernity at large engage in various purification projects in order to keep the feared and chaotic forces of contamination at bay. For one thing, the contamination of body, emotion, feeling, brain and mind maintained by Spinoza, together with contemporary neuroscientists, has troubling implications for Freudian psychoanalysis too. Žižek – perhaps the most important contemporary Freudian/Lacanian theorist – has recently raised a red flag over what he calls the reductive materialism of neurologists à la Damasio. Žižek's point of contention is self-proclaimedly progressive: the neurologists abandon their Kantian position and retreat to a 'naive' pre-critical perception of life. Poking fun at Damasio, Žižek articulates his 'problem with this easy and clear solution: reading the cognitivists, one cannot help noting how their description of consciousness at the phenomenal–experiential level is very traditional and pre-Freudian' (Žižek 2012: 716). Later on, Žižek makes it clear that he actually understands 'pre-Kantian' by his expression 'pre-Freudian' (Žižek 2012: 716). Here it is important to attend to what Žižek refers to as 'this easy and clear solution'. Without referencing her new book *The New Wounded: From Neuroscience to Brain Damage*, Žižek mentions Catherine Malabou – whose work on Hegel he keeps praising – for having advocated a dismissal of Freudian or Lacanian psychoanalysis in favour of contemporary neuroscience:

> Only with today's brain science do we have the true revolution, namely that, for the first time, we are approaching a scientific understanding of the emergence of consciousness. Catherine Malabou draws a radical consequence from the cognitivist standpoint: the task is not to supplement the Freudian unconscious with the cerebral unconscious, but to replace the former with the latter – once we accept the cerebral unconscious, there is no longer any space for the Freudian version. (Žižek 2012: 715)

As we will see, Malabou does not advocate abandoning Freudian psychoanalysis. She does, however, take issue with the Kantian residue of the mind's autonomy in Freud's writing and thought. It is this critique of an idealist unconscious in Freud's conscious and outspoken attack on Kant's notion of a mind that is in full possession of itself (Mack 2003: 136–54) which provokes Žižek's censure of Malabou's position.

Rather than doing justice to Freud's complex position between Spinoza and Kant, Žižek reads Freudian psychoanalysis as yet another version of Kantian autonomy. His fondness of paradox brings Žižek to declare that radical Cartesian (Descartes's *cogito*) and Kantian (Kant's autonomy) idealism coincide with the radical materialism of Marx, Lenin and Stalin. For pure idealists as well as pure materialists, there is no such thing as matter, brain, mind or selfhood. Rather than being embodied (as Spinoza and contemporary neuroscience maintain), we are disembodied, substance-less subjects: minds or organs without bodies. This insight into the non-substantial or non-corporeal foundation of human existence is what Žižek understands by 'Freudian'. According to Žižek the progressive 'Freudian' or Kantian position is one of 'purity', of the mind's autonomy from any contamination with the pathologies of the environmental natural or embodied world.

This modern purification project rejecting the figure of contamination actually derives not from Freud but from Descartes, Hume and Kant, as Žižek makes clear later on: 'while Hume endeavours to demonstrate how there is no Self (when we look into ourselves, we only encounter particular ideas, impressions, etc. – no 'Self' as such), Kant claims that this void *is* the Self' (Žižek 2012: 720). The emptiness of the empirical or embodied self serves as the foundation of Kantian autonomy. On account of the self's void, it is able to disregard empirical, embodied and contingent conditions of the merely natural (i.e. non-rational) world and legislate in an autonomous manner.

The self's void justifies the rule of a mind that is here even more radically than in Descartes's *cogito* completely independent of corporeal or material conditions. This independence from matter establishes the mind's autonomous rule over the material or embodied world. As Žižek has put it:

> The post-Humean critical-transcendental idealists, from Kant to Hegel, do *not* return to the pre-critical, rock-like, substantial identity of the Ego – what they struggled with was precisely how to describe the Self which has no substantial identity (as was stated by Kant in his critique of Descartes's own reading of *cogito* as *res cogitans* 'a thing that thinks'), but nonetheless functions as irreducible point of reference – here is Kant's unsurpassable formulation in his Critique of Pure Reason: '[. . .] Through this I or he or it (the thing) which thinks, nothing further is represented than a transcendental subject of the thoughts=X'. (Žižek 2012: 720–1)

According to Žižek, neuroscience returns to a pre-Freudian position, because his understanding of pre-Freudian is pre-Kantian or Spinozan (critical of both Descartes's and Kant's autonomy of the thinking thing). Kant has emptied thought of any substance. In his critique of the material vestiges of Descartes's *cogito* he has banished the matter implicit in the Cartesian notion '*res cogitans*': 'Kant thus prohibits the passage from "I think" to "I am a thing that thinks": of course there has to be some noumenal basis for (self-)consciousness, of I must be "something" objectively, but the point is precisely that this dimension is forever inaccessible to the "I"' (Žižek 2012: 721). The inaccessibility in question here is epistemological.

Kant's epistemological critique sets the stage for his metaphysical redefinition of the body. The presupposition of scientific knowledge in this Kantian context is premised on notions of purity. Only pure entities are objects of scientific insight. According to Kant, the messy, contaminated or 'pathological' matter of the embodied world lies beyond the grasp of categorisation, representation and meaning. Given that we do not know the possible meaning of our contaminated embodiment, it also could not be said with certainty that bodily contingency has any relation to a transcendent ground that would bestow on it some form of value. Our pure rational activity, which is supposedly unexposed to the pathologies of the contaminating force of our environment, operates as the true source of moral validity.

Kant's idealism does not deny the existence of matter, but maintains that matter has no right to exist except as material base for the mind's autonomous constructions. Precisely because the intrinsic value of matter is inaccessible, the mind can rule it without restrictions. The scandal of Spinoza's mind–body parallelism and that of contemporary neuroscience lies in the fact that corporeal matter here is no longer inaccessible to mental insight but, on the contrary, the very survival of the mental depends on corporeal materiality.

This takes us to the precarious existence of the mind, according to contemporary neuroscience. The mind's dependency on the body – or, in other words, the mutual contamination of the mental and the environmental – has serious implications for the survival or the eternity of the cerebral, because the mind is subject to corporeal mortality. In her new book, Malabou focuses on precisely this issue. She argues that cerebral plasticity not only denotes the donation and reception but also the destruction of life. She does not dismiss Freudian or Lacanian psychoanalysis – as Žižek claims she does. She asks, however, whether Freudian thought can imagine the mortality of psychic life. Addressing the question of whether Freud allows for the radical negativity of death as part of mental life, Malabou first points out that psychoanalysis defines mental illness not in terms of mortality but in terms of regression:

> Freud thus underscores two fundamental characteristics of pyschopathologies: They always entail both regression and destruction, and they only destroy that which stands in the way of regression. Destruction only bears upon the 'later acquisitions and developments' that Freud compares to a garment or envelope. These superstructures are thus designed to cover over the essential – the nature that breaks through our 'hard-won morality' – the nudity of the primitive psychic stratum, which becomes the aim of regression. *Destruction is merely the most effective manner of uncovering or revealing the indestructible.* (Malabou 2012: 59)

In establishing a link between mental illness and regression, Freud reiterates crucial tenets of Victorian psychology. As Sally Shuttleworth has recently shown, from roughly the mid-nineteenth century onwards childhood became a trope for nervous excitability and madness: 'Mental disorder, the loss of intellectual or emotional control, is thus defined as a form of a heightened state of childhood' (Shuttleworth 2010: 50). The state of childhood no longer offered glimpses of a qualitative leap back or forwards towards innocence (as some of the Romantics proclaimed) but was seen as regression to a primitive or irrational state: 'This shift in perception of the child marks a turning point, for it is now possible to see in the child's freedom from adult mental constraint the grounding of insanity' (Shuttleworth 2010: 50). According to Freud, madness is a regression to an infantile state, either at an onto- or phylogenic level. The past contaminates present and future. This fusion of the different levels of time makes not for immortality (so that individuals should die) but for a sense of eternity (the contamination of the past with the present and the future ensures that certain aspects of life keep being passed on).

Death's role is not very active here, as the dead can still pass on their heritage to the future generation. The indestructible is not death but the death drive. The death drive never comes to an end but turns around death – returning to the primitive pasts of childhood and the evolutionary beginnings of humanity before the stage of restrictive mental life, of civilisation. According to Freud, the psyche operates autonomously, as an inward drive, progressing and regressing ontogenetically to the childhood of a given individual as well as polygenetically to the savage origins of mankind, to the murder of the primeval father by the brothers who envy their progenitor's exclusive possession of women. Oedipus is itself a regression to this primal scene of savage patricide.

Nothing seems to get lost in psychic life: the same events keep returning in human history. This is what Malabou means by Freud's indestructibility of the psychic life. This indestructibility contrasts sharply with contemporary neuroscientific findings of the mind's dependence on bodily growth and mortality: the brain of an Alzheimer's patient, for instance, does not regress to childhood.

On the contrary, rather than growing like a child's, it incrementally closes down and retreats from an affective engagement with the outside world. As Malabou shows in her book, Freud vehemently denied that psychic life could shut down and cease to exist. From this perspective, Freud clings to a notion of psychic autonomy:

> The psychical regime of events, for Freud, is autonomous; it does not depend on any organic causes – especially not upon any cerebral cause. This autonomy manifests itself precisely through the independence of fantasmatic work whose only creative resources come from the psyche and not the brain. Once again, the concepts of scene, fiction, and scenario are foreign to any neuronal organization that, according to Freud, does not possess an apparatus of representation. (Malabou 2012: 98)

Malabou here confuses Freud's position with that of Lacan. As Alain Ehrenberg has shown (Ehrenberg 2010), Lacan turns Freud's account of the psyche's contamination with embodied drives (i.e. the libido) into one of the mind's state of purity in a linguistic, symbolic sphere that operates independently from any environmental factors. Indeed, Freud's notion of the death drive elevates the traditionally demoted notion of embodied or bare life to prospects of eternity. He does so by precisely contaminating the body with the recurring traits of mental life which, as we have seen above, keep occurring from the mythical times of the primeval father to the modern Oedipus complex.

There is a so far underappreciated bio-political dimension to Freud's scientific work: his new science contaminates visible, organic life with the invisible and eternal forces of psychic life. This contamination of the mortal body with the eternity of the mind or psyche makes for a sense of indestructibility (in other words, eternity) which Malabou has rightly noted. Malabou misreads Freud in a Lacanian manner when she argues that such a sense of eternity disregards the mortality of the body.

Rather than purifying the mind from the body, Freud contaminates the organic with the indestructability of the death drive, the libido. By contaminating the eternal forces of the psyche (pervading the prehistoric, the historic, the modern and the contemporary) with the organic, Freud endows bare life with philosophical validity which modern purification projects have tried to deny. The contaminating force operating in Freud's new science helps us discover a fusion of the mental and the embodied which Miguel Vatter, following Esposito, has recently appraised as the affirmation of merely embodied 'bare life' (*zoé*) as follows:

> I am interested in pursuing Esposito's suggestion that a conception of the power of life that escapes thanatopolitics depends on interpreting 'life's relationship with politics philosophically' (2008: 150). I understand this claim in the following sense: philosophy becomes truly political when it provides a conception of life (*zoé*) that is immediately theoretical or contemplative. Philosophy is political, or political philosophy exists, only where biology is philosophical. Philosophy is to be understood in the traditional sense of contemplating what is most real and actual, what never perishes, what is eternal. Thus eternal life would be a conception of a contemplative *zoé*. (Vatter 2011: 218)

Freud indeed contaminates his new science of psychoanalysis with political philosophy when he offers a conception of life that is theoretical, mental or, in other words, psychological. For Freud, as for Spinoza, the mind is the idea of the body. As such the psyche attempts to map or represent the organic state. According to contemporary neuroscience too, the brain engages in works of representation. These representations are, however, creative rather than mimetic in a flat or replicating way.[1]

As Damasio has shown, the brain's mapping of the external world 'is not a mere copy, a passive transfer from the outside of the brain to the inside' (Damasio 2010: 64). Instead, the 'assembly conjured up by the senses involves an active contribution offered from inside the brain, available from early in development, the idea that the brain is a blank slate having long since lost favor' (Damasio 2010: 64). Mental mappings are therefore not full representations of the objects concerned; they are creations:

> But the correspondence is not point-to-point, and thus the map need not be faithful. The brain is a creative system. Rather than mirroring the environment around it, as an engineered information-processing device would, each brain constructs maps of that environment using its own parameters of internal design, and thus creates a world unique to the class of brains comparably designed. (Damasio 2000: 322)

These different and divergent representations of the world constitute part of our subjectivity and create difference of perspective, different takes on things.

At first glance Freud seems, however, to be close to Žižek's image of him: he appears to dismiss any talk of material, embodied objects as imperious to the autonomy of psychic life. There is no such thing as external reality, only the hallucinations and fictions generated by the void which is psychic life:

> The gap that separates the quantum level from our ordinary perceived reality is *not* a gap between ultimate hard reality and a higher-level unavoidable-but-illusory hallucination. On the contrary, it is the quantum level which is effectively 'hallucinated,' not yet ontologically fully constituted, floating and ambiguous, and it is the shift to the 'higher' level of appearance (appearing perceived reality) that makes it into a hard reality. (Žižek 2012: 726–7)

Our sense of 'hard reality' is itself a product of fiction whose basis is psychic life. This makes Freud appear as a Kantian who rejects contamination and transposes Kant's notion of autonomy or purity into the workings of the psyche. How can we then account for Freud's repeated criticism of Kant's philosophy?

Freud's new science

Indeed Freud defines his new science as a science of contamination. He thus establishes his *differentia specifica* from Kant's understanding of the scientific as, in the words of Latour (see Chapter 2), the modern purification project.

Freud ironically characterises Kant's Copernican revolution as 'old science'. What makes it old is its presumption of purity and intra-human omniscience and omnipotence. Contra Kant, Freud argues that our world is not pure but contaminated – contaminated to the extent that we are not masters in our own house. Instead of being purely one entity, our ego or our psyche is split into competing claims and commandments of which we can rarely gain control. Significantly, Freud undermines the Kantian notion of autonomy as mastering one's own house and world, when he locates the psychoanalytical revolution in the historical context of both Copernicus and Darwin: both have inflicted contaminating wounds on humanity's narcissism. Psychoanalysis deals a third and decisive blow to this kind of anthropomorphism:

> Humanity had to endure two big wounds of its naïve self-love as inflicted by science over the ages. First when it learned that our earth is not the centre of the world, but a tiny part of a much bigger and unimaginable system of the world. This wound is associated with the name of Copernicus, although Alexandrinian science has pronounced something similar. The second: when biological science rendered null and void the presumed privilege of creation of man by referring to both his descent from animals and to the inerasable nature of his animalistic constitution. This re-evaluation has taken place in our time under the influence of Charles Darwin, Wallace and their predecessors [i.e. Spinoza, Herder, and Goethe], which have been met not without the fiercest resistance of their contemporaries. The third and most severe wound, however, human megalomania has to endure from psychological research, which proves to the ego[2] that it is not even master in his own house, but remains dependent on pathetic information derived from something which takes place unconsciously in the life of its soul. (Freud 1975 Vol. 1: 283–4)[3]

Here Freud clearly places his new science in a historical trajectory of maverick scientists who have radically rejected humanity's conception as pure and uncontaminated.

The Copernican revolution has questioned the pure, quasi-divine place of the earth as the centre of the universe, and Darwin and his predecessors Spinoza, Herder and Goethe have shown how humanity has always been exposed to being contaminated by its natural–corporeal environment. From the scientific perspective of both Spinoza and Darwin, nature does not cunningly perform a higher cerebral purpose. Instead the contaminating forces of chance and contingency govern its operations. As Gillian Beer has put it:

> 'natural selection' is a pithy rejoinder to 'natural theology'. Instead of an initiating godhead, Darwin suggests, diversification and selection have generated the history of the present world. Instead of teleology and forward plan, the future is an uncontrollable welter of possibility. (Beer 2000: xviii)

Within a Spinozan trajectory Darwin disrupts the divide between nature and society, contaminating one with the other. As will be discussed in Chapter 2, the construction of a harmonious, proportional and predictable natural world serves to justify punitive and exclusionary measures in politics. The assumed teleology of nature contrasts with the incalculable and unpredictable intricacies of human psychology. First Spinoza and then more outspokenly Darwin dismantle the theory of a nature's proportionality and teleological rationality.

The fatal blow to human pride which Freud attributes to psychoanalysis has to do not so much with issues of humanity's unpredictable psychic life as with the Cartesian doctrine of the mind's control over the mere extension, the mere matter of the body. In this way the most severe wound to humanity's anthropomorphic concept of God and the universe is still inflicted by Freud's new science. Why is this so? The preceding revolutions had to do with the strictly biological (Darwin) and astrological (Copernicus) spheres, while only minimally touching upon the sphere of the mind. This is why Kant is part of the Copernican revolution: with Copernicus he acknowledges the periphery of the astrological position of our habitat, the earth, but he nevertheless reclaims the autonomous mastery of humanity within its post-Copernican limits (i.e. the limits of the sublunar world).

Freud's new science is radical, because it assaults this last remaining bastion of purity: the mind. Rather than guaranteeing humanity's resistance to any contaminating, embodied forces, the mind is 'not master in his own house but remains dependent on pathetic information derived from something which takes place unconsciously in the life of its soul'. This indefinite 'something' (*von dem, was*) makes nonsense of any claim to an unambiguous, uncontaminated or pure self-knowledge. It therefore strongly undermines the Kantian position concerning transcending the empirical world, because of the autonomy of the rational mind.

According to Kant, reason shapes the material world in a pure, a priori manner, and as a result is capable of freedom from natural conditions (Mack 2003: 23–41). In Freud's *Introductory Lectures* of 1933 Kant appears as the godfather of philosophers, who argues that 'time and place are necessary forms of psychic activities' (Freud 1975 Vol.1: 511). Far from being able to create uncontaminated structures of space and temporal rhythms, the mind easily turns mindless when it removes the ego from the flow of time and also from the flow of life. This removal from time and space is consubstantial with a loss of reality which characterises various forms of psychosis.

In undermining Kant's conception of autonomy, Freud's new science refashions Spinoza's conception of the mind contaminated by its environment (the mind as the idea of the body). As Suzanne R. Kirschner has pointed out, Freudian psychoanalysis analyses 'the limitations of modernity's emphasis on rationality and autonomy' (Kirschner 1996: 199). Freud's new science enmeshes cultural with natural history. According to Freud we cannot overcome embodied condition and attain Kant and Hegel's state of freedom where natural impulses are suspended. Psychoanalysis focuses on damage caused precisely by such suspension. Rather than emphasising a future state of reason and freedom, Freud's new science tries to persuade us to commemorate a 'savage' (i.e. premodern) past which, if not brought to consciousness, determines our presumably modern and civilised way of life.

The death drive

As Gillian Beer has shown, Darwin writing about nature 'displaces the absoluteness of man's power of reason as an instrument for measuring the world' (Beer 2000: 92). His description of nature lacks, however, any ethical component and is thus removed from Spinoza's social agenda in his *Ethics*. Freud seems to intensify this naturalistic bleakness when he discusses the death drive: 'A strange drive', he exclaims, 'that is bent on the destruction of its own organic home!' (Freud 1975 Vol. 1: 538).[4] Distinguishing his approach from Schopenhauer's, Freud argues that far from being opposed to life, the death drive is actually the very foundation of our ability to survive. As we have seen in the preceding section, Freud sees psychic life as eternal, thus pervading the whole of natural and human history, rather than immortal, with the individual being subject to death.

The death drive only turns deadly if it has been cut off from an organism's erotic circulation, to which it originally belongs. This reliance on the corporeal organism contradicts Žižek's take on psychoanalysis in terms of a Kantian radicalisation of Descartes's *cogito*. As Malabou has shown, 'Freud dismisses any suggestion that an organic cause could have etiological autonomy' (Malabou 2012: 112). In this way he denies that mental illness can ever result from injury to the organ of the brain. His denial of the etiological autonomy of an organic cause does not, however, mean that Freud invalidates the significance of organic, material and embodied life and the psyche's interaction with the external world. Malabou does justice to Freud when she emphasises that he 'in no way minimizes the importance of external threats or perils' (Malabou 2012: 123). Oedipal phantasies and castration anxieties refer back to substantial and embodied events such as the trauma of separation taking place at birth and the baby's dependence on parental support later on: 'Castration anxiety (the third form of separation) is itself a substitute for the fear of punishment – punishment by the mother who threatens to withdraw her love for the child (the second form of separation); and this punishment anxiety, in turn, is the expression of an even older anxiety linked to the trauma of birth (the first form of separation)' (Malabou 2012: 125). The paradoxical position of the death drive – confirming life while driving beyond it – results from the deeply ambiguous, contaminated constitution of embodied life from birth onwards.

Freud's Spinozan contamination

The death drive certainly forms part of the libido and as such it is life preserving. In this way, Freud speaks of 'the way in which the two drives [i.e. of life and of death] interconnect and how the death drive is placed at the services of Eros' (Freud 1975 Vol. 1: 540).[5] This contamination of the constructive and destructive represents another shift within a Spinozist conception of an interconnected universe. The name Spinoza seems to be conspicuous by its absence in Freud's *oeuvre* – as he is frequently referred to indirectly. The absence of a direct reference to Spinoza points to the indirection or, we may say, the shift that Spinoza's thought is capable of inspiring. Freud only directly addresses his debt to Spinoza when he is asked to do so. In this way Spinozist Dr Lothar Bickel requested of the late Freud an acknowledgement of his intellectual reliance on Spinoza. Freud's reply (28 June 1931) is affirmative:

> *I readily admit my dependence on Spinoza's doctrine.* There was no reason why I should expressly mention his name, since I conceived my hypotheses from the *atmosphere* created by him, rather than from the study of his work. Moreover, I did not seek a philosophical legitimation. (Yovel 1992: 139)

The term 'atmosphere' denotes a contaminating force in which we cannot pinpoint a pure source. What Freud seems to have in mind is what he has in common with Spinoza, namely being affiliated while at the same time being disaffiliated with the contemporaneous Jewish community and with Jewish history. Both Freud and Spinoza are double outsiders: they are not part of their own community in terms of religious affiliation though they are perceived as Jews by the non-Jewish majority of their respective societies; moreover, being seen as typically Jewish, they are automatically associated with the Kantian fear of the 'pathological', the negative of Hegelian dialectics, and with the anxiety of contamination – the threatening, the savage, or, in Spinoza's case, the Satanic. This perception of their ethnicity is then reinforced through the subject matter of their writing and thought, which undermines in different but nonetheless related ways the conception of humanity as pure representations of God.

In his letter to Bickel Freud downplays the way in which he was an actual student of Spinoza's work. As a later communication makes clear, this lack of systematic study does not mean that he was not shaped by Spinoza's thought. While declining to contribute to a volume dedicated to Spinoza's 300th anniversary, Freud nevertheless emphasises his intellectual debt to the Dutch Jewish philosopher: 'Throughout my long life', he writes, 'I [timidly] sustained an extraordinarily high respect for the person as well as for the results of the thought [*Denkleistung*] of the great philosopher Spinoza' (Yovel 1992: 139). Here Freud implicitly conceives of Spinoza not as a single and isolated figure; rather, he sees in the name Spinoza an intellectual constellation of thinkers and writers who, from Herder and Goethe to Darwin, have introduced various shifts in the way we see humanity, not as a quasi-divine representative on earth, but as contaminated by the environmental forces of nature.

It may well be that it is due to this contaminating, non-definable, super-individual influence of Spinoza's work that Freud avoids mentioning his name in his various psychoanalytical studies. Freud sometimes alludes to Spinoza by referring to Heine as his non-religious coreligionist (*Unglaubensgenossen*).[6] This is precisely the term Heine employs in order to describe his affinity with Spinoza. Significantly, Heine focuses on Spinoza's critique of anthropomorphism in both philosophy and theology. Heine is often ingenuously right by saying something that is blatantly wrong: he does this, for instance, when he claims that Spinoza never denies the existence of God but always the existence of humanity.

Heine's *avant-là-lettre* posthumanist take on Spinoza has recently been supported by Vatter's interpretation of Spinoza as scientist and political philosopher not of a mentalist conception of humanity but of bare life's (*zoé*) eternity. 'I shall therefore', writes Vatter, 'call Spinoza's account of life "providential" insofar as the struggle to keep alive that characterizes the duration of every being rests on something other than itself, namely, on the eternal life that perseveres in it and through which it receives what it struggles to preserve' (Vatter 2011: 224). Breaking with notions of scientific purity, Spinoza confronts us with a world that is eternally contaminated, where the *conatus* (preservation) is not a question of single or pure entity but the product of infinite contaminations of one with the other. One may die but the other may persevere, and what perseveres is precisely a contaminated rather than distinct or pure entity.

Implicitly contradicting the seventeenth- and eighteenth-century charge of atheism and the twenty-first-century appraisal of Spinoza as atheist, Heine writes:

Nothing but sheer unreason and malice could bestow on such a doctrine the qualification of 'atheism.' No one has ever spoken more sublimely of Deity than Spinoza. Instead of saying that he denied God, one might say that he denied man. All finite things are to him but modes of the infinite substance; all finite substances are contained in God; the human mind is but a luminous ray of infinite thought; the human body but an atom of infinite extension: God is the infinite cause of both, of mind and of body, *natura naturans*. (Heine 1986: 72)[7]

What Heine refers to in this important quotation is precisely the topic on which I want to focus the discussion of encounters between psychoanalysis and neuroscience: namely, the shift Spinoza introduces away from thought centring on the priority of the mind over merely embodied matter. In other words, Spinoza's philosophy corrects a problem which will be discussed in the next chapter: the modern divide between the mind's 'natural order' and the irrational deviance from this order in human society and psychology (criminals, outcasts and so forth). Freud reinforces this Spinozan shift when he distinguishes his new science from the presumptuous claims of both religion and philosophy. By contaminating the psychological with the organic or embodied, Freud is not so far removed from a neuroscientific approach as Žižek in his critique of Malabou would make us believe.

Freud's new science of contamination

We can better understand Freud's conception of his 'new science' by attending to his polemics against religion. In a highly ironic manner Freud argues that religion renders God anthropomorphic by endowing humanity with quasi-divine notions of purity. As has been discussed above, Freud clearly characterises his new science as an affront to Kant's conception of an autonomous mind that is capable of shaping its own world and history.

Why does Freud, despite his nineteenth-century background in anthropological evolutionism (i.e. Frazer and Tylor), base his conception of psychoanalysis on the non-progressivist footing of contamination, of lack (or incompletion), and the insufficiency of civilisation and its morals (or on aggression and savagery as the original foundation of morals and civilisation)?

To address this question it is worth drawing attention to Eric L. Santner's brilliant discussion of a sense of 'too muchness' in Freud's writing and thought. Santner's term 'too muchness' evokes images of contamination, of a vessel overflowing and thus contaminating what surrounds it. The confrontation with this topic stipulated the composition of Santner's *On the Psychotheology of Everyday Life*. Here Santner speaks of his 'sense that Freud's mostly negative assessments of religion are in some way undermined or at least challenged by what I can't help but characterise as the "spiritual" dimension of the new science he founded' (Santner 2001: 8). This 'spiritual dimension' is precisely the contamination of physiological with a psychic energy of excess (or too muchness):

> Psychoanalysis differs from other approaches to human being by attending to the constitutive 'too muchness' that characterizes the psyche; the human mind is, we might say, defined by the fact that it includes more reality than it can contain, is the bearer of an excess, a too much of pressure that is not merely physiological. The various ways in which this 'too much,' this surplus of life of the human subject seeks release or discharge in the 'psychopathology of everyday life' continues to form the central focus of Freudian theory and practice. Now the very religious tradition in which Freud was raised, his protestations of lifelong secularism notwithstanding, is itself in some sense structured around an internal excess or tension – call it the tension of election – and elaborates its particular form of ethical orientation to it. For Judaism (as well as for Christianity), that is, human life always includes more reality than it can contain and this 'too much' bears witness to a spiritual and moral calling, a pressure toward self-transformation, toward goodness. (Santner 2001: 8)

This excess is paradoxically humanity's limitation: it is so overwhelmed by various pressures and conflicting demands that it is incapable of mastering its own house. This sense of 'too muchness' contaminates the ego, splitting it apart into at least three incompatible force fields: one is the demand to attend to the hardship imposed by external reality (what Freud calls *Lebensnot*: Freud 1975 Vol. 9: 186), the second is the realm of aggressive or sexual drives (the so called *id*), and the third, equally overwhelming and potentially destructive, is the valid, but sometimes non-significant, moral imperative imposed by civilisation (the superego).

In his works on religious history, Freud attempts to show how the superego or civilisation are themselves contaminated by the aggression and obscenity of the drives, of the id. Instead of a narrative of progression here we clearly have an account of how qualitative leaps emerge only thanks to what they apparently oppose, and into which they could easily regress yet again. According to Freud, civilisation begins not with the promulgation of moral doctrines but with the murder of the primeval father by his sons, who are so envious of his exclusive sexual possession of women that they kill him in a fit of rage. How is murder responsible for morality? It evokes a sense of guilt. The excessive and contaminating demands of psychic and physiological drives thus give way to the too much of self-destructive feelings of guilt. As Santner puts it in the excerpt quoted above, it is due to this contamination of guilt that we attempt to be 'good'.

This sense of goodness, however, can easily turn into an anthropomorphic conception of God: through our moral consciousness we may feel identical with God. In this way religion does not bring about humility but megalomania. So Freud's critique of religion is in fact a Spinozist one that criticises human self-aggrandisement out of which we construct notions of pseudo-scientific purity. The spectre of anthropomorphism looms large when Freud argues that religious folk are the most hubristic imaginable because they feel at one with the limitless power of God. It is this conviction of being a representative of divine purity that provides the foundation for the thanatopolitical exertion of power over bare life (see the discussion of posthumanism and biopolitics in Chapter 7). According to Freud, religious folk:

> give the name of 'God' to some vague abstraction which they have created for themselves; having done so they can pose before all the world as deists, as believers in God, and they can even boast that they have recognized a higher, purer concept of God, notwithstanding that their God is now nothing more than an insubstantial shadow and no longer the mighty personality of religious doctrine. Critics persist in describing as 'deeply religious' anyone who admits to a sense of man's insignificance or impotence in the face of the universe, although what constitutes the essence of religious attitude is not this feeling but only the next step after it, the reaction to it which seeks a remedy for it. The man who goes no further, but humbly acquiesces in the small part which human beings play in the great world – such a man is, on the contrary, irreligious in the truest sense of the world. (Freud 1964: 53)

Freud argues that it is not an awareness of humanity's contaminations with its natural environment but a sense of quasi-divine purity that characterises religion. He makes it clear that his way of thinking here is idiosyncratic, if not ironic. This is so because we usually define religious character in the opposite manner: not in terms of anthropomorphically occupying the place of the divine but, on the contrary, in terms of accentuating human lack in the face of God or nature. According to Freud, in contrast, this sense of contamination and incompletion shapes not the world view of religion, but that of science.

Freud's notion of science is indeed new – not least because it reverses the role traditionally attributed to religion with that of his 'new science'. Rather than delineating the triumphal progress of the mind's 'natural order', Freud's new science analyses the way in which the cerebral remains contaminated by an embodied loop which it cannot overcome without imperilling its existence. Progress remains dependent on an awareness of a savage or regressive history (that of the primal scene or that of Oedipal conflict and incest). Here we encounter the opposite of a triumphal narrative of progression.

Freud's 'new science' focuses on contamination, on our lack of self-mastery, proving that we are not even masters of our own house. Radicalising Spinoza's analysis of the self as being contaminated by the other, Freud denies that we are unified entities. Rather than forming a consistent whole, our psyche is torn by a whirlpool of excessive demands, commands and urges. It is due to this internal strangeness, or, in other words, this experience of being contaminated by competing drives and desires and aspirations, that it is so difficult for us to take account of what is actually happening in the external world. Psychic illness results from an overflow of internal pressures so that the ego cannot see anything in its environment but an intensification or mirror image of its mental conflicts. This is, of course, what Spinoza criticises as anthropomorphic distortion of nature or God according to the life of our internal appetites or passions. This distortion is nothing but a psychotic loss of reality where we cannot accurately recognise that our self is always exposed to its environment and various contaminations that constitute selfhood as a fluid entity that can rarely reach a point of autonomy or purity.

This loss of coordination between self and other brings about destruction as self-destruction. As Malabou has pointed out, psychoanalysis focuses on the point where the distinction between internal and external danger collapses, where the 'ego doubles itself, and this scission opens the psyche to the horizon of its own disappearance' (Malabou 2012: 128). Freud attributes equal significance to the materiality of the external world and to the immateriality of psychic life. The material presence of the external world which contaminates the psyche is the Spinozan heritage of psychoanalysis. It is from this corporeal or material perspective that Freud criticises the lofty aspirations of Kantian moral philosophy.

In his *Ethics*, Spinoza provides a philosophical guide for a sustainable integration of the self within the world at large. From a Kantian perspective, Spinoza's notion of preservation (*conatus*) would appear to be 'pathological' in its connection with the external world: the self perseveres within the eternity of a diverse environment where it is fused and yet contaminated by it. According to Spinoza, we achieve an eternal state of contamination through the realisation that we are part of what is ostensibly not us. Spinoza calls this contaminating force of the other the third kind of knowledge or the intellectual love God, an immanent force that keeps us eternally enmeshed with our constantly changing embodiment and environment. Vatter has analysed how Spinoza does not distinguish between the immanence of the embodied mortal and yet eternal other and the traditionally demoted existence of bare life (*zoé*):

> In short, Spinoza's doctrine is that human life, or the divine contemplation (for these are the same), brings God down from the Height of his Throne, where the tradition said He ruled over the world like a King. A (philosophical) life is providential, therefore in the sense that in and through it, God is entirely 'among' things and in no way separate from them: for in a (philosophical) life, there can be no more sacred precincts, spaces, and times absolved from the profane, where God or his representatives come to stand in judgment over the becoming of life. From this point of view, God's life as the eternal living contemplation refers to the state of things in which everything is connected with everything else in exactly such a way as to allow it to persevere in its most singularizing being. (Vatter 2011: 244–5)

Spinoza contaminates contemplation and material existence, body and mind, self and environment. He discusses immanence not as a self-sufficient entity *sub species aeternitatis* but rather as contaminated by the intellectual love of God. Freud, too, develops his new science of psychoanalysis within a Spinozan atmosphere of contamination.

According to Freud, 'truth consists in the agreement with the actual external world'.[8] Spinoza tackles the passions and appetites and Freud attends to the surreal reality of various drives and hyper-moral commandments to prepare for an accurate perception of the actual world surrounding us. Spinoza's passions and Freud's various libidinal urges and demands cause a distorted or anthropomorphic reading of nature or God. Significantly, the two thinkers take these distortions seriously, because the loss of reality brought about by the passions importantly shapes the life of human society. According to Spinoza, reason has to collaborate with the passions to change social practices.

Rather than imposing a categorical framework on the affects, Spinoza encourages us to conduct an ethical life that is not at war with the passions but makes use of their constructive rather than their destructive potential. In a similar vein, Freud's new science criticises the deleterious effects of a morality that attempts to destroy the passions. This attempt at destruction is in actuality self-destructive. Rather than advocating resistance and warfare, both thinkers of modern science plead for reframing what has traditionally been demoted as inferior, negative, unhealthy or pathological and dangerous: the boundary traversing force of contamination. In order to prepare for such revaluation of values, the traditional system of morality has to be emptied of various hierarchies and boundaries. Both Freud and Spinoza undermine the quasi-divine status of moral commandments. Spinoza shows how our understanding of good and evil reflects our appetites and so we call good what we desire and evil what we loathe. These categories therefore reflect our psychic and physiological state but they distort the object that they are supposed to denote.

In Spinozist fashion Freud's 'new science' questions 'morality which God has presumably given to us'.[9] Morality as gift from God is of course an anthropomorphic construct. Significantly, Freud sees anthropomorphism as operative not only in religion but also in philosophy – and that nowhere more than in Kantian moral philosophy. To illustrate his discussion of an anthropomorphic deity as foundation of morality, Freud refers to Kant's famous parallelism between the mind and the starry heavens above:

> Following the famous sentence by Kant, who connects our conscience with the starry heavens, a pious person could be tempted to venerate the two as masterpieces of creation. The stars are certainly marvellous but as regards conscience, God has done an uneven and careless job [. . .]. We do not fail to appreciate the bit of psychological truth that is contained in the claim that conscience is of divine origin, but the sentence requires interpretation. If conscience is something 'in us', then it is, however, not so from the beginning. It is quite a counterpart to sexual life which is really there straight from the beginning of life and is not superadded only later.[10]

Rather than following Kant and becoming a pious person, Freud follows Spinoza and Nietzsche when he uncovers the appetites as the ground of morality. By turning upside down the anthropomorphic narrative of conscience or reason as original divine endowment, Freud ironically translates the contaminating force of sexual drives into the point of origin of all human values. The excessive contamination of sexual drives limits rather than aggrandises humanity's position in the universe. Instead of confirming the quasi-divine status of morality, Freud naturalises all aspects of human society. This naturalisation is so all-encompassing that it includes the realm of cultural and intellectual achievements.

Intellectual or spiritual achievements are not the offspring of a divine gift mirroring the sublimity of the stars, but rather they emerge from the plasticity of the libido. The plasticity of the libido is at once organic and cerebral: 'In Freud "plasticity" mainly designates two essential phenomena: on the one hand, *the vitality of the libido*, its capacity to change its object and resist fixation; on the other hand, *the indestructible character of psychic life*. Within the psyche nothing is forgotten; traces have an indestructible character' (Malabou 2012: 18). Malabou sees, however, in Freud's notion of indestructibility the danger of a new form of religion or immortality.

Does Freud's understanding of the plasticity of the psyche and the libido give rise to a quasi-religious assumption of life beyond death? Malabou criticises Freud for not taking into account the destructive connotations of 'plasticity': 'If brain damage creates a new identity, this *creation can be only a creation through the destruction of form*. The plasticity at stake here is thus destructive plasticity' (Malabou 2012: 17). Does Freud's notion of the death drive not describe precisely destructive plasticity? Surely Freud does not propound a new theory of human immortality which would reinstate the anthropomorphism of God, which is the point of his critique of religion. He perceives in religion the main enemy of his 'new science', because it does not allow for human finitude and precludes an unsavoury view of humanity's intellectual achievements. Freud does not take issue with art and literature, because they do not presume to be anything else but illusions.

Freud contaminates science with literature and the arts. His 'new science' is indeed heavily indebted to works of art and literature. One could even say that he takes their purported illusion to be a true reflection of psychic reality. A striking example is the Oedipus complex. Freud believes in the actual truth of the Oedipus myth. The Oedipus myth articulates our unacknowledged desires. They are unacknowledged because any acknowledgement of their actuality would be an intolerable offence to humanity's quasi-divine self-image (surely as images of God we must not have any unconscious desire to be so depraved as to want to kill our father and to sleep with our mother).

Freud values art for 'not daring to make any encroachments into the realm of reality'.[11] As his reading of the Oedipus myth illustrates, Freud does, however, employ the self-professed illusion of art for a better understanding of psychic reality. In Beverley Clack's words, 'engagement with Freud's work is fruitful precisely because he takes seriously the power that phantasy has to shape one's experience of the world' (Clack 2008: 209). Freud's new science is far from being positivistic in so far as it attends to dreams and other forms of consciousness such as religious narratives or myths that are ostensibly illusory and cannot be proven in any quantitative way. In what is pertinent for the discussion in the following chapter, Freud's new science contaminates the visible with the invisible, presence with absence, evidence with what is evidentially not there, and yet exerts a graspable impact on a given society (such as religion, myth and fiction).

Freud's method, however, is empiricist: he observes the details of an illusory reality in a way similar to the way a physicist or chemist depicts the progress of an experiment. The crucial point here is that Freud's new scientist dedicates such time and energy to the observation of false consciousness because it forms a substantial part of our psychic condition. In Spinozist terms, false consciousness is a lamentable but necessary ingredient of humanity. Spinoza's rationalism consists in recognising falsehood. Both Spinoza and Freud take issue with theology and philosophy, because these two disciplines tend to focus on the mind's perfection while paying scant attention to where and when it makes mistakes. Psychoanalysis, on the contrary, focuses on the mind's blind spots. It is, however, not judgemental but treats mental failures as inevitable or, in Spinoza's terms, necessary aspects of our humanity with which we have to reckon (rather than dismiss them as unworthy of scientific discussion).

It is then unsurprising that, next to the anthropomorphic conception of God as found in various religions, Freud should discuss the discipline of philosophy as hostile to his 'new science'. Like religion, philosophy proclaims to be promulgating nothing less than the truth. One of its illusions, however, consists in its claim to 'proffer an unbroken and consistent world view'.[12] Freud's new science contaminates philosophical consistency with the inconsistency that shapes our embodied mortal but also communally eternal life (the individual dies and yet individual traits persevere in the ongoing life of society at large – this is what Vatter described earlier as Spinoza's mortal and yet eternal realm of immanence).

According to Freud, philosophy's methodology is even more questionable, because it 'overrates the cognitive value of our logical operation'.[13] Philosophy shares with religion the illusion of an omniscient quasi-divine mind. Similar to the way that Spinoza warns against electing either philosophy or theology as the key to a full understanding of biblical texts, Freud differentiates his 'new science' from the lofty sphere of the pure mind as found in secular form in philosophy and in spiritual shape in religion. Rather than endowing our cognitive capacities with an infallible, quasi-divine power, Freud asks us to be mindful of our mind by contaminating the mental with the corporeal, the psychological with the organic.

Freud makes the mind mindful of its origination within the dark and unsavoury sphere of the drives. The drives are themselves a product of the contamination between the psychological and the organic. Attending to these contaminations helps bring to the fore repressed memories. Freud sees a resistance to this work of remembrance not so much in the relatively small world of philosophy, but in the larger ambience of religion, particularly in Christianity. 'Philosophy, however', Freud writes, 'does not have an immediate influence on a large amount of people; it only catches the interest of a small number, and of that small number only a tiny elite of intellectuals; and philosophy is unfathomable for everyone else.'[14] Religion, on the other hand, shapes the lives of most people. Freud considers in particular Christian and Jewish salvation narratives in which he sees the nucleus of endowing morality with a quasi-divine force. Those who conceive of intellect and will as pertaining to God transcribe human values and human cognition into the sphere of Divinity.

This unduly aggrandises the mind. The divinisation of humanity's intellect prevents a critical engagement with the way the mind assists rather than checks the destructive and self-destructive life of the passions. Abstractions veil what is actually occurring at the interface that contaminates the cerebral with the emotive. Malabou denies Freud's knowledge of an interconnection between the cerebral and the affective: 'Could it be that psychoanalysis hasn't said everything on the subject of psychic suffering? Could it be, precisely, that it ignores the suffering of the brain and along with it, the emotive and emotional dimension of the brain?' (Malabou 2012: xiii). Clearly Freud's new science does not invalidate or deny the mind's reliance on emotions.

Conclusion

As we have seen in this chapter, following Spinoza (and also Nietzsche) Freud takes issue with both theology and philosophy for covering the often unsavoury aspects of the emotive life of the brain or mind with grandiose abstractions. These abstractions precisely constitute the resistance to psychoanalysis. Those who dismiss Freud's new science in fact reject critical engagement with how the mind is itself contaminated by spectres of corporality. Our sexual constitution certainly refers to embodied existence. As we have seen, the cerebral and the organic meet in the Freudian notion of drives.

Rather than ignoring the brain's suffering – as Malabou claims – Freud discovers the contamination of our psyche with the passions of our embodied life. He certainly did not dismiss neuroscientific attempts at understanding the brain as embodiment of the mind. Indeed, as Eric R. Kandel has pointed out, 'a keen student of the anatomy of the brain, Freud had written repeatedly about the relevance of the biology of the brain to psychoanalysis' (Kandel 2006: 45). What Freud sees as 'resistance to sexuality' (Pfister 1963: 63) results from an anthropomorphic conception of God, which, in Cartesian fashion, prioritises the mind over the body (the brain). Freud's psychoanalysis radicalises Spinoza's demand to be mindful of the mind; that is to say, to attend to the ways in which the corporeal contaminates the cerebral. Resistance to such mindfulness originates in a loss of reality, where the mind has assumed the position of omniscience and omnipotence attributed to God by theology.

The incompatibility of neuroscience and psychoanalysis is thus not to be found in (according to Žižek) the demoted pre-critical Spinozism of the former and the assumed Kantianism of the latter. Rather than being incompatible, psychoanalysis and neuroscience contaminate each other. As we have seen earlier, Freud does not conceptualise the self as substance-less, non-organic, non-biological entity. Instead he tries to evaluate when and how the 'I' loses a sense of her material conditions (the reality principle). To prevent such loss, Freud attempts to weaken resistance to the scientific insight into our contaminated constitution wherein mind and body, psychology and biology, psychoanalysis and neuroscience are enmeshed with each other.

This chapter has analysed how in different ways both Spinoza and Freud try to re-evaluate demoted forms of what Agamben (see Chapter 7) would later call 'bare life'. Here demoted life is a matter of the body and nature. There are, however, also constructions of an order of nature which establish hierarchies between the natural and the societal. These constructions contrast the posited purity of nature with the deviance of human psychology. Even though this mentally constructed order of nature operates under a different nomenclature (the natural here represents the perfection of the cerebral as opposed to the irrationalism of the human psyche), here too the opposition of pure binaries is liable to eventuate in violent forms of resistance and confrontation rather than in the contamination and reconciliation of two purportedly irreconcilable aspects of our constitution.

The following two chapters will thus discuss the larger historical context of a new scientific paradigm of contamination which was critiqued by Bruno Latour as modernity's purification project. As analysed by Latour, this project constructs a divide between the natural and the human, between nature and society, which can of course never be put into practice, because, as the discussion in the current chapter has shown, the human mind is itself embodied (as brain) and the natural and the societal are deeply interwoven. In this context the following shows how the divide between nature and humanity turns deleterious at the point at which the unpredictability of the human psyche is seen to contrast sharply with the transparency and predictability of 'nature'.

In what ways has a mental construction of nature as harmonious and predictable (from the economic and medical discourse of François Quesnay and his fellow physiocrats onwards) become the model for an ideal or virtuous human society? Here we encounter a utopia that turns out to be a dystopia: an ideal societal order that would mimetically replicate the mentally constructed order of nature in that it would have overcome deviance and other forms of human unpredictability. Revising Latour's thesis, the following chapter argues that the divide between nature and society serves to create theories of human inadequacy and worse still (later in the twentieth century) exclusion, criminalisation and genocide. Modernity's purification project (as theorised by Latour) denies various contaminations. First, it posits an order of nature in terms of visibility and predictability. It then proceeds to contrast this construction of an ordered natural sphere with the supposed unpredictability, the deviance and the unnatural or perverse nature of certain groups of people (ethnic, religious or occupational).

How can we explain that the first modern attempt to subjugate the self under the homogeneous rule of the state proceeded under the concept of natural affect? Far from abandoning a Cartesian mind–body divide, Robespierre refers to emotions as the visible concretisation of virtue. As a result of such reduction, ethics becomes naturalised, a matter to be measured by the mind. The reign of terror followed the concept of natural order first established by the physiocrats. The following two chapters will also analyse how certain literary works of the mid-nineteenth century which refer to the guillotine and the reign of terror question the reduction of our embodied nature to what is measurable, monolithic and predictable, here anticipating the argument of Antonio Damasio and other leading contemporary neuroscientists.

Notes

1. For a critique of what I call flat mimesis see Mack (2012).
2. Translating Freud's *Ich* as 'ego' can be misleading: the term *ego* seems to be related to the notion of egoism. Freud's *Ich* does not encompass such semantic associations. However, I refer to the common translation of 'ego' for *Ich* in order not to confuse the reader.
3. 'Zwei große Kränkungen ihrer naiven Eigenliebe hat die Menschheit im Laufe der Zeiten von der Wissenschaft erdulden müssen. Die erste, als sie erfuhr, daß unsere Erde nicht der Mittelpunkt des Weltalls ist, sondern ein winziges Teilchen eines in seiner Größe kaum vorstellbaren Weltsystems. Sie knüpft sich für uns an den Namen Kopernikus, obwohl schon die alexandrinische Wissenschaft ähnliches verkündet hatte. Die zweite dann, als die biologische Forschung das angebliche Schöpfungsvorerecht des Menschen zunichte machte, ihn die Abstammung aus dem Tierreich und die Unvertilgbarkeit seiner animalischen Natur verwies. Diese Umwertung hat sich in unseren Tagen unter dem Einfluß von Ch. Darwin, Wallace und

ihren Vorgängern nicht ohne das heftigste Sträuben seiner Zeitgenossen vollzigen. Die dritte und empfindlichste Kränkung aber soll die menschliche Größensucht durch die heutige psychologische Forschung erfahren, welche dem Ich nachweisen will, daß es nicht einmal Herr ist im eigenen Hause, sondern auf kärgliche Nachrichten angewiesen bleibt von dem, was unbewußt in seinem Seelenleben vorgeht' (Freud 1975 Vol. 1: 283–4). My translation.

4. 'Ein sonderbarer Trieb, der sich mit der Zerstörung seines eigenen Heims befaßt!' My translation.
5. 'Wie sich die beiden im Lebensprozeß vermengen, wie der Todestrieb den Absichten des Eros dienstbar gemacht wird.' My translation.
6. Freud called Heine an *Unglaubensgenossen* in the *Future of an Illusion* (Freud 1975 Vol. 9: 183). And in his monograph on *Jokes and their Relation to the Unconscious* he quotes the Heine excerpt where Heine uses the term *Unglaubensgenosse* as synonym for Spinoza: ' "Mein Unglaubensgenosse Spinoza", sagt Heine' (Freud 1975 Vol. 4: 75).
7. 'Nur Unverstand und Böswilligkeit konnten dieser Lehre das Beiwort "atheistisch" beilegen. Keiner hat sich jemals erhabener über die Gottheit ausgesprochen wie Spinoza. Statt zu sagen, er leugne Gott, könnte man sagen, er leugne die Menschen. Alle endlichen Dinge sind ihm nur Modi der unendlichen Substanz. Alle endliche Dinge sind in Gott enthalten, der menschliche Geist ist nur ein Lichtstrahl des unendlichen Denkens, der menschliche Leib nur ein Atom der unendlichen Ausdehnung; Gott ist die unendliche Ursache beider, der Geister und Leiber, natura naturans' (Heine 1968: 95).
8. 'Diese Übereinstimmung mit der realen Außenwelt heißen wir Wahrheit.' (Freud 1975 Vol. 1: 597). My translation.
9. 'Die Moralität, die uns angeblich von Gott verliehen wurde' (Freud 1975 Vol. 1: 500). My translation.
10. 'In Anlehnung an einen bekannten Ausspruch Kants, der das Gewissen in uns mit dem gestirnten Himmel zusammenbringt, könnte ein Frommer wohl versucht sein, diese beiden als die Meisterstücke der Schöpfung zu verehren. Die Gestirne sind gewiß großartig, aber was das Gewissen betrifft, so hat Gott hierin ungleichmäßige und nachlässige Arbeit geleistet, denn eine große Überzahl von Menschen hat davon nu rein bescheidenes Maß oder kaum so viel, als noch der Rede wert ist, mitbekommen. Wir verkennen das Stück psychologischer Wahrheit keineswegs, das in der Behauptung, das Gewissen sei göttlicher Herkunft enthalten ist, aber der Satz bedarf einer Deutung. Wenn das Gewissen auch etwas in "in uns" ist, so ist es doch von nicht von Anfang an. Es ist so recht ein Gegensatz zum Sexualleben, das wirklich von Anfang des Lebens an da ist und nicht erst später hinzukommt' (Freud 1975 Vol. 1: 500). My translation.
11. 'wagt sie kein Übergriffe ins Reich der Realität' (Freud 1975 Vol. 1: 588). My translation.
12. 'ein lückenloses und zusammenhängendes Weltbild liefern zu können' (Freud 1975 Vol. 1: 588). My translation.
13. 'sie den den Erkenntniswert unserer logischen Operationen überschätzt' (Freud 1975 Vol. 1: 588). My translation.
14. 'Aber die Philosophy hat keinen unmittelbaren Einfluß auf die große

Menge von Menschen, sie ist das Interesse einer geringen Anzahl selbst von der Oberschicht der Intellektuellen, für alle anderen kaum faßbar' (Freud 1975 Vol. 1: 588). My translation.

Contaminating the Visible with the Invisible: From Einstein via H. G. Wells to Hannah Arendt, Luhmann and Derrida

'You are invisible now'
        Bob Dylan, 'Like a Rolling Stone' (1965)

Introduction: Einstein's and Latour's contamination of objectivity with subjectivity

In what ways does the Cartesian division between mind and body reinforce hostility to what is invisible and immeasurable? According to Descartes, the body is matter and as such subject to measurement and control by a sovereign mind. The mind, however, remains invisible and cannot be measured. We cannot grasp the mind as an external object. How can we then claim to know that it rules sovereign over the bare life of the body? The invisibility of the mind also denotes the lack of a clear definition distinguishing or separating it from the corporeal. As we have seen in the preceding chapter, new neuroscientific findings have shown that the mind is linked to the body in an inseparable loop.

However, this interconnection between the corporeal and the cerebral does not solve the mystery of the mind's invisibility: the brain may be the material foundation for mental activities but these activities cannot be grasped through any empirical measurements of the grey matter and the skull. As we shall see below, the division between mind and body had particular resonance in the nineteenth century, because Victorian brain-worship in its striking positivism proved inconclusive, especially in semi-para-natural disciplines like phrenology.

Avant-garde twentieth-century science began to take issue with notions of certainty and objectivity which preoccupied nineteenth-century positivism. As Lorraine Daston and Peter Galison have recently shown, 'many early twentieth-century scientists increasingly concluded that subjectivity could never be extirpated. Some frankly espoused the need for subjective judgment in the production and use of scientific images; objectivity without subjectivity was, they concluded, an ultimately self-defeating ambition' (Daston and Galison 2007: 190). Twentieth-century science consciously and conscientiously contaminated the subjective with the objective, recognising that nineteenth-century positivism tried to expurgate the subjective element through an effort of the will.

The paradigm governing science from the mid-nineteenth century to the early twentieth century was what Daston and Galison have called 'mechanical objectivity': 'By *mechanical objectivity* we mean the insistent drive to repress the wilful interventions of the artist-author, and to put in its stead a set of procedures that would, as it were, move nature to the page through a strict protocol, if not automatically' (Daston and Galison 2007: 121). While these 'protocols aimed to let the specimen appear without that distortion characteristic of observer's personal tastes, commitments, or ambitions' (Daston and Galison 2007: 121), they were themselves the product of a subjective desire to supress the will.

We could define positivism's mechanical objectivity as the will's wilful self-extirpation. Rather than being purely 'objective', a certain interpretative and Kantian moral perspective shaped the operations of mechanical objectivity: 'Only the "good" will, which acted solely in accord with the "objective laws" ordained by reason, was genuinely autonomous, insofar as the will was also swayed by personal inclinations and interests, "as it really is with humans," it remained less than free' (Daston and Galison 2007: 210). Twentieth-century avant-garde science, by contrast, contaminated objectivity with subjectivity, truth with relativity.

A case in point is Einstein's relativity and unified field theory: 'Einstein took special relativity to shatter the objectivity that seemed to characterize time by itself. Time could be defined objectively only alongside space' (Daston and Galison 2007: 302). Rather than being pure, time's objectivity is always contaminated by the subjective position of those who find themselves in a specific space:

> In the special theory of relativity two events simultaneously in one constantly moving reference frame are not simultaneous in another: as Einstein says, '"Now" loses for the spatially extended world its objective meaning. It is because of this that space and time must be regarded as a four-dimensional continuum that is objectively irresoluble, if it is desired to express ... objective relations without unnecessary conventional arbitrariness.' In other words, two observers will disagree as to the separation of two events in both space and time – there is no unique division between differences in space and differences in time that will be shared by all observers. (Daston and Galison 2007: 302)

Einstein redefined scientific objectivity in terms of contamination: 'Einstein did not take objectivity itself to be purely objective' (Daston and Galison 2007: 303). Rather than being a pure entity, the objective cannot be grasped apart from being contaminated by the subjective:

> In the case of relativity, Einstein took subjective time to be the beginning of our construction of objective, coordinated time. That subjective starting point, alongside what he always insisted was a *conventional* method for coordinating clocks, showed very clearly how inextricable the subjective and the objective were within a theory. (Daston and Galison 2007: 303)

Einstein implicitly introduced the figure of 'contamination' into science by showing how scientific objectivity cannot be purified from its purported opposite – the subjective element of interpretation. This does not mean that Einstein plays off the subjective against the objective. On the contrary, he undermines the certainty of our Kantian synthetic judgements which remain mired in our own subject position and fail to take into account the complexity and uncertainty of our environment.[1]

As Daston and Galison have argued, Einstein's insight into the mutual contamination between objectivity and subjectivity has been largely ignored in our contemporary obsession with positivist certainty that clings to the purported evidence of what can be measured as opposed to what remains immeasurable or invisible: 'The suspicion of the individual, the private, the sectarian, and the ineffable has, if anything, deepened: the positive ideal of objective knowledge as that which remains invariant under the transformations of any and all perspectives is still current' (Daston and Galison 2007: 305–6). Rather than allowing for a contamination of the quantitative with the qualitative, the objective with the subjective, current public opinion pitches one against the other, and as part of this purification project the assumed objectivity of science seems to remain incompatible with the taken for granted subjectivity of the arts (the humanities, literature and cinema and so forth).

In the meantime, literary and cultural theory in the mid-twentieth century has come to be wrongly associated with the promotion of a distorted image of the humanities and arts wherein they have abandoned all pretensions to objectivity or universality. Objectivity and universality seem to be the exclusive precinct and prerogative of the sciences. The figure of contamination – as evoked in this book – tries to unsettle such firm or purified classifications. As Einstein has shown in his relativity theory, the subjective might well be the cornerstone of what we have come to see as the objective.

Rather than laying claims to either subjectivity or objectivity, we should allow for a contamination of both. Contamination here is as much physical as it is conscious and conscientious: it is one where we are aware of the pitfalls and limitations of both the subjective and the objective. In this way it would be as distortive to reject positivistic elements in the arts and humanities as it would be deleterious to banish interpretative and critical efforts from our scientific endeavours.

There might be ways of contaminating positivism and interpretation not only in the arts but also in the sciences. One striking proponent of such contaminating work is indeed Albert Einstein. As Jeroen van Dongen has recently shown, Einstein gradually distanced himself from Ernst Mach's positivism which shaped his early philosophical point of view:

> The empiricist attitude of Ernst Mach, prominent in the late nineteenth century, implied that one should remain as close as possible to the experimental facts: one should confine oneself to searching out the most economic statements of relations of observation. Broadly speaking, one can say that Einstein moved from Mach's empiricism, earlier in his career, to a strong realist position later on. But at no given moment can one decisively put him in either camp. (Dongen 2010: 37)

Einstein's position in-between the metaphysics of realism (realism 'has maintained that the claims of scientific theories are true of a reality independent of us': Dongen 2010: 37) and the positivism of empiricism allows for a contamination of the factual with what remains out of our reach and thereby 'invisible'.

Twentieth-century field theory departs from holders of certainty and measurability which influence the mutually opposed approaches of empiricism and realism. As Timothy Morton has recently put it: 'Quantum theory extends the non-mechanism inherent in relativity theory' (Morton 2013: 41). Field theory as well as quantum physics overturned traditional notions of modern science as formulated by Newton and then by Kant: 'The great appeal of Kant's system had been that it warranted the feeling that geometry, arithmetic and the fundamental principles of Newtonian kinematics were too certain to be based merely on generalization from experience' (Dongen 2010: 46). In this way Kant read Newton's empiricism in terms of a realist position, of a priori established laws and truths:

> Contra Hume, Kant argued that there are such necessary and more than merely inductive laws. Kant found examples of these in the principles of Newtonian mechanics, i.e. the law of conservation of matter or the equality of action and reaction. These are synthetic a priori principles: human understanding guarantees the a priori truths of these principles. Our understanding

can further elevate inductively established rules to necessary and universal laws. (Dongen 2010: 45)

Einstein, however, 'felt that the fundamental principles of geometry and physics cannot be grounded in some a priori fashion. Instead, he emphasized that they are "free creations of the human mind"' (Dongen 2010: 46). By rejecting the Kantian version of Newtonian physics (i.e. 'Kant's a priori necessary truths': Dongen 2010: 46), Einstein allows for the non-predictable and uncertain, for what may be invisible now but might become visible later on.[2]

Van Dongen emphasises the uncertain and revisable character of Einstein's approach to not only what is visibly or measurably there (and so following a positivist approach) but also to what theory posits in a certain or a priori manner (realism) about what remains (to us at least) invisible: 'But one could never be certain that a theory is correct: there is always the possibility that additional observation would prove it wrong' (Dongen 2010: 53). Einstein departs from the dogmatism of nineteenth-century positivism while remaining wary of a priori notions of certainty which, in Kantian manner, translate empirical laws into metaphysical ones. At the same time he does not abandon metaphysics as such: 'I believe that every true theorist is a kind of tamed metaphysicist, no matter how pure a "positivist" he may fancy himself' (Einstein 1950: 13).

In some ways learning from the mistakes of nineteenth-century science, twentieth-century field theory and string theory as well as some strands within contemporary neuroscience refrain from claiming to have discovered crudely positivist explanations of intellectual work. What neuroscience makes visible is the corporeal ground of the mind's invisible operations.

The question of the invisible, immeasurable and the non-territorial has been a constant reason for provocation and irritation for secular or modern attempts to solve the riddles of the universe. Here the nineteenth century again plays a crucial role for a conception of scientific modernity with which we are still trying to come to terms. As Bennett Zon has clearly put it:

> The liminal state between mind and body, the unmeasurable and the measurable, was no further advanced by the Victorians, but it did go some way to paralysing modernity with uncertainty and fear. Determination to objectify the mysteriously invisible – in effect to make the invisible visible – caused great anxiety. Darwin tried it with modification by descent, otherwise known as evolution. When exactly is an evolutionary change observable? The fact is that evolution is invisible, yet measurable over intangibly vast stretches of time.[3]

Focusing further on various contaminations of what have traditionally been depicted as incompatible entities (the visible and the invisible, mind and body, and so forth), Chapters 3 and 4 will discuss how the inability to materialise and rationalise invisibility also led to sexual aggression (in Nathaniel Hawthorne) and violence (in Hermann Melville). This chapter will analyse how the damage resulting from such frustration and aggression caused disenchantment with our experience in the world – or in other words a secular loss of the world, which philosopher Hannah Arendt describes in her book *The Human Condition*. Arendt responds to the conundrum of nineteenth-century positivism in her critique of science and secularisation. Positivism held out the promise of making us more at home in the world by illuminating what had so far been dark or invisible. Rather than making our planet more homely, however, a preoccupation with the merely visible and measurable has reduced and diminished our horizon for diverse encounters in a multidimensional sphere which goes under the name 'world'.

Arendt's and Einstein's dissatisfaction with positivism is not entirely new. In her novel *Middlemarch* George Eliot demonstrated the absurdity of positivist claims to find the key to the enigmas of both the human mind and the embodied natural world. One aspect of the novel illuminates the futility (Edward Causabon) of finding the key to all mythologies (the mind). Dr Lydgate's search for a route towards understanding the origins of nature and the body proves fruitless too. In her scientific scepticism Eliot responds critically to the positivist promise to discover a universal and objective formula capable of explaining and predicting the future, targeting in her critique various assumptions of certainty.

This chapter discusses how the obsession with a world purified of all uncertainty has led to various pitfalls in modern science and politics. As Akira Mizuta Lippit has recently pointed out, expectations of rendering the invisible visible and the uncertain certain were frustrated rather than encouraged by new scientific discoveries at the end of the nineteenth century: 'X-rays and cinema, along with the technique of psychoanalysis, established in 1895 new technologies for visualising the inside, for imagining interiority; but they also transformed the conditions of visuality as such' (Lippit 2005: 30). In this way, the scientific preoccupation with the invisible does not endorse positivist notions of certainty, transparency and visible evidence. Thus, the X-ray does not eradicate the invisible. It merely allows us to see what is inside us and what nevertheless remains obfuscate: 'Not so much an exposure as a disclosure, the X-ray reveals secret visibility as a mode of secret visuality, showing what nonetheless remains invisible, without operation or accident' (Lippit 2005: 32). In a similar way, the scientific technique that operates cinematography removes from presence what it ostensibly illuminates:

> A secret sign and homonym that signifies in two registers, bringing together ashes and movement. To *cinefy*: to make move, to make cinema and to incinerate, to reduce to ashes. Traces and residues of movement, and the movement of ashes. *Cinefaction*. Like the true story of your death, a secret cinema, registered in the unimaginable depths and interiority of the Library of Babel at the end of the universe. Burning and disappearing, atomic ...'
> (Lippit 2005: 33)

From the *fin de siècle* onwards modern scientific discoveries reveal the paradoxes of sight, movement and enlightenment. Light does not only illuminate, but it also blinds and incinerates.

Radical twentieth-century science – such as Einstein's new approach to physics and quantum physics – has overturned traditional scientific notions of hierarchical dichotomies and clear separations between supposedly incompatible fields (including the supposed incompatibility of the subjective and the objective).[4]

As N. Katherine Hayles has pointed out, 'One of the important points of continuity between Romanticism and the field concept [i.e. as encountered in twentieth-century physics] is the appearance of inherent limits on sequential, logical analysis' (Hayles 1984: 9).[5] In a related way, contemporary neuroscience has discovered a parallelism between body and mind. In so doing, it has also analysed how such discoveries pose a challenge to traditional science (or natural philosophy) from Descartes to Žižek.

The following analysis of a paradoxical secular retreat from the world prepares for the discussion of a possible source for such loss of immanence in the worship of virtuous affect that justifies Robespierre's enlightened reign of terror (see Chapter 3). This and the following chapter attend to the conundrum of a scientific loss of the secular, by interrogating the ways in which modern literature has questioned mind–body distinctions as a response to – on a political level – Robespierre's reign of terror and the ensuing scientific positivism of the mid-nineteenth century.

Literature has proved resistant to such illusions of all-encompassing visibility and measurability, not least because one of its subject matters is subjectivity, which is another word for what goes on in our mind. Literature illuminates the ways in which what we take to be subjective is already contaminated by the objective. Conversely, it sheds light on the subjective foundations of what has been categorised as objective. This is also the point of Sylvia Plath's poem 'Daddy', which deflates the image of an objective father figure – representing 'all there is' – to a bizarre and obscene, highly biased representative of Nazi ideology: a German WWII Panzermann.[6]

This is not to deny objectivity but to alert us to the ways in which the objective is implicated in the subjective (see Mack 2014). In order to gain a more truthful or nuanced view we need to take seriously biased positions which claim to represent the universal and objective but which are in fact parochial. As Daston and Galison have shown, from its scholastic origins the term objectivity has been exposed to contaminations with subjectivity, albeit here the two words go with a reversed order of meaning:

> From the very beginning, it [i.e. objectivity] was always paired with *subjectivus/subjective*, but the terms originally meant almost precisely the opposite of what they mean today. 'Objective' referred to things as they are presented to consciousness, whereas 'subjective' referred to things in themselves. (Daston and Galison 2007: 29)

It was Kant who introduced derogatory connotations into the term subjective by associating subjectivity with the illusory and inferior sphere of our relationship with the empirical world which is our external environment (heteronomy): 'And his habit of using "subjective" as a rough synonym for "merely empirical sensations" shares with the later usage only the sneer with which the word is intoned' (Daston and Galison 2007: 30). When 'sometime *circa* 1850 the modern sense of "objectivity" had arrived in the major European languages, still paired with its ancestral opposite "subjectivity"' (Daston and Galison 2007: 31), both terms 'had turned 180 degrees in meaning' (Daston and Galison 2007: 31).

Now objectivity had become a scientific ideal whereas subjectivity was to be avoided at all costs in any quest for accuracy and truth:

> Objectivity the thing was as new as objectivity the word in the mid-nineteenth century. Starting in the mid-nineteenth century, men of science began to fret openly about a new kind of obstacle to knowledge: themselves. Their fear was that the subjective self was prone to prettify, idealize, and, in the worst case, regularize observations to fit theoretical expectations: to see what it hoped to see. Their predecessors a generation or two before had also been beset by epistemological worries, but theirs were about the variability of nature, rather than the projections of the naturalist. (Daston and Galison 2007: 34)

From now on science laid claim to objectivity, whereas literature and the arts were seen to be confined to the epistemological limitations and distortions that go with subjectivity: 'The scientific self of the mid-nineteenth century was perceived by contemporaries as diametrically opposed to the artistic self, just as scientific images were routinely contrasted to artistic ones' (Daston and Galison 2007: 37). However, such radical contrast between scientific objectivity and artistic subjectivity neglects how these opposed terms contaminate each other. Some aspects of mid-nineteenth-century literature highlight how investigations into the subjective sphere of the mind illuminate where presumptions of scientific objectivity create new distortions rather than new truth.

The theoretical discussion of this chapter prepares the ground for the analysis of literary works from the mid-nineteenth century which react not only – as Eliot's *Middlemarch* does – to the positivism in the social and natural sciences, but also to the quest for certainty in the everyday praxis of politics and economics. One striking case is how long before contemporary neuroscience that literature discovered the human mind as embodied and yet invisible.

Meanwhile, neuroscience has had to abandon models of explanation which claimed to have fully grasped the workings of the mind through quantifiable evidence: from nineteenth-century phrenology – which professed to make the mind fully measurable through the study of the skull – to the twentieth-century neuroscientific doctrine of the fully grown and static brain of adults. As John Lehrer has put it, 'the Cartesian impulse to worship the brain and ignore the body gave rise to the new "science" of phrenology' (Lehrer 2007: 3). Following Descartes, the neuroscientists of the nineteenth century 'looked for the soul solely in the head, desperate to reduce the mind to cranial causes' (Lehrer 2007: 5). In the twentieth century the doctrine of the measurability of the brain gave way to Pasko Rakic's 'theory of the fixed brain' (Lehrer 2007: 39), maintaining that 'a human was born with a complete set of neurons' (Lehrer 2007: 38) which after infancy remain incapable of change or further development. Far from being assessable through skull measurements and far from ever reaching a measurable state of full growth, the mind constantly generates itself. Contemporary neuroscience has discovered that neurons renew themselves and thus form the plasticity of the brain. The brain's plasticity also reinforces its resistance to measurement. How can we measure and depict in visible terms something like the mind-brain which keeps changing its composition? Our brain and our mind cannot be pinned down to a visible, measurable manifestation. Rather than being either one thing or another, the cerebral undergoes contaminations with the corporeal, mutating from visible (neurons) to invisible operations (such as thought and emotions). Plasticity denotes precisely such mutations wherein visibility and invisibility contaminate each other.

Contaminating the Visible with the Invisible 59

We can see the operations of the mind in various manifestations but its substance remains invisible. As this brief account of the pitfalls of neuroscientific attempts to make visible and measurable the working of the mind has shown, issues of the not-to-be-fully-grasped and the immeasurable persist in our current culture, which defines science (as Daston and Galison have shown) in purely positivistic terms.

One could indeed say that a split between the measurable and the non-demonstrable distinguishes modernity (and our current form of high modernity) from what preceded it. Bruno Latour has described this gap between facts and subjects, between visibility and the obscure, in terms of the conceptual gulf between nature (non-humans) and humanity (culture, politics, society), which he sees as foundational for modernity's self-understanding. As we shall see, in this split between the natural and the societal – replicating the Cartesian mind–body divide – society has been cast in a rather problematic setting, because human psychology cannot be fully measured and controlled.

Nature, by contrast, holds out the promise of full control, order, harmony, transparency and measurability. Conversely, mind could be associated with society and body with nature. This is so because the conception of nature in terms of order is itself a mental construct. Mental constructions are superimposed on what is perceived as mere matter, mere embodiment or, as Giorgio Agamben puts it, the 'bare life'. According to Agamben, the various divisions of life (i.e. into mind and body, societal and natural, and so forth) are themselves symptomatic of how our culture avoids establishing definitions of what constitutes 'life': 'everything happens as if, in our culture, life were *what cannot be defined, yet, precisely for this reason, must be ceaselessly articulated and divided*' (Agamben 2004: 13). In other words, the political duality between a natural order of the mind and the potential disorder of the extended societal body furthers social divisions between those who come to represent the posited order of nature – which turns out to be a mentally constructed order – and those who are seen to embody the potential disorder of society at large.

According to Latour we have never been modern for the reason that the modern purification project – premised as it is on the radical separation between nature's supposed order and society's potential disorder – has actually never been put into practice. Where theories proliferate that posit the existence of pure entities – such as objectivity versus subjectivity – mutual contaminations between these notional oppositions are in fact prevalent.

Latour thus argues that the division between 'here, on the left, [where there] are things themselves; [and] there on the right, [with] the free society of speaking, thinking subjects, values and signs' (Latour 1993: 37) does not work, because the two separated spheres of non-human fact and human consciousness require mediations. He continues in such terms: 'Everything happens in the middle, everything passes between the two, everything happens by way of mediation, translation and networks, but this space does not exist, it has no place. It is the unthinkable, the unconscious of the moderns' (Latour 1993: 37). Latour calls this excluded middle of mediation between the objective and the subjective, between science and politics, between fact and its social usages, either network or translation.

This mediating work is unconscious because modernity's constitution denies its existence. The term contamination, by contrast, awakens to consciousness various mediations which the modern purification project has relegated to unconsciousness. The figure of contamination acts by dint of its scandalous connotations that evoke an array of medico-cultural horrors ranging from the abject, to the defiled, the infected and the impure.

By radically separating science from society, the modern constitution proclaims, however, the purity of objective visibility, which it separates from the vagaries that accompany social and political life. Following Stephen Shapin and Simon Schaffer's revolutionary account of the history of science, Latour points out that the objective visibility of scientific fact is itself a construction of science's modern setting: the laboratory.

Modernity ignores, or more radically still, flatly denies the element of subjective construction in both scientific as well as socio-political representations of what is purportedly objective: 'Boyle and his countless successors go on and on both constructing Nature artificially and stating that they are discovering it; Hobbes and the newly defined citizens go on and on constructing the Leviathan by dint of calculation and social force, but they recruit more and more objects in order to make it last' (Latour 1993: 31). In this way both nature and society are rendered objective, while the work of subjective construction officially remains invisible, unacknowledged, or as Latour puts it in the quote above, 'unconscious'.

The figure of contamination brings to the level of consciousness the fusion of the objective and the subjective, the visible and the invisible. Further developing Latour's analysis one could define modernity as the repression of the invisible or as *the unconscious of the invisible*. Modernity falls prey to delusions when it denies the existence of invisible factors constituting the workings of our minds. Denial may give rise to repression or to aggression. The focus on forcing the invisible into the visible and on reducing the immeasurable to what can be measured in this chapter prepares for an analysis in Chapter 3 of both the frustration and the aggression that accompanies such attempts. As we shall see there, in a discussion of key texts from the mid-nineteenth century, literature explores the ways in which the self-deluding or fictitious aspects of the modern constitution first deny or repress (sexuality in Hawthorne's *The Scarlet Letter*) and then attack (the obsessive and violent quest for the white and quasi-invisible whale in Melville's *Moby Dick*) what remains hidden, invisible or ghostly sensory (the result of the first violent encounter with the whale which leaves Captain Ahab with the invisible sensation of his amputated leg).

Approaches to secularisation and Hannah Arendt's critique of a scientific loss of the world

Whereas (according to Latour) the unrealisable project of modernity disputes the validity or, more radically still, the existence of the invisible, premodern forms of social and scientific thought appear to leave some space for the non-demonstrable. Here we may sometimes encounter an acknowledgement of the actual contamination of the visible with the invisible, of the objective with the subjective and of the biological with the psychological.

In a variety of ways religion permeates different forms of premodern society. The religious does not necessarily denote belief in god or gods but it also refers to a sphere beyond full empirical proof (i.e. full measurability and visibility). This non-empirical sphere may go under the name theology or the numinous, the ghostly, the religious, the sacred, the totem or taboo. There is nothing surprising about the premodern, albeit parochially Western/Christian inclusion of – or perhaps, more accurately, focus on – the empirically ephemeral concept of the otherworldly. Modernity shifts this focus away from the other-worldly to the worldly – or so it seems.

Firstly, the following discusses two contrasting theoretical narratives about the shift from the religious to the secular in European societies. It then discusses how Hannah Arendt refers to more nuanced sociological and philosophical discussions of the emergence of modernity when she formulates her intriguing analysis of the ways in which the worldly and the other-worldly are contaminated in supposedly pure conceptions of the modern scientific.

Let us first turn to Carl Schmitt's famous secularisation theory, which does not argue for a break but rather for the continuity of the theological from the premodern to the modern. Here the secular appears to remain entangled with the religious or theological – that is to say, with empirically not to be substantiated concepts and creeds.

Schmitt's most striking example is that of modern sovereignty: secular modern politics still invests the leader or the ruling elite with the arbitrary and unjustifiable power to decide over the state of exception wherein norms are suspended. The power to declare this state of exception does not have an empirically visible ground. It is as ephemeral as the power with which theology invests God. The secular merely turns from the other-worldly sphere of God to the worldly precinct of the sovereign or ruling elite. The grounds which establish the prerogatives of secular sovereignty are as ghostly as belief in non-verifiable other-worldly forces. According to Schmitt, however, the theological does not contaminate the political. Instead, modern politics reinstates the purity of theology in new, modern form.[7]

Taking issue with this reading of the secular as being identical with the theological, Hans Blumenberg asserted the break of the modern with what preceded it. Here the secular does not mean the persistence of traditional theology within an immanent context. On the contrary, the modern proclaims the liberation of the worldly from the other-worldly context of theological premodernity. While Schmitt celebrates the purity of the theology that goes under the modern name of sovereignty, Blumenberg argues that modernity is a pure break with premodernity. Even though their arguments differ, both thinkers deny the presence of contamination in their respective theories of the theological (concerned with what is sometimes invisible and measurable) and the political (the visible manifestation of social and political structures).

The persistence of the immeasurable, invisible, non-graspable, other-worldly, or even non-worldly flies in the face of efforts to legitimate modernity's break with the premodern, such as Blumenberg's famous defence of the modern age's (*Neuzeit*) legitimacy. Blumenberg insists on modernity's purity (or on what Latour calls modernity's purification project). In doing so, he attempts to invalidate Schmitt's secularisation thesis (first published in 1922) according to which 'all precise notions of the modern state are secularised theological notions' (Schmitt 1990: 49). Writing in post-World War II West Germany, Blumenberg set out to show – in painstakingly researched and highly nuanced scholarly studies – that modern politics and science are not merely different translations of various theological paradigms or notions, as the Catholic 'crown jurist of the Third Reich' Schmitt had claimed before: 'For Blumenberg, secularization constituted a "category of historical injustice". It denied the legitimacy of the modern age, which made it seem derivative and somewhat inferior' (Müller 2003: 159). Rather than showing the infinite reach of theological or other-worldly concepts, Blumenberg tried to prove the allure of modern, worldly notions as far back as medieval scholastic thought.

This process of modernisation reaches a culmination in Descartes's *cogito* in which 'the provocation of the transcendent absolute at the point of its most extreme radicalization reverts into the unveiling of the *immanent* absolute' (Blumenberg 1974: 209).[8] Whereas Schmitt's secularisation thesis detects in the most striking secular features of the modern age, theological concepts at their purest, Blumenberg follows the opposite methodological procedure: he sees in Descartes's religiosity the point where theology turns radically non-theological, radically immanent and secular. As has been intimated in Chapter 1, by radicalising the mind–body divide, Descartes philosophically prepares for the scientific measurement of the world which characterises modernity:

> Particularly in his [i.e. Descartes's] *Geometry*, the distinction Aristotle proposed between the mode of connection of units and points, between arithmetic and geometry is collapsed, thus rendering the material, external world – *res extensa* – as amenable to calculation and division. (Elden 2006: 10)

Modern science promises the rationalist transparency of the world. How do societal obsessions with visibility, transparency and the measurable develop from the philosophical constellations of a Cartesian mind–body divide? The body denotes the world. Body and world are matter. The mind, however, constitutes immaterial and yet immanent sovereignty which fully knows and directs the matter under its control. By rendering the matter of the world visible and all comprehensive, the role Descartes allocates to the mind performs the promise of modern science. Blumenberg argues that the theology behind Descartes's mind–body divide is itself modern and scientific.

Rather than being contaminated by the theological, Blumenberg argues that Descartes's thought is purely scientific and modern. He sees in the divide between sovereign immateriality which forms and makes visible the material world – and from which it is, like God, hierarchically distinct – modern science's emergence uncontaminated by the theology which supposedly preceded it.

In advancing his thesis of scholasticism's modernity, Blumenberg struggles with a number of thinkers and scholars (especially Karl Löwith) who propound a contrasting thesis about the modern.[9] Moreover, Blumenberg ignores the fact that at least some practitioners of twentieth-century science have changed its modus operandi with regard to traditional notions of order and hierarchical dichotomies such as the

Cartesian mind–body divide. As has been intimated above (and as will be further developed in the following chapter), avant-garde twentieth- and twenty-first-century science has taken nineteenth-century literature seriously, together with its critique of positivist approaches to order, hierarchy, visibility, measurability and certainty.

As Sally Shuttleworth has clearly shown, 'it is certainly not the case that literary texts simply drew on emerging scientific theories. Indeed, the reverse can be shown to be true, with key literary works playing a formative role in the development of the frameworks of nineteenth-century psychiatry' (Shuttleworth 2010: 3). As we shall see in Chapter 3, literature has played a significant role for a newly emerging scientific paradigm in late nineteenth- and early twentieth-century science (one that includes but is not restricted to the field of child psychiatry as analysed by Shuttleworth).

From this historical perspective it is not surprising that Blumenberg's thesis of modern secular science's independence from the theological should remain an isolated and controversial thesis. Contrasting with Blumenberg's approach, in different but related ways, Max Weber, Walter Benjamin and Karl Löwith maintain that scholasticism has not given rise to modernity but that the latter is, in Derrida's opinion, a differing and differentiating trace of premodern theological ideas. No surprise then that Blumenberg should take issue with Löwith's thesis according to which the modern concept of progress is nothing but a slightly altered version of theological redemptions (Löwith 1949). Löwith, Benjamin and Weber prepare the ground for Hannah Arendt's argument that the modern cannot be understood as uncontaminated by what preceded it.

It is Arendt's thesis of the secular as contaminated by its supposed opposite, the other-worldly, which offers an alternative to secularisation theories which, even though they develop contrasting arguments, share a structural preoccupation with pure entities. In opposed ways, Schmitt and Blumenberg are concerned with pure manifestations: for the former the modern is purely theological, whereas for the latter it is purely rational. In contrast to Schmitt, Blumenberg attempts to prove modernity's legitimacy as the horizon of rational measurability and transparency.

This horizon of rational measurability and transparency describes what the sociologist Niklas Luhmann calls functionality: 'that the transition from traditional societies to modern society can be conceived as the transition from a primarily stratified form of differentiation of the social system to one which is primarily functional' (Luhmann 1986: 5). Luhmann's systems theory approach radicalises Blumenberg's notion of a secular autonomy from a transcending realm of the theological.

Luhmann thus translates the biologists' terms of autopoiesis into the cultural sphere of meaning:[10] Luhmann claims 'that human consciousness and human societies are also autopoietic systems that do not produce life as biological systems do, but instead operate in terms of meaning, whether this is part of communication, or internally, in a mind' (Thomsen 2013: 20). However, the visible functions of measurable systems do not merely reproduce themselves. In their autopoietic operations of self-reproduction systems also create obfuscate hybrids.[11]

The purity of either the theological or the secular disintegrates within both systems theory and deconstruction. Here the figure of purity gives way to the figure of contamination. In a fascinating itinerary of thought, Blumenberg's autonomy of the secular undergoes a transformation when Luhmann contaminates the biological notion of autopoiesis with exposure to the cultural sphere of interpretation.

Less striking are the subtle differences between Schmitt's secularisation theory and Derrida's project of deconstruction. Where Schmitt insists on tracing purely theological terms within the secular, Derrida in a more formal way develops an approach to culture, society and politics which is premised upon the contaminating traces of remnants. Comparable to the invisibility of the trace in Derrida's deconstruction, however, Luhmann's Blumenbergian secular-functionalist systems theory paradoxically produces non-functionalist remnants of the invisible.

According to Derrida the invisible emerges as 'irrepressible difference whose unavoidability and unmasterability deconstruction aims to bring to light and sustains' (Wolfe 2010: 14). Similarly, Luhmann argues that in 'systems theory, however, this radical heterogeneity is handled within an adaptive and operational framework, as a fundamental evolutionary *problem* for autopoietic systems that have to reproduce themselves in the face of overwhelming difference' (Wolfe 2010: 14). The difference to systems is their environment.

By isolating itself from its environment, a given system becomes paradoxically contaminated by this same environment from which it attempts to reproduce itself as a pure, uncontaminated, autonomous entity: 'In the form of meaning, then, we find that systems increase their contacts with their environments paradoxically by *virtualizing* them' (Wolfe 2010: 18). This virtualisation of their environment constitutes the immanent transcendence of systems – thus calling into doubt positivist assumptions of scientific visibility and measurability.

In some ways anticipating the figure of contamination in Luhmann's system and Derrida's deconstruction theories, Hannah Arendt diverges from Schmitt's and Blumenberg's contrasting accounts of the secular. As we have seen, even though they are opposed to each other, Blumenberg's and Schmitt's respective approaches to secularisation nevertheless share a triumphant element – in Schmitt's case it is the purity and resilience of theological sovereignty (which in Derrida becomes a figure of contamination – i.e. the past or its trace) and in Blumenberg's it is the triumph of the secular. Arendt, by contrast, deprives both the theological and the secular of their purported purity. Her writing and thought in fact contaminates the worldly with the other-worldly. According to Arendt, modernity reaches the Archimedean point of nature's absolute transparency and measurability, but this very high-point of the secular backfires: by gaining a full and translucent account of the world it paradoxically loses it. The Archimedean point turns back on itself and thereby forms a knot.

This perspective on the modern is modernist: not as continuation of triumphant teleological movements (either that of Schmitt's political theology or that of modernity's worldly progress), but as regressing and contaminating knot. It embodies what Maud Ellmann has recently called *The Nets of Modernism*: 'Like the Delphic omphalos, hollow in the middle and encased in knotted nets, the navel is both seam and fissure, knot and not' (Ellmann 2010: 5). More radical than Ellmann's discussion of the nets in Joyce's modernist novel and navel, Arendt's knot is a not. It is a modern qualitative leap (reversing, however, the teleological moment implied by this Hegelian term) forward, which at the point where it comes into the full visibility of its target or goal flips over and accelerates backwards to a point of not just invisibility but darkness: the not – or the loss of the world which it so desperately tried to grasp and illuminate in the first place.

Arendt's modernist-existentialist writing and thought has been shaped by that of her mentor Heidegger. Heidegger's brief infatuation with Nazism did not dampen Arendt's admiration for his philosophy. She was not, however, an uncritical follower of his philosophical insights.[12] She took issue with his reinterpretation of contingency in eschatological and teleological terms (the *Geworfenheit* or the teleological trajectory towards death), which she confronted with her notion of natality, and what I have called her philosophy of birth (Mack 2012: 62–71).

Heidegger's critique of the calculable and measurable in the Cartesian model of modern science, in contrast, deeply impressed Arendt. Heidegger identifies in Descartes's mind–body divide the philosophical justification for a modern interpretation of both politics and science in terms of the visible, measurable and calculable: 'Descartes' understanding of "space" as extension – and, moreover, of the material world as something extended in three dimensions of which geometry is the science that best allows us access to – has more than merely mathematical implications. It is behind his overall ontological casting of the world as calculable, which, in Heidegger's account paves the way for modern machine technology' (Elden 2006: 10). In the wake of Heidegger's critique of modern science, Arendt's is not so much concerned with secularisation as such but with the experience of the secular in terms of the worldly. A Cartesian reduction of the world to what is purely visible and measurable has put at risk the viability of contamination, which would allow for a blurring between the visible and the invisible. Such contaminated rather than pure entities permeate the plurality of lived worldly experience with which Arendt's political and scientific thought is concerned.

It is in this context of contamination that we can explain Blumenberg's irritation with Arendt's work. Clearly Arendt does not argue that the modern is 'nothing new' and just a transformation of premodern theology. Arendt's idiosyncratic position within theories of either modernity's trace (Derrida, Benjamin, Weber and so forth) or its autopoiesis – i.e. break with and independence from what preceded it (Blumenberg and Luhmann) – has not been sufficiently appreciated. Crucially, her point is that the modern does not constitute a repetition but rather an intensification of a quasi-religious, quasi-theological loss (what in Christian theology has been called kenosis) or renunciation of the worldly.

Arendt discovers the contamination of theology and modern science in what she calls the alienation from the world. Blumenberg gives Arendt's 'reluctant modernism' (Benhabib 2003) short shrift, writing that the 'notion "world" is not a stable one but subject to historical change' (Blumenberg 1974: 15–16). Arendt would not deny this and Blumenberg has not succeeded in invalidating her approach. Arendt's point is that the world at hand – in other words, what Blumenberg would call the current world as it is present to us – becomes reduced to the zero point of its existence in modern purification projects.

Arendt's critique of modernity is precisely that it reduces our plural and contaminated experiences of the world to a point of purification instantiating a radicalisation of traditional notions of the other-worldly. This would also confound Blumenberg's thesis, according to which the modern break with an irrational past may be found in premodern scholasticism and Cartesian theology. Arendt's oxymoronic definition of the secular in terms of the loss of the world also questions Schmitt's claim that secularisation simply translates the old truth claims of theology. Far from positing continuity between the premodern and the modern (as Schmitt, Löwith and others argue), Arendt demarcates modernity's break with what preceded it (this is exactly Blumenberg's concern).

In contrast to Blumenberg's account of *Neuzeit*, however, Arendt idiosyncratically argues for an interruption so forceful that it actually breaks itself and thus turns into a contaminating trace. According to Blumenberg, modernity emerges as a pure entity. For Arendt, however, modernity's break with what preceded it is so radical that it changes the way we experience the world to an unprecedented zero-point of existence and significance. It erases meaning by doing away with the contaminating forces of plurality and difference. Modernity's measurement of the world shrinks what it measures to a tiny spot of insignificance:

> Only now has man taken full possession of his mortal dwelling place and gathered the infinite horizons, which were temptingly and forbiddingly open to all previous ages, into a globe whose majestic outlines and detailed surface he knows as he knows the lines in the palms of his hand. (Arendt 1998: 250)

The Cartesian ideals of measurability, transparency, control and order instigate a loss of experience and meaning. Mid-nineteenth-century literature attends to the paradox in question here which Arendt and Luhmann theoretically analyse in terms of the instability of autopoietic systems. As will be discussed in the next chapter, Melville's *Moby Dick* confounds the identification of scientific truth with autonomy, proportionality, visibility and surveillance. The novel helps us discover the illusions of purportedly modern conceptions of science.

From the perspective of Arendt's analysis, by taking 'full possession' of the globe modernity paradoxically loses the world. Descartes's all comprehensive knowledge of matter gives rise to a new and increased sense of immateriality. A given system's autopoietic isolation from its environment produces virtual, invisible environments. The visibility and measurement of matter – what Arendt calls the world – eventuates in a loss of sight and experience. Having argued that the now fully measured and comprehended vastness of the world shrinks to the visible and yet tiny 'lines in the palm' of a hand, Arendt further reduces the possibility of secular experience within the surveyed confines of modernity. The hand and what is in its proximity has become obsolete:

> It is in the nature of the human surveying capacity that it can function only if man disentangles himself from all involvement in and concern with the close at hand and withdraws himself to a distance from everything near him. The greater the distance between himself and his surroundings, world or earth, the more he will be able to survey and measure and the less worldly or earth-bound space be left to him. (Arendt 1998: 251)

By measuring and controlling the world of matter, the Cartesian mind severs its connection to embodiment as such (what Arendt calls 'worldly or earth-bound').

As we have seen, the mind–body divide shapes Latour's critique of what he calls the modern purification project, which separates nature from society. Nature or the body are the objects of society's mental comprehension and control. It is crucial to emphasise that for Arendt modernity goes further than simply translating or tracing a theological distance to and demotion of embodiment and matter: it empties our corporeal world from any remainder of worldliness by precisely reducing the space for a contamination of various supposedly opposed entities (such as the visible and the invisible or the objective and the subjective). In short, the paradox of a secular loss of the world shrinks the contaminating complexity of life to questions of measurement and thus denies the presence of the immeasurable, the subjective and the invisible.

While explicitly following the secularisation thesis of Max Weber, Arendt implicitly analyses the presumed translation of a theological into a secular praxis as a disturbing break away from life's habitat within an earth-bound, embodied world. The secular is not secular as Blumenberg and secularisation theorists à la Schmitt and Weber proclaim. The secular in Arendt's usage does not denote what it usually does: the worldly. More radically still, Arendt turns the word secular upside down so that it means the opposite of what it proclaims to signify. While evoking Weber and the secularisation theory, she undermines the semantics of the very term 'secular':

> The greatness of Max Weber's discovery about the origins of capitalism lay precisely in his demonstration that an enormous, strictly mundane activity is possible without any care for or enjoyment of the world whatever, an activity whose deepest motivation, on the contrary is worry and care about the self. World alienation, and not self-alienation as Marx thought, has been the hallmark of the modern age. (Arendt 1998: 254)

The full comprehension of the globe paradoxically gives rise to a sense of the other-worldly that has lost any sacred or spiritual connotations. Arendt here seems to evoke Weber's disenchantment thesis. Modern scientific knowledge deprives us of a sense of wonder. The loss of the capacity to wonder about the world turns our globe into a dreary and tiny substance from which we retreat. The world has become a dead object which we exploit in our capitalist quest for wealth creation.

Conclusion: the contaminating force of Arendt's, Kafka's and H. G. Wells's modernism

Following Weber's approach, Arendt's methodology is modern through and through: she separates nature (the world) from human society, politics and economics. This part of her argument could be subjected to Latour's charge of an illusory purification project – radically separating nature from society, the mind from the body – by which he defines what is modern. Arendt's notion of a loss of worldliness assumes, however, that there once had been a contamination of the natural and the social, the corporeal and the cerebral. She calls humanity's sense of a fusion with the natural or earth-bound 'love of the world'. Indeed our reliance on nature characterises our human condition: we are, as Arendt puts it, 'still bound to the earth through the human condition' (Arendt 1998: 262). Her recognition of the illusory or impossible (as Latour would put it) foundation of the purification project that lies at the heart of modernity turns Arendt from a modern thinker into a modernist.

Michael Levenson has recently defined modernism as 'a radically alternative practice that presented a counterhistory for modernity' (Levenson 2011: 12). This 'counterhistory' of modernity was 'seen as dangerous and contagious' (Levenson 2011: 5). The contagion contaminates what the modern purification project attempts to keep as separate entities (nature and society, environment and system, immanence and transcendence, and so forth):

> In this view, the telling events were not the text, the painting, the film, or the quartet, no matter how extreme, but the artifacts as emblems of a widening counterworld. The growing perception, as conspicuous in the dominant press as in avant-garde journals, was that these formidable artifacts exemplified rival forms of life, other styles of thinking and feeling. (Levenson 2011: 12)

One way to define modernism is to say that it both analyses and questions the modern attempt to purify the societal from the natural and the mental from the embodied. Arendt's methodology is at once modern and modernist: she first thinks on the basis of the modern purification project and then proceeds to turn around this line of thought and to undermine the purification project with the contaminating force of what she calls worldliness – a term that combines seemingly opposed entities (nature and society; body and mind, and so forth).

Crucially, Arendt refers to literature when she reverses her methodological procedure and calls into question the traditional scientific (which includes also the social science of Weber's sociology) attempt to compartmentalise mind from world and society from nature. The case in point here is one of Kafka's aphorisms which frames the opening of the last chapter in *The Human Condition*: 'He found the Archimedean point, but he used it against himself; it seems that he was permitted to find it only under this condition' (Arendt 1998: 248). Kafka's aphorism illustrates modernism's critique of the modern purification project.

By forcing the realisation of the impossible or illusory denial of the natural within the societal, modernity's 'purity' turns self-destructive. The ideal of an Archimedean point of view refers to the rationalist distrust of the senses which informs not only Descartes but also Spinoza's modern philosophy. Like their ancient scientific-philosophical ancestor Archimedes, Spinoza and Descartes had ample justification to distrust bodily senses and intuitions, which, according to them, tend to be misleading. Spinoza's *differentia specifica* from Descartes's rationalism is, however, that he implicates the mind in the illusions of bodily intuitions. According to Spinoza, the mind is the idea of the body and this means that our minds are unavoidably bound up with the input received from the body.

As we have seen in Chapter 1, Spinoza's philosophy anticipates the current neuroscientific discovery of a loop that binds the corporeal to the cerebral. Spinoza's rationalism admonishes us to be mindful of our minds: to falsify any potential distortions and hallucinations that arise in the mind as it receives misleading sensations from our corporeal existence in its entirety. In contrast to Spinoza, the conventional scientific outlook has opted for a radical separation from the merely natural or embodied. This is exactly what Arendt sees in Kafka's vision of an Archimedean point of view: 'the Archimedean wish for a point outside the earth from which to unhinge the world' (Arendt 1998: 262). According to Spinoza and Latour, this would be like wishing for the impossible. In Arendt's interpretation of Kafka, however, modernity realises the impossible by damaging not only nature but also society: 'the [Archimedean] wish would be granted only provided that we lost reality' (Arendt 1998: 262). This loss of reality (the world) is self-destructive: Kafka's Archimedean point of view resides outside of nature, and this distance to the object under investigation preconditions the measurability and potential transparency of the world. The very precondition of this scientific triumph, however, also seals the fate of the subject who achieves this feat of science, because we cannot ever leave the world or its corporeal ground without giving up our life.

Kafka is not the only writer who may alert us to humanity's autoimmune uses of science. In the last part of H. G. Wells's *The Time Machine*, the narrative voice abandons grand hopes for moral and educational progress which scientific advances might have helped to achieve. Instead the conquest and subjugation of nature goes hand in hand with humanity's self-destruction:

> The great triumph of Humanity I had dreamed of took a different shape in my mind. It had been no such triumph of moral education and general cooperation as I had imagined. Instead, I saw a real aristocracy, armed with a perfected science and working to a logical conclusion the industrial system of today. Its triumph had not been simply a triumph over Nature, but a triumph over Nature and the fellow man. (Wells 2005a: 49)

As Marina Warner has pointed out, it is so-called 'degeneration' rather than class struggle which brings about humanity's self-destruction ('Wells abandoned this kind of agitprop for science, his true interest, and took a very long view. Extinction, not renewal, was to be the ultimate outcome': Wells 2005a: xxvi). Degeneration simply implies the passing of time. In Wells, however, the future also alludes to progress – to scientific progress to be precise.

Paradoxically, it is within this narrative of progression that humanity degenerates and self-destructs. The divide between nature and society ends up turning humanity into nothing but matter – a natural object to be consumed: in the quote above Wells writes of 'a triumph over Nature and the fellow man'. Degeneration does not happen through the neutral medium of a mere lapse in time. Rather there are societal and cultural dispositions which create degeneration. These preconditions are paradoxically the opposite of the degenerate: they are progressive.

As Simon J. James has argued recently, Wells contaminates the cultural with the biological through his 'scientific romances [which] evaluate culture and morals as a function of biology, only as enduring as biological reality will allow them to be. Biology, the parent, must always dominate over and even ironise culture' (James 2011: 120). Biology ironises the cultural construction of history's assumed progress by contaminating it with its anonym (i.e. regression or degeneration). Progression works for degeneration and this not only on a biological but also on an intellectual-scientific level.

How could this be possible? The scientific parameters of modernity first establish a divide between nature and society, and then within this construction of nature as radically separated from human society, scientific progress reduces every form of embodied life (whether human or non-human) to a measurable object which is almost transparent in its visibility.

What remains provocative is, however, the invisibility and plurality of the mind, together with human psychology. In order to extinguish this last bastion of the invisible, progress promises to turn humanity into a measurable, fully transparent object. The hopes and dreams invested by public opinion in science are bound up with the desire for security as promised by science's promise of predictability and certainty – by the secure and clear vision which transparency and measurability seem to proffer.

In Lippit's words, 'global visibility: a universal archive, in which everything in the world is visible, everything is visible to the world' (Lippit 2005: 47). Full transparency, however, may coincide with a form of vanishing and thus with invisibility. In 1895 Röntgen's discovery of the X-ray rendered the invisible visible, and yet the visibility which such scientific innovation yielded came at a cost: 'At work from the X-ray to the VHP is also a form of destructive visuality, a visuality born from abstraction' (Lippit 2005: 48). Scientific sight indulges in the longing for clarity and measurability but then it also creates new anxieties about how the transparency of its objective view has been produced.

In the case of Röntgen's X-rays, the translucent images they afford are those of the living body reduced to dust: 'The X-ray situates the spectacle in its context as a living document even when it depicts, actually and phantasmatically, an image of death or the deterioration of the body that leads to death. A living image of death and the deathly image of life are intertwined in the X-ray' (Lippit 2005: 47). From Darwin's invisibly visible traces of evolution to Röntgen's discovery of the X-ray onwards, modern science has thwarted expectations of clarity, measurability and visibility.

Modern techniques of rendering the invisible visible produce new remnants of darkness, the phantasmal, and the immeasurable. Darwin's invisibly visible evolutionism, Röntgen's X-rays, the invention of photography as well cinema and Freud's new science of psychoanalysis share a peculiar fusion of the visible and the invisible, the measurable and the immeasurable, the conscious and the unconscious, the factual and the fictive: 'Like the X-ray image, Freud's dream confuses art and science, phantasy and fact, imagination and observation. Like psychoanalysis itself. The lines between those orders have been blurred' (Lippit 2005: 41). Science's quest for visibility and measurability brought to the fore the blurring of opposites – the disorder merely presenting the fiction of order. The enlightenment and modern, cutting edge science illuminates the illusions produced by light, the delusions spurned by illusions of measurability. Traditional ideals of order and clarity pertain to the surface: 'The Enlightenment project always was, perhaps, an attempt to move toward the surface, to search for that locus in which the subject would be annihilated by the glare of an intensive radiation, one that moves resolutely toward intensity and interiority' (Lippit 2005: 80). The sight of interiority, however, dissipates what it illuminates.

Here the process of hypostasising humanity in terms of measurable matter goes so far as to render it consumable and digestible. At this point progress clearly becomes regressive and most spectacularly so in the societal practice of cannibalism. Here humanity has literally found the Archimedean point to wrest the measurable and fully visible from the last bastion of invisibility. It achieves this illusory triumph of transparency by turning the embodied mind into a fully knowable feast for the digestive organs. This is the moment when the psyche has fully turned into visible and measurable nature: into a culinary object on the kitchen table:

> His prejudice against human flesh is no deep-seated instinct. And so these inhuman sons of men – ! I tried to look at the thing in a scientific spirit. After all, they were less human and more remote than our cannibal ancestors of three or four thousand years ago. And the intelligence that would have made this state of things a torment had gone. Why should I trouble myself? These Eloi were mere fat cattle, which the ant-like Morlocks preserved and preyed upon – probably saw to the breeding of. (Wells 2005a: 62)

Humanity uses its knowledge against itself to the point of preying on itself. What makes this more than regressive state of cannibalism ('more remote than our cannibal ancestors') possible is a certain socio-scientific process, which reduces human diversity into visible states of one homogeneous entity: at one extreme we encounter nothing but sheer delicacy – the 'mere beautiful futility' (Wells 2005a: 58) of the Eloi – and, as polar opposite we confront the Morlocks who are purely 'mechanical' (Wells 2005a: 57). Far from being ineluctable, degeneration is the product of a modernity that is obsessed with the reduction of not only the non-human but also the human world to visible and measurable states of homogeneity – as Wells succinctly puts it elsewhere: either 'feeble prettiness' or 'mere mechanical industry' (Wells 2005a: 79). The reduction of human diversity to two binary opposed characteristics – futile delicacy versus mechanical industry – deprives humanity not only of intelligence and creativity but also of subjectivity. Wells's grisly vision of a degenerate modernity confronts us with the paradox of a world which has been reduced to the zero-point of visible, objective matter – ready for consumption. It is a society which no longer allows for a contamination between the measurable and the immeasurable, the visible and the invisible.

Wells's *The Time Machine* describes the structure of totalitarian societies wherein plurality has been sacrificed to what can be identified as uncontaminated, as pure: the Eloi are purely delicate and the Morlocks are solely mechanical. Here we indeed encounter the practice of homogeneity in these purely opposed specimens of either the merely artistic (Eloi) or the purely technological (Morlocks).

There is no room for deviation from the norm of constituting a single-minded, pure entity. Here we are confronted with the radical lack of contamination and difference: there is nothing approximate which could be the divergence of subjectivity and individuality. The following chapter discusses how some early modernist texts from the mid-nineteenth century tackle the problem of humanity's quasi-scientific political reduction to visible and measurable assemblies of the homogeneous.

Notes

1. Timothy Morton has recently described Einstein's departure from both Newton's and Kant's notions of science: 'It is a false cliché that we have grasped the meaning of relativity. Far from it. In our daily social and psychological practices, we are still Newtonians, still in awe of infinite space. At most we see infinity and space as transcendental categories, as Kant does. [. . .] it is Einstein who continues the Copernican legacy, by showing how time and space emerge from objects, not from synthetic judgments that preunderstand being to be thus and so' (Morton 2013: 62).
2. As Morton has pointed out: 'Nuclear radiation is not visible to humans' (Morton 2013: 38).
3. Bennet Zon's email from 9 May 2014 in response to an earlier version of this paper presented at the inaugural conference launch of the *Centre for Nineteenth-Century Studies* at Durham University (10 May 2014).
4. As Dongen has put it, 'Generally speaking, one could say that the quantum program initially introduced principles and rules that were in opposition to "classical" physics, yet depended on classical physics to be formulated' (Dongen 2010: 158).
5. As Dongen has shown, Einstein's approach has been shaped by the literature and thought of German romanticism: 'No lesser figures than Alexander von Humboldt and Johann Wolfgang von Goethe, the latter in particular through his Faust figure, had emphasized the striving of science for simplification on the one hand and the ultimate unity of nature on the other. While the origins of these ideas are located in romantic and natural philosophy of the early nineteenth century, Einstein likely absorbed them for the first time through the works of popular science writers like Ludwig Büchner and Aaron Bernstein (who had in fact considered themselves critical of the natural philosophers)' (Dongen 2010: 60). Goethe and other writers indeed questioned the ideas of order which were part of the classical science of the natural philosophers. See Mack (2010: 139–67).
6. For a detailed discussion of this point see Mack (2014).
7. As Roberto Esposito has recently argued, Schmitt's political theology outdoes or neutralises the political in terms of the theological. His political

theology is dialectical and does away with the secular as a negation of the negation. This triumph of theology in Schmitt's espousal of sovereignty follows Hegel's dialectics which does away (*Aufhebung*) with what it encounters as resistant or negative, thus recuperating traditional theodicy's proof of God's and the world's goodness: 'The very concept of the Hegelian *Aufhebung*, for that matter, as the overcoming of evil by encompassing it, demonstrates the survival of the language of theodicy after it seemed to have been exhausted by Kant's downgrading it to a transcendental illusion' (Esposito 2011: 78).

8. My translation.
9. As Esposito has shown, Blumenberg does not circumvent the theological in his juridical argument contra Löwith: 'But the eminently juridical argument that he [i.e. Blumenberg] uses, especially against Karl Löwith, attests more than he cares to admit to the crucial function performed by the theologically informed lexicon of immunization in the constitution of modernity' (Esposito 2011: 78).
10. As Mads Rosendahl Thomsen has recently pointed out: 'The theory of autopoiesis was originally developed by biologists Humberto Maturana and Francisco Varela as a way of defining life, and to better describe how self-identity may be maintained over time in a system that changes its elements over time' (Thomsen 2013: 20).
11. 'Luhmann's gambit is based from the outset on replacing the theory of closed systems with a theory of open systems; the system only lives in relation to the environment from which it draws the stimulus towards increasing complexity, which it reproduces in continually more developed forms. But this relationship is a closed one, since systematic communication with the environment is, in principle, impossible, other than through a progressive inclusion of its exteriority. This means that the system is open only to its own closure; or that closure is a condition for any form of openness' (Esposito 2011: 47).
12. See Vatter (2006: 137–59) as well as Mack (2009: 35–60).

Contamination of Nature with Society: The Collapse of Natural Order from Melville to Wells and Ellison

Introduction: Kandel's contamination of modernism with biology

> Modernism began in the mid-nineteenth century as a response not only to the restrictions and hypocrisies of everyday life, but also as a reaction to the Enlightenment's emphasis on the rationality of human behaviour. The Enlightenment, or Age of Reason, was characterized by the idea that all is well with the world because human action is governed by reason. It is through reason that we achieve enlightenment, because our mind can exert control over our emotions and feelings. (Kandel 2012: 11)

In the quotation above, Eric R. Kandel locates the beginning of modernism in the middle of the nineteenth century. At that time the dark side of the Industrial Revolution had already become apparent, and with it the ambiguity of modernity's – or, in other words, the enlightenment's – claim that reason's controlling position over the body and the emotions guarantees unambiguous progress: 'The modernist reaction to the Enlightenment came in the aftermath of the Industrial Revolution, whose brutalizing effects revealed that modern life had not become as mathematically perfect, or as certain, rational, or enlightened, as advances in the eighteenth century had led people to expect' (Kandel 2012: 12). Kandel further substantiates his claim that modernism begins not at the end but at the middle of the nineteenth century by pinpointing the then emerging rise of biology as a radical break with modernity's/the Enlightenment's intellectual anchorage in physics and astronomy: 'As astronomy and physics inspired the Enlightenment, so biology inspired modernism. Darwin's 1859 book *On the Origin of Species* introduced the idea that human beings are not created uniquely by an all-powerful God but are biological creatures that evolved from simpler animal ancestors' (Kandel 2012: 12). Far from claiming (see the concluding section to this chapter) that mid-nineteenth-century works such as Büchner's *Danton's Death*, Hawthorne's *Scarlet Letter* or Melville's *Moby Dick* are classic modernist works of literature *avant là lettre*, the following chapter nevertheless argues that in their concern with the potential modern loss of worldliness and diversity these texts are less about their historical subject matter than about the fears for a future where subjectivity has been subjected to bio-political visibility and measurability.

Natural order as terror and social invisibility: Wells's *The Invisible Man* and Ellison's *Invisible Man*

Kandel's socio-historical point of orientation is the Industrial Revolution. In terms of intellectual history, he mentions the Enlightenment as furthering the general hope that science would facilitate a global society turned secular and uncontaminated by irrational interference – in short, a new polis that is fully at home with the world. The flip side of these enlightened expectations for a secure and autonomous secular order emerged when the French Revolution morphed into Robespierre's reign of terror.

The title of Wells's *The Time Machine* (1895) evokes the mechanisation of life in the wake of this revolution. In his next novel, *The Invisible Man* (1897), Wells frequently refers to Robespierre's reign of terror in order to highlight the ambiguity of the Enlightenment's promise to render the world visible and measurable in a peaceful or non-violent manner. This novel accentuates the paradox of the great expectations public opinion had previously invested into science for rendering the world less dangerous and more secure, measurable, and predictable. The novel's scientist, Mr Griffin, retreats from London into a remote village (the secluded village of Iping) in order to embark on an experiment that would render him invisible. As Akira Mizuta Lippit has pointed out, this experiment is premised on an axiom that pushes the Cartesian demotion of corporality to a point where 'the human body is like paper, a network of fibres and essentially transparent' (Lippit 2005: 89). Lippit reads Wells's Mr Griffin in the 1895 context of Röntgen's groundbreaking scientific discovery: 'Griffin experiences his vanishing body like an X-ray image' (Lippit 2005: 90).

Discussions of *The Invisible Man* have so far focused on its immediate historical setting, neglecting its crucial references to the French Revolution and to Robespierre's reign of terror in particular.[1] In the novel, however, Griffin's fellow scientist Doctor Kemp does not see the quest for invisibility as an innovative scientific endeavour but, on the contrary, as a repetition of the terror that precipitated the collapse of the French Revolution. Kemp insists: 'He [i.e. Griffin] dreams of a reign of terror! A reign of terror, I tell you' (Wells 2005b: 127). In his missive to Kemp, Griffin announces his quasi-scientific resurrection of Robespierre's rule:

> There is nothing for it, but to start the Terror. This announces the first day of the Terror. Port Burdock is no longer under the Queen, tell your Colonel of Police, and the rest of them; it is under me – the Terror. This is day one of year one of the new epoch, – the Epoch of the Invisible Man. I am Invisible Man the First. To begin with the rule will be easy. The first day there will be one execution for the sake of example, – a man named Kemp. Death starts for him today. He may lock himself away, hide himself away, get guards about him, put on armour if he likes; Death, the unseen Death, is coming. (Wells 2005b: 143)

Griffin, the invisible man, has become a ghost, the ghost of the French Revolution that has turned into a reign of terror.

Like Robespierre, Griffin announces the beginning of a new calendar, a new time. The irony is of course that there is nothing new here, that Griffin's experiment is a modernisation of the previous rule of terror. Griffin's 'new epoch' produces a scientifically enhanced and modernised version of the 'new era' inaugurated by the guillotine's death-dealing mechanism. Death is indeed the destination: just as Robespierre has his fellow revolutionist killed – as Büchner's Damton puts it: 'the revolution is like Saturn, it devours its own children' (Büchner 1993: 21)[2] – Griffin sets out to kill his fellow scientist Kemp. The references to the French Revolution do not, however, have a political agenda or horizon.

Indeed, Wells's 1897 novel is not so much about politics as it is about science.[3] In this context, science, however, becomes a question of politics (the term politics here understood rather narrowly as the quest for power). The interaction between the scientific and the social is problematised in the novel. For some critics Griffin's fate illustrates how society can potentially lose a talented scientist. As Steven McLean has pointed out:

> Since *The Invisible Man* is the first of his [i.e. Wells's] scientific romances in which 'we are shown a recognizable society', it is through the grotesque figure of Griffin that Wells most thoroughly investigates the factors which can lead potentially to the scientist's alienation from the community, and thus to the loss of outstanding scientific capacity which could be of far greater benefit to society as a whole. (McLean 2009: 66)[4]

The focus of the novel is, however, not on the loss of scientific capacity for the greater benefit of society, but on the way in which science can become deleterious for society once it attempts to 'revenge', and at the same time free itself from its supposedly contaminating natural and socio-political environment.

Griffin employs 'science' to wage a 'war' against society or, as the novel puts it, 'the world'. This combative posture evokes the reign of terror's declaration of war against what preceded its 'new epoch', its 'new calendar'. Unlike Robespierre, however, Griffin does not announce a political programme. Rather than envisioning a new social order, Griffin tries to enhance his own personal sense of omnipotence. The repeated evocation of the French Revolution within a work of science fiction has, however, serious implications for reconfiguring the relationship between the scientific and the socio-political.

Anticipating Latour's analysis of the actual contamination of what the modern purification project theoretically separates (i.e. the supposed opposition between natural sciences and society), Wells's *The Invisible Man* highlights the politics of science. First of all, there is the power struggle between two scientists (i.e. Griffin and Kemp). Kemp has gained recognition for his work and is not interested in excessive forms of power. Griffin, however, employs his scientific work in order to eliminate not only his competitors in his specialist field but also to wage war against the embodied world *tout court*.

Becoming invisible seems to depend on losing one's corporality by becoming 'pure' mind. Like Latour, Wells questions the validity of modern purification projects. Griffin learns to do without food so that he can morph into an invisible entity: 'I was fasting; for to eat, to fill myself with unassimilated matter, would be to become grotesquely visible again' (Wells 2005b: 114). Here indeed Arendt's unearthly, unworldly immateriality preconditions the attainment of the Archimedean point where science could fully illuminate the world.

The illumination of the world paradoxically causes the loss of the world. We witness the return of the supernatural and the medieval with the arrival of miracle-working science. In Kemp's words, 'One might think we were in the thirteenth century' (Wells 2005b: 70). The crucial point here is that science's potential indifference to the vulnerability of the embodied world is itself political. The fusion of scientific ambitions and political megalomania emerges as social concern in *The Invisible Man*. Griffin's science attacks the world with the motto '*contra mundum*' (Wells 2005b: 135). His is a political 'last great struggle against the world' (Wells 2005b: 133). *The Invisible Man* accentuates the risk of how the Enlightenment and scientific reason may turn into what it set out to overcome: the alienation from the world in premodern preoccupations with the supernatural and the other-worldly. Wells's novel establishes parallels between the secular political project of the French Revolution and the rapid progress in science. Revolution may become more regressive than what preceded it; and secular science may deprive us of worldly experience in a way more severe than a polis governed by a theological idea.

The so far neglected political references to the French Revolution in Wells's early scientific novel come fully to the fore in Ralph Ellison's mid-twentieth-century *Invisible Man* (1952). Ellison's novel 'shares its name with Wells's novel but without the definite article' (Lippit 2005: 98). What has so far been neglected is the way in which Ellison redirects the focus on science in Wells's *The Invisible Man* and inverts it with one on politics. In his 'Author's Introduction' (1981), Ellison invokes the scientific preoccupation in Wells's novel. Here, however, it is not so much concerning nature as the social sciences. Ellison sets out to correct pseudo-scientific delusions about visibility and he takes pains to distance himself from science fiction à la Wells:

> And all the more so because the voice seemed well aware that a piece of science fiction was the last thing I aspired to write. In fact, it seemed to tease me with allusions to that pseudoscientific concept which held that most Afro-American difficulties sprang from our 'high visibility': a phrase as double-dealing and insidious as its more recent oxymoronic cousins, 'benign neglect' and 'reverse discrimination,' both of which translate 'Keep those Negroes running – but in their old place.' My friends had made wry jokes out of the term for many years, suggesting that while the darker brother was clearly 'checked and balanced' – and kept far more checked and balanced – on the basis of his darkness he glowed nevertheless, within the American conscience with such intensity that most whites feigned moral blindness toward his predicament; and these included the waves of late who refused to recognize the vast extent to which they too benefited from his second-class status while placing all the blame on white southerners. (Ellison 2001: xxxiii)

Whereas invisibility is a question of scientific potentiality and power in Wells's novel, in Ellison's *Invisible Man* it turns into an issue of perception.

Whom does society grant the privilege of being visible and as being thereby socially recognised? This is a socio-political concern. Literature here corrects the politically fraught misconception of the social sciences: 'Thus despite the bland assertion of sociologists, "high visibility" actually rendered one *un*-visible' (Ellison 2001: xxxiii). The societal neglect of 'high visibility' evidences wilful ignorance: the refusal to grant social recognition. This refusal of social recognition flies in the face of the Enlightenment presupposition of human brotherhood on which the French Revolution and, in its wake, the American Constitution had been founded at the end of the eighteenth century. Ellison implicitly indicts the social sciences for a political refusal to recognise non-recognition – in other words, the societal construction of invisibility – in the supposedly 'enlightened' and democratic culture of the American East Coast in the mid-twentieth century.

What is problematic in the (social) sciences is that they remain too positivistic. They are too much taken in by what is factually, visibly and measurably there but they are unable to attend to the invisible and yet always present questions of the mind – of perception, consciousness and conscience. As Ross Posnock has shown, Ellison's concern with invisibility counteracts notions of cultural and biological purity: 'Ralph Ellison and Albert Murray pondered a pragmatist pluralism that, borrowing Murray's words, thrives on "complexity and confusion" and is allergic to whatever "has any presumptions of purity"' (Posnock 2010: 185). Here the sciences have much to learn from literature.

According to Ellison, literature has the capacity to alert us to the contamination of the invisible and the visible, the interpretative and the positivistic. In this context Ellison singles out Henry James as the discoverer of mental deeds which operate in an invisible sphere and nevertheless take visible manifestations in the social and scientific sphere of facts: 'Henry James had taught us much with his hyperconscious, "Super subtle fry," characters who embodied in their own cultured, upper-class way the American virtues of conscience and consciousness' (Ellison 2001: xxxii). Ellison presents his African-American protagonist with precisely such 'virtues of conscience and consciousness' that had so far been the prerequisite of wasp American society.

His novel thus does justice to scientific as well as political questions (which the social sciences had misconceived): he integrates those kept on the margins of our social and intellectual horizon by pseudo-scientific and political forces. Literature's work of social and cognitive integration brings to the fore the Enlightenment's view on social interdependence, which neither the French Revolution nor the American Revolution were capable of uncovering.

Ellison declares that it is art which fulfils the democratic promise of equal social visibility which is truly non-exclusive:

> Here it would seem that the interests of art and democracy converge, the development of conscious, articulate citizens being an established goal of this democratic society, and the creation of conscious, articulate characters being indispensable to the creation of resonant compositional centers through which an organic consistency can be achieved in the fashioning of fictional forms. (Ellison 2001: xxxiii)

The work of the imagination is integrative and achieves the unification which is the modern ideal of the sciences (most prominently of course Einstein's unified field theory): 'The human imagination is integrative – and the same is true of the centrifugal force that inspires the democratic process' (Ellison 2001: xxxiii). Literature's 'victory of conscious perception' (Ellison 2001: xxxix) brings about the universalism and the fraternity about which the enlightened thinkers of the French Revolution could only theorise:

> So my task was one of revealing the human universals hidden within the plight of one who was black and American, and not only as conveying my personal vision of possibility, but as a way of dealing with the sheer rhetorical challenge involved in communicating across our barriers of race and religion, class, color, and region – barriers which consist in many strategies of division that were designed, and still function, to prevent what would otherwise have been a more or less natural recognition of the reality of black and white fraternity. And to defeat this national tendency to deny the common humanity shared by my character and those who might happen to read of his experience, I would have to provide him with something of a worldview, give him a consciousness in which serious philosophical questions could be raised, provide him with a range of diction that could play upon the richness of our readily shared vernacular speech and construct a plot that would bring him in contact with a variety of American types as they operated on various levels of society. Most of all, I would have to approach racial stereotypes as a given fact of the social process and proceed, while gambling with the reader's capacity for fictional truth, to reveal the human complexity which stereotypes are intended to conceal. (Ellison 2001: xl)

Ellison's novel works within the theoretical framework of the Enlightenment, the French Revolution and the American Constitution. Crucially, he shows how enlightened, scientific truth becomes a lie when it denies the existence of what does not fit into its theoretical schema. Here revolution turns into regression.

Invisible Man sheds light on the darkness of an Enlightenment that belies itself. The novel does so while fully depicting the high visibility of what has been wilfully ignored: social divisions that persevere in a supposedly democratic and liberal society. Literature confronts social and scientific discourse with the contaminating complexities of experience. These complexities are paradoxes, which Ellison's narrator has the courage to render visible, perceptible, so that we can change our conscience and consciousness.

The narrator's grandparents embody these paradoxical and contaminating complexities: 'About eighty-five years ago they were told that they were free, united with others of our country in everything pertaining to the common good, and, in everything social, separate like the fingers of the hand' (Ellison 2001: 15). On a scientific or theoretical level the end of slavery guaranteed inclusion of the freed slaves into the common good of American society.

Yet the truth in question here is a lie, because on a practical and socially embodied level African-Americans had still been excluded from integration. The 'high visibility' of the narrator's grandparents kept them invisible, forced into a state of social invisibility. Ellison shows how the truth of scientific visibility covers the invisibility of its lie: 'Perhaps the truth was always a lie' (Ellison 2001: 498). The truth of certain scientific theories turns out to be lies when they impose invisibility on those whom they prefer not to recognise: 'Well, I *was* and yet I was invisible, that was the fundamental contradiction. I was and yet I was unseen' (Ellison 2001: 507). The same contamination of truth with a lie holds true for Brother Jack's revolutionary ideology:

> What if Brother Jack were wrong. What if history was a gambler, instead of a force in a laboratory experiment, and the boys his ace in the hole? What if history was not a reasonable citizen, but a madman full of paranoid guile and these boys his agents, his big surprise! His own revenge? (Ellison 2001: 441)

The figure of contamination confronts the purported truth held dear by science and society with its opposite: the lie morphs into what is considered to be true. This reversal of perspectives on socially approved truths as lies only emerges when we are able to question representations of stable and pure identities.

The reign of terror or the collapse of nature's order

Ellison's novel inverts the scientific focus of Wells's *The Invisible Man* by showing how whole segments of society have become subjected to political, societal and scientific invisibility. Here invisibility concerns a general state of affairs for a demoted group within the 'common good' – hence the definite article is missing from Ellison's title (not Wells's *The Invisible Man* but less definitive, more general *Invisible Man*). In doing so, however, Ellison further develops and accentuates Wells's critique of the power struggle that takes place in various social-scientific arenas.

Within this scientific–societal constellation, around which both Ellison's *Invisible Man* and Wells's *The Invisible Man* revolve, the French Revolution is a crucial historical turning point. The French Revolution is a turning point because it promised to translate central Enlightenment concepts of order and rationality into socio-political practice. The revolution's mutation into a reign of terror, however, highlights the actual instability of eighteenth-century ideas about stability and order.

We may come to understand modernity's conceptual framework through an analysis of what it means to be secular. The Secular is concerned with immanence: the sphere of what is visibly and measurably there – in other words positivist, or, as Heidegger would say, *zuhanden* (graspable, 'at hand'). The rationality of the natural order, however, becomes surreptitiously the model of both, on a collective level, a stable society and, as concerns individuals, a well-balanced psyche.

Nature here turns into a space wherein reason plays out its progress: the worldly or immanent movement towards a fully rational, clear and visible world which has abolished biological impulses that have become closely associated with the opposite of the rational – the merely embodied or animal sphere of 'bare life'. Modern and contemporary literature attempt to do justice to this demoted realm of our embodied or animalistic constitution which we cannot overcome through scientific and philosophical concepts of order, predictability and efficiency.

What goes under the name 'modern' has certainly not come into being with modernism. Instead perhaps some of the most intriguing aspects of modernist art, music and literature counter stifling and homogeneous tendencies within the modernity of the eighteenth, nineteenth and early twentieth centuries. As we have seen in the preceding chapter, these less appealing facets of the modern could – as Hannah Arendt and H. G. Wells feared – turn hostile towards invisible and immeasurable instantiations of our thoughts and emotions.

Reason is indeed closely bound up with the less predictable workings of emotions. This is the result of new neuroscientific findings which have proved right William James's intellectual treatment of feelings. William M. Reddy has summed up these recent neuroscientific discoveries, pointing out that 'research in cognitive psychology has also shown that emotions are virtually indistinguishable from cognition itself' (Reddy 2001: 321). Against this background, Reddy takes issue with the lack of attention which the emotions have received in scholarly and intellectual discussions: 'I insist that emotion is the one concept that has most needed theoretical interrogation, that has most – and most mysteriously – suffered from theoretical neglect in our long Western examination of the self' (Reddy 2001: 319). Reddy holds the French Revolution – and its reign of terror in particular – responsible for an otherwise inexplicable avoidance of theoretical engagement with the emotions in the nineteenth and twentieth centuries.

Why the French Revolution? Because the French Revolution may have been the first modern event whose actors tried to mobilise political affects in order to channel these into the assumed rationality and efficiency of the body politic. Instead of allowing for animal-like instincts and impulses in human emotions, the leaders of the French Revolution saw in sentiments evidence of humanity's participation in a rational – rather than animalistic – natural order.

According to Reddy, the French Revolution took the originally literary form of sentimentalism as an aesthetic and formal model for the practice of politics. It divided the polis into citizens with either good or evil sentiments: 'suspicion of the insincere gave a tinge of Manichaeism to the political thinking of the period, a sense that goodness was locked in conflict with evil. After the French Revolution got underway and sought to establish the rule of sentiment, its leaders had great difficulty distinguishing between reasonable dissent and evil, dissembling opposition' (Reddy 2001: 326).

In her 1963 (contemporaneous with the publication of her study of totalitarian mentality, *Eichmann in Jerusalem*) book *On Revolution*, Arendt pinpoints in Robespierre's reign of terror the early beginning of a totalitarian concept of history which helps to justify the suppression of both diversity and dissent by invoking the overruling force of 'historical necessity'.

Whatever does not homogeneously fit into this supposedly necessary order of history becomes relegated to non-existence or, as Ellison would put it, invisibility. The figure of contamination makes visible how we reduce the divers and plural into invisibles when they are seen as not cohering with specific representations of what nature or history should be like.

According to Arendt, the French Revolution paradoxically progressed towards a regressive replacement of truly revolutionary freedom with totalitarian constructions of historical necessity and natural order:

> Yet the point of the matter is that all those who, throughout the nineteenth century and deep into the twentieth, followed in the footsteps of the French Revolution saw themselves not merely as successors of the men of the French Revolution but as agents of history and historical necessity, with the obvious and yet paradoxical result that instead of freedom necessity became the chief category of political and revolutionary thought. (Arendt 1973: 52–3)

The turn away from the stifling protocols of the *ancien régime* towards political affect and sentiment did not establish a breakaway from despotism and oppression.

Knot-like, progress here does not move towards new beginnings, but either repeats old forms of subjugation or regresses beyond them to even worse forms of terror. How, however, can we explain that the first modern attempt to subjugate the self under the homogeneous rule of the state proceeded under the concept of natural affect or sentiment? Far from abandoning a Cartesian mind–body divide, Robespierre refers to emotions as the visible concretisation of virtue.

As a result of such reduction, ethics becomes naturalised and as such turns into 'matter' measurable by the mind. The reign of terror followed the concept of natural order first established by the Physiocrats. As has been discussed in Chapter 2, the Physiocrats developed an economic as well as disciplinary theory in eighteenth-century France. In some ways anticipating Adam Smith's interpretation of economics in terms of a rational and harmonious conception of nature, they argued that the economy not only represents but also replicates purported rational operations of the natural order. The Physiocrats were not the first to refer to the concept of natural order – a concept reaching back to Aristotle – but 'they became known as the most vocal defenders of natural order' (Harcourt 2011: 89). In their usage the concept of natural law reconciles individuals with the economic system (which is here part of nature): 'According to this logic, natural law and its orderliness alone can reconcile the perfect liberty of the individual with the determinism of an autonomous economic system' (Harcourt 2011: 89). Here we first encounter what Arendt would see developing further from the French Revolution onwards to the extreme violence which characterises totalitarianism in nineteenth- and twentieth-century political thought and praxis: the suppression of diversity under the dictum of an all necessitating or all determining force – be that the economy, nature or history.

Crucially, necessity first goes under the name of nature and nature itself is here strongly affiliated with reason, order and virtue. The natural order is indeed a product of the mind. Whatever lies outside it is deviant, irrational, unnatural, insane or criminal. Here the sphere of deviance is not nature (even though within another mentally constructed framework it could easily be classified as such) but the unpredictability and potentially non-conforming diversity of human society and psychology. The latter bears a troubling resemblance to the opposite of rational predictability and efficiency – the 'bare life' ('bare' because it is deprived of mental capacities such as language which seem to be prerogatives of the human) of animals.

The order of nature, by contrast, is visible, predictable and measurable and must not be interfered with. According to the *OED*, the term 'order' was coined around 1225 to denote both the theology of angels ('any of the nine grades of angels, according to medieval angelology') and the immanent management of worldly affairs. The word thus combines theological hierarchies with connotations of classifying and managing the contaminating diversity of the secular (the worldly). Order safeguards against the contamination of the predictable with the unpredictable, the measurable with the immeasurable, and the visible with the invisible. Building on the classifying and hierarchical connotations of the thirteenth-century term 'order', modern disciplinary thought and practice endows the economic sphere with nature's perfection, which contrasts with the unpredictability, the deviance, and worse still the 'perversion' from the norm that goes under the names of contamination and hybridity: the consuming and impure psyche of the human animal. Let me explain.

As Bernard Harcourt has recently shown, the leading Physiocrat François Quesnay was a medical doctor as well as a founding father of the modern discipline of economics: 'The economic domain, Quesnay believed, was governed by natural order and constituted an autonomous, self-regulating system that required no external intervention – no administration, no police' (Harcourt 2011: 78). According to Quesnay, economics was part of a natural order which we can understand perfectly well, in the same way that we are in a position to acquire full knowledge of the human body through medical research. Nature's and economy's rationality contrasts sharply, however, with the unruliness, plurality, unpredictability – in short, irrationality (in terms of non-measurability) of human society and the human psyche.

Here we see how the divide between nature and society – which, as we have seen, Latour has analysed as modernity's prime paradigm – is intricately bound up with a Cartesian mind–body divide. How so? Nature's rationality partakes of the mind, whereas human society and psychology are here seen to bear the characteristics of the traditionally sinful, potentially ill and mortal body. Like the body, society requires control, oversight and discipline. The split between economic freedom and societal incarceration which characterises the free market society of modern America (which is of course the setting of Ellison's *Invisible Man*) constitutes a socio-political version of the dualism between mind and body.

This socio-political split between a rational natural order of economics and an embodied, plural and potentially deviant society first crystallised in the divide between economic rationality and political despotism of Quesnay and his fellow Physiocrats:

> The idea of natural order, Quesnay would explain in 1767, inexorably led to a political theory of despotism. Natural order in the autonomous economic sphere demanded, first, that there be no human intervention in terms of positive law in the economic realm and, second, that positive law limit itself to punishing the deviant. (Harcourt 2011: 93)

As Harcourt convincingly shows, this split between nature, economic reason, on the one hand, and body, society, psychology, on the other, characterises social thought from the Physiocrats via the French and American Revolutions to the neoliberal paradigm of a rational free market.

Against this background of partial demotion of our constitution, we can better understand why in a post-Enlightenment, liberal society such as Ellison's mid-twentieth-century East Coast America, whole social groups are still subjected to invisibility, to non-recognition. No wonder that the narrator of *Invisible Man* insists on having not only a body but also a mind: 'I am a man of substance, of flesh and bone, fibre and liquids – and I might even be said to possess a mind. I am invisible, understand, simply because people refuse to see me' (Ellison 2001: 3). As we have seen in the preceding section, invisibility here is a question of perception, of the societal refusal to recognise the existence of someone or a group.

The reason for this refusal reaches back to various Platonist, Christian, humanist as well as Cartesian scientific paradigms which construct our constitution along the lines of a mind–body divide. In this division mental capacities (foremost language) are allocated to the human and an indifferent, as good as invisible body to the animal. As Derrida has put it:

> It is as if the men representing this configuration had seen without being seen, seen the animal without being seen by it, without being seen seen by it; without being seen seen naked by someone who, from deep within a life called animal, and not only by means of the gaze, would have obliged them to recognize, at the moment of address, that this was their affair, their lookout [*que cela les regardait*]. (Derrida 2008: 14)

Derrida's perhaps rather awkward 'seen seen' phrase describes the mutuality of social recognition whose absence describes Ellison's social-scientific notion of invisibility. Thinking matter is what characterises the human: as Derrida has shown, radicalising a Christian as well as humanist mind–body divide, 'Descartes proposes abstracting from his "I am", if I can put it this way, everything that recalls life' (Derrida 2008: 72). The body becomes irrelevant and might as well be non-existent, invisible. Racist stereotyping identifies a given ethnic group with the demoted body that stands in for the animal as the occlusion (hence 'invisibility') and exclusion of the human. As a result of such demotion it is no longer seen to be human but animalistic.

In this way the narrator of Ellison's *Invisible Man* loses his scholarship and with it his place at his school because he had ventured with his College's white philanthropist (Mr Norton) to the slum neighbourhood of Jim Trueblood. Why is this encounter with poverty disturbing to the wasp benefactor? Because it confirms white racist stereotypes of African-Americans as animals: the narrator and his classmates fear 'the crude, high, plaintively animal sounds of Jim Trueblood' (Ellison 2001: 47). Paradoxically, African-Americans only become invisible when they reach the 'high visibility' of Trueblood. Trueblood is scandalous: 'Norton literally goes into shock when he is exposed to the squalid poverty and moral depravity of the rural blacks who lead lives that discredit the reassuring message of the College's tranquil gentility' (Scheingold 2010: 149). While still being socially visible – apparently due to the social and financial support of the white benefactor and his school – the narrator and his classmates are embarrassed by the presence of Trueblood just outside the precincts of their educational institution:

> I didn't understand in those pre-invisible days that their [i.e. his school's] hate, and mine too, was charged with fear. How all of us at the college hated the black-belt people, the 'peasants', during those days! We were trying to lift them up and they, like Trueblood, did everything to pull us down. (Ellison 2001: 47)

His school makes the narrator genteel and visible. Hence his College days are 'those pre-invisible days'. He becomes invisible when his school expels him, rendering him contaminated and scandalous. Then he falls in with the demoted sections of society who, like Trueblood, due to their scandalous 'high visibility', do not get granted social recognition and thus submerge into the 'invisibility' of overlooked animal life. Here society's poverty comes to represent a threat to nature's posited order: the contamination of the animal with the human, of what should be invisible with what is proudly visible.

The predicament of *Invisible Man* illustrates that the problem is no longer the external, natural world (which after Descartes and Kant has become visible, measurable, manageable matter), but the invisible and immeasurable intricacies of psychology and society. Here we need disciplinary rules and regulations to punish those who violate the posited natural order of economics.

As Harcourt and Derrida have shown, this preoccupation with the potential animal-nature of society emerged in the seventeenth century in the wake of Descartes's and Hobbes's scientific and social thought. Derrida has argued that Hobbes's sovereign is a beast, precisely because the state has to be prepared to deal with its subjects as if they were beasts.

The art of statecraft is monstrous, is beastly: 'Art is here, like the institution itself, like artificiality, like the technical supplement, a sort of animal and monstrous naturality' (Derrida 2009: 27). The nature of the beast Leviathan is unnatural due to its societal frame of reference: 'but this absolute sovereignty is, as we shall see, anything but natural; it is the product of mechanical artificiality, a product of man, an artifact; and this is why its animality is that of a monster as prosthetic and artificial animal, like something made in the laboratory' (Derrida 2009: 27). Politics is a product of a social laboratory set up to tame or purify the beast or monster of society.

This is why there exists a close correlation between the criminal and the sovereign: the sovereign has to beat the criminal at his or her own game. The police employ violence and sovereignty to impose the state of exception in order to make what is perceived to be beastly disappear into thin air – to render it invisible. In this sense Derrida writes, 'there is between sovereign, criminal, and beast a sort of obscure and fascinating complicity, or even a worrying mutual attraction, a worrying familiarity, an unheimlich, uncanny reciprocal haunting' (Derrida 2009: 17). The social sciences engineer the beast of absolute sovereignty so as to counteract and thereby turn invisible what has been all too visible in feared states of lawlessness and bawdry. As Derrida has pointed out, the beast of absolute sovereignty operates through producing fear in the populace – fear that accompanies Robespierre's reign of terror: 'Leviathan is the name of an animal-machine designed to cause fear or of a prosthetic and state organon, a state as prosthesis, the organ of a state prosthesis, what I nickname prosthstatics, which runs on fear and reigns by fear' (Derrida 2009: 39–40). The social scientist adopts the radical and potentially violent procedure of a physician or surgeon.

As a physician, the economist or political/legal theorist refers to artificial prosthetic measures in order to cure the assumed unnatural monstrosities that are seen to be societal insufficiencies (such as criminal behaviour or mental illness). Quesnay was a court physician to Madame de Pompadour and later to Louis XV and was clearly part of the ancien régime. As the Encyclopaedia Britannica has stressed, the free trade theory – based as it is on an equation between natural order and economic law – had, however, a huge influence on the French Revolution:

> Their [i.e. that of the Physiocrats] free-trade theories were, however, embodied in the Anglo-French commercial treaty of 1786 and in the Revolutionary decree of Aug. 29, 1789, freeing the grain trade. The land tax established by the Revolutionary Constituent Assembly on Dec. 1, 1790, also followed physiocratic precepts.[5]

Similarly, Harcourt refers to Tocqueville who 'famously noted, in *La ancien régime et la Révolution*, that the Physiocrats were the first writers who sounded most truly revolutionary toward the end of the *ancien régime*' (Harcourt 2011: 210–11).[6] Robespierre and St Just extended the notion of a natural order from the economic sphere to that of society, politics and ethics as whole. As Harcourt has shown, Quesnay and the Physiocrats advocated legal despotism in the face of deviance from the natural order of economics.

The reign of terror's totalitarianism consisted in extending this visible and 'manageable' sphere of natural order from economics to society as a whole. This raises the question whether the 'naturalisation' of not only economics but also the societal in its entirety resulted in the dissipation of the modernist purification project. Once humanity has been completely naturalised, the need for a compartmentalisation (or purification) of nature and society seems to be lost. This, however, did not eventuate.

On the contrary, Robespierre and his fellow practitioners of terror did not declare human society to be contaminated with, or indistinguishable from a rational and virtuous state of natural order. The purported split between nature and society only increased, because of society's perceived deviance and defiance in the face of what it should 'naturally' (or 'sentimentally') be: i.e. virtuous. (In a different historical context, this is also the predicament of Ellison's *Invisible Man*, who has been deprived of his pre-invisible days; as has been discussed above.) What has been economics according to the Physiocrats becomes terror in the hands of St Just and Robespierre: an instrument of the natural order which is at once free and disciplinarian, chopping off the heads of those who do not conform to virtue's affect.

Büchner's play *Danton's Death* pivots around this equation of terror with the natural order as opposed to the perversity of human society set, as it is posited here, against nature. Terror does not only work for the natural order – it is its own manifestation. Büchner's St Just identifies social with natural order, justifying the reign of terror as follows:

> Nature follows her own laws, calmly, irresistibly; man is destroyed wherever he comes into conflict with them. A change in the composition of the air, a burst of subterranean fire, a shift in the equilibrium of a mass of water – an epidemic, a volcanic eruption, a flood kills thousands. And what is the outcome? An insignificant, scarcely perceptible ripple on the surface of the physical world that would almost have disappeared without a trace were it not for the jetsam of corpses. I ask you now: should *moral* nature be any more considerate in her cataclysmic revolutions than *physical* nature? Does an *idea* not have just as much right as a law in physics to destroy whatever stands in its way? (Büchner 1993: 42)[7]

Here terror establishes the identity of the order of nature with the social order of virtue. The contextualisation of Büchner's *Danton's Death* in the mid-nineteenth century thus links it not only with the historical past of the French Revolution, but also with what the equation between rational nature and historical necessity (as discussed by Arendt above) may hold out for modern politics. As we have seen, the French Revolution and Robespierre's reign of terror were important components of an emergent modern and yet violent equation of natural with social order. In the following we will see how not only Büchner but also Melville and Hawthorne complicate timeless conceptions of both nature and society.[8]

Melville's *Moby Dick* and the birth of twentieth-century science

In a similar way to *Danton's Death*, Melville's *Moby Dick* was published in the middle of the nineteenth century, articulating fears about modernity's future while ostensibly being concerned with the past. Effectively, the historical background of *Moby Dick* indirectly encompasses the French Revolution. How does Melville achieve this? As Charles Olson has discussed in some detail, the novel traces and depicts the ways in which whale oil was utilised to produce a certain type of light – a light that contributed to a growing readership's conception of an emerging modernity shaped by enlightenment ideas as well as practices of early globalisation (in the form of colonialism and imperialism; see Olson 1967). Derrida correctly argued that the French Revolution gave rise to both the Enlightenment idea of human rights and the Leviathan-like absolute sovereignty that operates within Robespierre's reign of terror: 'the modern name "terrorism" coming initially, as you know, from the Terror of the French Revolution, of a Revolution that was also at the origin of all the universal declarations of human rights' (Derrida 2009: 30). As we shall see below, following Derrida, Žižek has recently emphasised the close correlation between the light of the enlightenment and the darker elements of terror.

Žižek, however, pays little attention to the fact that in Robespierre's reign of terror Enlightened rationality gave way to a delirious combination of terrifying affect and strategic thinking. Robespierre appealed to the emotions of his audience in order to establish a break with the cool or detached government of the *ancien régime*. A quasi-religion of the affects emerges where feelings overcome the calm of the unemotional whose coldness has come to signify a profound lack of virtue. Affect has thus turned into the cornerstone of the revolution's continual dissatisfaction with the status quo: 'Do they really feel', Robespierre asks, thus highlighting the leading role of the emotions, 'the full weight of that sacred mission, those who, in answer to our justified complaints, are content to say coolly: "With all its faults, our constitution is still the best that has ever existed"' (Robespierre 2007: 8). Žižek nevertheless mentions the *raison d'être* behind this mobilisation of the emotions: the willingness to risk one's life for the greater good of virtue and the revolution.

The emotional espousal of sacrifice preconditions the virtuous independence from worldly or material interests and concerns: 'It is against the background of this topic of the sovereign acceptance of death that one should reread the rhetorical turn often referred to as the proof of Robespierre's "totalitarian" manipulation of his audience' (Žižek 2007: xv). Žižek abstains from questioning the totalitarian character of such emotive endorsement of sacrifice, and he refers to Kant's transcendental philosophy, premised on such metaphysics of a loss of embodied life: 'The argument only works if, in a Kantian way, one presupposes a pure transcendental subject unaffected by this catastrophe – a subject which, although non-existing in reality, *is* operative as a virtual point of reference' (Žižek 2007: xvii). The term 'catastrophe' here refers to the loss of world (through ecological crises or other types of destruction and violence) which is the theme of Arendt's critique of modern science: its aspiration to reach the Archimedean point of view from which the world becomes fully visible. By not only illuminating our condition but rendering it completely translucent modern science also risks harming humanity and its environment. Light here might act as a magnifying glass, incinerating what it illuminates. Conversely, the social and scientific preoccupation with visibility might lead to treating those who are, on account of their societal demotion, highly visible as if they were invisible – the subject matter of Ellison's *Invisible Man*.

Against this background, Žižek argues that from a Kantian metaphysical perspective the ambivalence of light and Enlightenment – at once illuminating and destructive (incinerating what it lights up) – disappears. This metaphysical vantage point is of course that of Kant's radicalisation of the Cartesian mind–body divide. No wonder that Žižek uses this opportunity to launch his attack on contemporary neuroscience (the more developed version of his attack has been discussed in Chapter 1), arguing that metaphysics remains the last bastion which could defend the mind's full supremacy over the philosophical irrelevance of embodied life.[9]

Here Žižek faces an unacknowledged problem: at the point at which philosophy meets politics, embodied social life cannot be easily overcome. The dark side of Robespierre's democratic enlightenment comes to view: terror's positive or substantial imposition of force onto those who are perceived not to conform to virtue and reason. Žižek asks 'how to translate/inscribe the democratic explosion into the positive "police" order, how to impose on social reality a *new* lasting order' (Žižek 2007: xxxv), avoiding to remain ensconced in the virtual sphere of Kantian transcendental philosophy.

Instead, he returns to political reality with a vengeance, appraising the mind's 'virtuous' reign over the mere body of society. In a satirical mode he sides with contemporary religious fundamentalists, who perpetuate Robespierre's affect-ridden espousal of virtue's reign of terror over what is deviant, and non-orthodox, the enemy of a democracy conceived in terms of a homogeneous group. In other words, they represent Carl Schmitt's fascist version of demos; manifested in totalitarian form as the ethnic or religious or class coherence of sovereignty: 'Happy we who live under cynical public-opinion manipulators, not under the sincere Muslim fundamentalists ready to fully commit themselves to their projects ... What better proof of the ethico-political misery of our epoch whose ultimate mobilising motif is the mistrust of virtue!' (Žižek 2007: xxxix). Without acknowledging it, Žižek resurrects the philosophical tradition of constructing natural order as model for the economy and society at large. The crucial point here is that nature has become a synonym for rationality. Nature as product of reason's construction rules over the unruliness of a potentially deviant, unruly, non-homogeneous social body – the traditional body politic which Hobbes clearly conceptualised in his *Leviathan*.

The way in which natural order manifests is still varied. As we have seen, in the context of the reign of terror, sentiments of virtue evidence natural justice. In his late novella, *Billy Budd, Sailor*, Melville narrates the working of natural order in a different ambience: that of the counter-revolutionary English navy. Here the harmless, loyal, good-natured and naive sailor Billy Budd arouses the suspicion of being in league with the French Revolution. As an apparent secret agent of the French Revolution he thus represents danger and the violation of the natural law of justice in the context of counter-revolutionary English naval politics.

As a 'dangerous man' (Melville 2001: 141), the harmless sailor turns into the opposite: rapacious and animalistic nature which disorders the order of natural law – which is of course the proper sphere of human reason. The construction of the innocuous as dangerous is ironically the product of a seemingly rational but in actual fact deeply irrational mind. Claggart, whose mind constructs such fictional but effective distortions (Billy Budd indeed acts the revolutionary by killing the accusing Claggart in a single blow), resembles the monomania of Captain Ahab in *Moby Dick*. Hidden emotions drive the irrational actions of an apparently rational mind:

> Though the man's even temper and discreet bearing would seem to intimate a mind peculiarly subject to the law of reason, not the less in heart he would seem to riot in complete exemption from that law, having apparently little to do with reason further than to employ it as an ambidexter implement for effecting the irrational. That is to say: Toward the accomplishment of an aim which in wantonness of atrocity would seem to partake of the insane, he will direct a cool judgment sagacious and sound. (Melville 2001: 128)

Whereas during the reign of terror the display of virtuous affect provided proof positive of rational justice, in the context of the English navy (fighting France and its revolution) coolness and the absence of emotions evidences a rational and just mind.

The element that triggers moral anxiety and panic remains, however, the same: the feared contamination of the animalistic with the human, which comes to represent the dreaded deviance from a natural order of either a revolutionary or counter-revolutionary conception of the mind.

As we shall see, the rationality of *Moby Dick*'s Ahab is a pretext for his emotional instability too: the economic quest for the profitable oil of whales covers the real motive of revenge. Ahab's monomaniacal desire for revenge quasi-naturally, or, in other words, 'organically', grows out of having his leg amputated by the whale. The latter will from then on bear the name 'Moby Dick' and the apprehended contamination of the human and the animal occurs – what Derrida has called 'the becoming-whale of Ahab in *Moby Dick*' (Derrida 2009: 69). Strikingly, Claggart's insane or obsessive evil is a product of nature too.

A reversal of the meanings of science and nature has taken place. According to Melville nature and its scientific exploration no longer presents a proportional, stable or predictable structure: 'Now something such a one was Claggart, in whom was the mania of an evil nature, not engendered by vicious training or corrupting books or licentious living, but born with him and innate, in short "a depravity according to nature"' (Melville 2001: 128). The narrator spells out that it is not human knowledge or habit or indulgence which causes Claggart's malevolence but nature. Crucially, in *Moby Dick* the whale symbolises nature, which here too provokes Ahab's violent rush for revenge.[10] In both *Moby Dick* and *Billy Budd, Sailor*, Melville dismantles or dismasts the architecture of natural order which, under the pretext of justice and rationality, justifies either emotive-revolutionary or cool counter-revolutionary violence.

In her intriguing reading of Melville's *Billy Budd, Sailor* Arendt exclusively discusses 'the men of the French Revolution' and 'their proposition that man is good in a state of nature and becomes wicked in society' (Arendt 1973: 83). She here clearly articulates the nature–society divide which (as has been discussed above) partakes of a Hobbesian and Cartesian mind–body opposition.

Perhaps the most astonishing of Melville's achievements is to have undermined the divide to which Arendt refers and which, according to Latour, establishes the impossible ground of modernity's purification project: the supposed purity of nature as opposed to the potential depravity of human society. Nature has traditionally been associated with the concept of science and up to the mid-nineteenth century the revealing term 'natural philosophy' denoted what we now understand by science. The ethics of Melville's literature questions the nature–society divide that has shaped our understanding of science.

The term 'science' too easily evokes the illusion of a natural and ordered sphere that has been freed from its messy societal context. What Arendt neglects, however, is that this divide between natural order and disorderly humanity does not only prove to be foundational for modern revolutionary but also modern conservative social thought: for instance, Melville critiques the natural order of political obedience and hierarchy in the figure of Captain Ahab.

Why, however, does a discussion of Melville's *Moby Dick* contribute towards establishing an innovative perspective on Latour's famous conception of a spurious construction which divides society from nature? As we have seen in the preceding chapter, this divide is bound up with another one: that between mind and body. Following Descartes, Kant established a new definition of freedom premised on the mind's autonomy from merely empirical or, in other words, embodied life. According to both Adorno's and more recently Derrida's analysis, Kant identifies embodied life with the animal (Adorno 1997: 80): 'Nothing, Adorno says, is more abhorrent, more hateful, more odious (*verhasster*) to Kantian man than the memory of a resemblance between human and animality (*die Erinnerung an die Tierähnlichkeit des Menschen*)' (Derrida 2008: 103). As Derrida goes on to make clear, 'Adorno takes things much further: for an idealist system, he says, animals virtually play the same role as Jews did for the fascist system' (Derrida 2008: 103). Kant indeed identified Jews with the opposite of freedom and autonomy (see Mack 2003: 23–41), becoming for him symbolic placeholders of heteronomy. In this context of excluding the animal from the human, Kant develops his notion of freedom in terms of the liberation from our (as he sees it animal-like) inclination to depend on objects in the empirical world.

Kant's notion of autonomy clearly has a liberating potential, because it can demystify as mentally constructed what we may have taken to be natural.[11] To say, as Judith Butler rightly does,[12] that the material or embodied is always already preconceived in a signifying system, does not, however, touch upon Kant's and Descartes's prioritisation of the mental over the corporeal and relatedly the demonisation of the societal body in the face of nature's assumed rationality and virtue. The latter is part of what preceded the foundation of modern science: natural philosophy.

Following Adorno, Derrida has highlighted the violence that goes with such opposition between the natural and the societal, between order and chaos, between man and animal: 'And as such a fascism begins whenever one insults an animal, even the animal in man. Authentic idealism (*der echte Idealismus*) consists in insulting the animal in the human or in treating the human as animal' (Derrida 2008: 103). This exclusion of the animal from concepts of the human is founded upon various oppositions between self and other – as they play out in the mind–body divide or in the contrast between natural order and societal chaos or, conversely, in the division between the merely empirical, chaotic matter of nature and the refined cerebral entity that goes under the name of culture. Throughout his work Derrida 'has been emphasizing the fragility and porosity of this limit between nature and culture' (Derrida 2009: 15). Melville's *Moby Dick* undermines this binary construction by highlighting the contamination of human and animal as epitomised by the whale.

Indeed, *Moby Dick* radically questions the tradition of natural philosophy or physical science which presupposes rational and virtuous conceptions of nature. At its very opening Ishmael, the narrator of the novel, acknowledges the irrationality or the 'spleen' of his constitution which makes him seek diversions by taking off to sea: 'It is a way I have of driving off the spleen, and regulating circulation' (Melville 1992: 3). In an as yet insufficiently appreciated irony, the narrator does not so much escape his internal spleen but rather confronts a much bigger form of madness in the figure of the captain of the ship whose crew he decides to join (Captain Ahab of the *Pequod*).

This pervasive sense of irony joins 'the problematic two-part structure' (Bryant 1998: 69) of the novel. Reviewing the literature on *Moby Dick*, John Bryant has maintained that given the novel's 'flip-flopping from Ishmael to Ahab – from comedy to tragedy and from lyric meditation to drama – scholars might locate the cause of the novel's structural oddities in its actual composition and assign differently structured sections to different phases of the composition' (Bryant 1998: 68). Departing from the scholarly consensus, the following shifts the focus of analysis away from the two main protagonists, Ishmael and Ahab, to nature which is the secret prime mover of the novel and of which 'the whale' is the symbol.

Crucially, the image of nature here differs from the natural order of traditional scientific discourse. In *Moby Dick* nature appears unhinged rather than ordered. The suicidal mental disorder of Ishmael and Ahab's self-destructive obsession with revenge meet not only in the generic term 'madness' but also in the inscrutable unpredictability of nature which is as unstable as the sea. Monomaniacal feelings of revenge drive Ahab to kill the whale which deprived him of one of his legs in a primal act of violent counteraction – a classic case of the hunted turned hunter:

> 'it was Moby Dick that dismasted me; Moby Dick that brought me to this dead stump I stand on now. Aye, aye,' he shouted with a terrific, loud, animal sob, like that of the heart-stricken moose; 'Aye, aye; it was that accursed whale that razeed me; made a poor pegging lubber of me for ever and a day!' (Melville 1992: 177)

Here natural philosophy's (from Descartes to Kant to Heidegger and Lacan) various divisions between man and animal collapse: humanity transmogrifies into the animal – the object of human exploitation – 'the heart-stricken moose'.

Ahab's feelings of pain and loss have later come to be classified in neuroscientific findings. Therein they have been categorised by the term 'sensory ghost'. Ahab still feels the presence of the leg which the whale took away. His self-characterisation as a 'pegging lubber' refers to his need of an artificial peg leg for which he summons a carpenter in chapter 108. The carpenter describes the predicament of the sensory ghost from what he heard by hearsay: 'how that a dismasted man never entirely loses the feeling of his old spar, but it will still be pricking him at times' (Melville 1992: 513). On a neuroscientific level, Ahab's bodily illusion of the presence of his missing leg causes his obsession with the quasi-intangibility and invisibility of the whale (as John Lehrer has shown, Melville here anticipates Weir Mitchell's medical discovery of the 'sensory ghost' symptom; see Lehrer 2007: 13). He commits to chasing the whale in a way that parallels his searing and searching pain caused by the persistent feeling of the leg of which Moby Dick deprived him. The past presence of the leg disturbs the present, which is that of the leg's absence. A disorienting and disordered blurring takes place which confuses and contaminates distinctions between animal and man, between the actual and the virtual, between present and past. Here we encounter nature as disorderly force – a force that mutilates and provokes tyrannical rule and obsession for revenge.

The whale Moby Dick in fact gives rise to a new conception of nature not in terms of natural order and physical laws but of intangible and unpredictable life (biology) which resides invisibly in the depth of the sea. Melville indeed makes clear his divergence from traditional scientific conceptions of nature, based as they were on the physics of natural philosophy:

> And when we consider that other theory of the natural philosophers, that all earthly hues – every stately or lovely emblazoning – the sweet tinges of sunset skies and woods; yea, and the gilded velvets of the butterfly cheeks of young girls; all these are subtle deceits, not actually inherent in substances, but only laid on from without, so all deified Nature absolutely paints like the harlot, whose allurements cover nothing but the charnel house within; and when we proceed further, and consider that the mystical cosmetic which produces every one of her hues, the great principle of light, for ever remains colourless in itself, and if operating without medium upon matter, would touch all objects, even tulips and roses, with its blank tinge, pondering all this, the palsied universe lies before us like a leper; and like wilful travellers in Lepland who refuse to wear coloured and colouring glasses upon their eyes, so the wretched infidel gazes himself blind at the monumental white shroud that wraps all the prospect around him. And of all these things the Albino whale was the symbol. Wonder ye at the fiery hunt? (Melville 1992: 212)

This important quotation highlights the collapse of a traditional scientific view which is based on the idea of natural order. What is crucial here is that the unmasking of the illusion of natural order preconditions Melville's egalitarian politics. The latter casts Ahab's political theology of revenge and unconditional fealty to the sovereign into the dark ambience of madness.

With Ahab's mad but effective calls for absolute authority – untouched by critical thinking – Melville parodies the famous medieval concept of the king's two bodies, which Schmitt argues still informs secular notions of sovereignty: 'There is one God that is Lord over the earth and one Captain that is lord over the *Pequod* – On deck!' (Melville 1992: 517). Ironically it is not Ahab the sovereign ruler over the ship but the intangible and disorderly creature of the sea which resembles divinity. We read of the whale's first appearance in the following revelatory terms: 'the grand god revealed himself, sounded, and went out of sight' (Melville 1992: 597). The intangibility of the whale – its appearance on and submergence below water – gives rise to a supernatural sense of ephemerality.

What enrages Ahab is the apparent invisibility of nature of which the whale is a symbol. At the point where natural phenomena turn disorderly, invisible or indecipherable they seem to call into question the political theology of the sovereign's apparent omniscience and omnipotence: 'Would now the wind but had a body; but all the things that most exasperate and outrage mortal man, all these things are bodiless, but only bodiless as objects, not as agent' (Melville 1992: 614). This invisible and yet embodied entity constitutes animal nature – nature beyond the grasp of the mind's construction of a natural order or natural law. The whale is clearly an embodied form of nature. Nature here, however, resembles the potential deviance of society, of the human mind that has not abandoned its animal constitution. The whale is an embodied agent of animal instinct and impetus but yet cannot be pinned down, cannot be the target of a hunt as a clearly visible object could. The whale, however, turns invisible when it submerges its body into the depth of the sea.

This bodily lack of visible objectification highlights the dangerous and at the same time sacred quality of untamed and untameable animal nature: it differs from ordered, controlled and controllable nature; in other words, it avoids becoming the 'matter' of Cartesian science. The novel endows Moby Dick indeed with an angelic aura of madness: 'but maddened by yesterday's fresh irons that corroded in him, Moby Dick seemed combinedly possessed by all the angels that fell from heaven' (Melville 1992: 618). The whale's madness in fact reflects that of Ahab.

Ahab's revenge on the whale turns out to be self-destructive, because the line dividing man and animal is illusory, is actually non-existent. This becomes amply apparent in the brilliant but so far unanalysed collation of Ahab's human cry earlier in the novel (below deck) and the whale's animalistic shriek towards its end: 'Ahab descried the spout again, and instantly from the three mast-heads three shrieks went up as if the tongue of fire had voiced it' (Melville 1992: 615). Within two lines the text enfolds humanity's 'descrying' with the shrieking of animals. The supernatural quality of the 'tongue of fire' bestows not so much the effect of order but of gothic disorder.

Melville's usage of the supernatural derives from his friend Nathaniel Hawthorne's gothic techniques of defamiliarisation. As Lauren Berlant has shown, Hawthorne's 'gothic semiotics of historical transmission' in his 'tales locates the power over the American historical materials in strange and deformed old crones, implying that the past is not our *heimlich* origin, but a place of potential exile from understanding, control, and identification' (Berlant 1991: 37). As is well known, the German word *heimlich* does not only refer to the noun 'home' but also to the order and security associated with being at home, in a secure, tangible, known and structured space. Melville, however, does not merely copy Hawthorne's gothic semiotics. Instead, he transfers from the historical context of Hawthorne's writings to the scientific matter which is the natural philosophy of 'the whale'. By describing nature in a gothic key, Melville transforms the traditional scientific (or natural philosophy) conception of nature from the orderly to the uncanny.

Rather than establishing a model of proportionality, rationality, health and sanity, the passage above illuminates the horrors lurking behind the façade of such illusions of colourful, beautiful, cohesive, and orderly nature to which human society should conform. As Harcourt has shown, this idea of a natural order informs not only scientific but also socio-economic practices from the eighteenth century onwards. Harcourt 'reveals how the notion of natural order from the eighteenth century evolved into one of market efficiency at its most sophisticated, erudite, scientific theorisation – the version that achieved multiple Nobel prizes, prizes that have validated and confirmed in the public imagination the superiority of the supposed unfettered market' (Harcourt 2011: 232). Melville's *Moby Dick* demystifies the orderliness and freedom of the market that produces, exchanges, and consumes whale oil.

Moby Dick does so not only in the figure of Ahab but more importantly in its depiction of nature (of which the whale is a symbol), which is far from guaranteeing the supposed order of free markets in the novel. As Harcourt has shown, free markets have become increasingly associated in the public imagination as orderly, proportional, 'natural', whereas the social has turned into a potential problem of deviancy and criminality – in need of discipline and punishment. In Melville's novel, by contrast, Ahab's revengeful and disproportional monomania does not deviate from nature (i.e. the whale). Rather Ahab's insanity develops from and radicalises the natural force to which it has been subjected (i.e. Moby Dick's amputation of Ahab's leg).

Conclusion: the collapse of natural order

Where the Enlightenment proclaimed modernity as the future promise of full knowledge, visibility, measurability and understanding, Melville's magnum opus narrates the 'collapse of knowledge and of understanding' (Peretz 2003: 30). Its main subject matter is the economic hunt for the oil of whales: 'In general, the mission of sperm-whale hunts is an economic one – to kill as many whales as possible in order to extract oil from their blubber, oil that will be used to light up the dark nights of the inhabitants of the land' (Peretz 2003: 42). As we have seen, this economic mission is also a rational and educational one, because it literally promises to enlighten darkness by dint of the exploitation of sperm-whale oil (producing the light that makes possible the reading of the novel at night). Yet Ahab's economic–rational quest – based on the enlightened mind's natural order – undergoes a collapse into the disorder associated with madness. Ahab obsesses about revenge rather than economic gain or an increase of intellectual light fuelled by nature's oil. It is this turn from self-proclaimed reason to monomaniacal violence which highlights the novel's anxiety about modernity's future. Peretz has recently emphasised this aspect of Melville's mid-nineteenth-century work:

> It is precisely in this remaining open of the enigmatic past beyond its own context that these historical events communicate and resonate even with chronologically 'later' events – the destruction of the Indians is linked to the disaster of the Jews, for example – and thus a book like *Moby Dick* can be said to testify to twentieth-century events, that is, to speak for them and to communicate the horrible excess beyond linear historical time which was revealed through their occurrence. It is because of this that there is no essential difference between *Moby Dick*'s testifying to 'literary' events and its testifying to 'historical' events. (Peretz 2003: 94)

The name of the ship *Pequod* refers to and commemorates the extermination of the Pequods. In doing so it also establishes an intertextual point of reference to Timothy Dwight's eighteenth-century poem 'The Destruction of the Pequods', 'which chronicles the annihilation of the Pequod tribe by the Puritans in a swamp just outside Fairfield in 1637, in response to the murderous activities of Indian "savages"' (Giles 2011: 63). In Melville's novel, the Pequods – bearing the name of the whaling ship – become associated with the 'whale' and thereby traverse traditional, distinct boundaries between man and animal. From the innovative perspective of Melville's magnum opus various distinctions collapse – whether they are those between nature and society or those between past and future. Ahab's cry portends disasters to come not only within the plot of the novel but also those which are visible on the historical horizon of the twentieth century. The namelessness of Ahab's quest also fuses with the white blankness of the animal – 'the whale' resembles 'a ray of light, to be sure without an object to color, therefore blankness itself' (Melville 1992: 220). Ahab's cry of light incinerates what it illuminates.

Another American novel of the mid-nineteenth century inscribes such a portentous cry: '*A scarlet letter or a scar(let) letter is the very definition of the cry*' (Peretz 2003: 58). According to Peretz, the cry in Melville's *Moby Dick* is addressed to Hawthorne, author of *The Scarlet Letter* (to whom the book is dedicated):

Indeed I would suggest that a certain vision of literary history is implied in this exchange of cries, a non-Bloomian vision of literary history, which is not structured as an Oedipal scene with the anxiety of influence inscribed in it, but rather as a history where the past calls out as a wound or a cry that can only be heard and transmitted to the future through a response in kind, through an additional wail. (Peretz 2003: 58)

Hawthorne's *The Scarlet Letter* and Melville's *Moby Dick* indeed share repeated evocations of shrieks and cries. Strikingly it is not the victim who has to bear the scarlet letter – Hester Prynne – but the priest Arthur Dimmesdale who succumbs to crying under the weight of unacknowledged guilt:

> Mr Dimmesdale was overcome with a great horror of mind, as if the universe were gazing at a scarlet token on his naked breast, right over the heart. On that spot, in very truth, there was, and there had long been, the gnawing and poisonous tooth of bodily pain. Without any effort of his own will, or power to restrain himself, he shrieked aloud; an outcry that went pealing through the night, and was beaten back from one house to another, and reverberated from the hills in the background; as if a company of devils, detecting such misery and terror in it, had made a plaything of the sound, and were bandying to and fro. (Hawthorne 1970: 130)

Within this scream the scarlet letter pierces through the surface of reality and permeates the world in its entirety: 'as if the universe were gazing at the scarlet token'. This reduction of our experience to one hue, as it were, is what Arendt has in mind when she writes about the loss of worldliness. Melville elaborates on this reduction of experience while discussing what he calls Captain Ahab's monomania. Monomania characterises the shrinking of our perception and experience of human and natural diversity to one interest, one characteristic, one mission or obsession (which is the subject matter of Don DeLillo's late twentieth-century parody of mathematics in his novel *Ratner's Star*). This reduction of diversity to homogeneity is the panicked response to our disorderly animal nature which cannot be fully or smoothly suppressed. The cry or shriek articulates the return of the repressed, violating the mind's construction of nature in terms of order and proportion.

The crucial point here is that it is not so much the phenomenon of madness – which binds the different personalities Ishmael and Ahab to one common characteristic – but a new perspective on nature which allows for vistas of despair in the face of violence. Both *Moby Dick* and *The Scarlet Letter* trace the societal mechanisms of violence to ideational constructions that establish sharp distinctions between animal nature and ordered nature, between sin (adultery in the Puritan context of

Hawthorne's *Scarlet Letter*) and purity. The collapse of natural order conceptually as well as formally preconditions a peculiar modernist style which ruins stable positions of either order or reliable perspective.

Notes

1. In this way Jack Williamson's study (1973) does not discuss Wells and the ideologies of progress which were the trademark of the Enlightenment as well as the French Revolution.
2. 'die Revolution ist wie Saturn, sie frißt ihre eigenen Kinder' (Büchner 1988: 84).
3. As Simon J. James has pointed out in a conversation with the author, the reason for neglecting politics and the French Revolution in Wells's early 1897 novel about science might well be that his later political works are rather disappointing. Critics tried to avoid questions of politics in Wells's better received earlier fictions on science so as not to evoke the later political novels which do not live up to the literary quality of his early *oeuvre* focusing on science (but which does not ignore socio-political questions).
4. McLean reads the novel in didactic terms as follows: 'The didactic purpose of Griffin's bizarre behaviour should be understood in the context of Wells's insistence that scientists must endeavour to facilitate effective communication with the rest of society, or else risk alienating the ever proliferating public sources of funding for scientific research' (McLean 2009: 87). Rather than being a didactic novel putting on public display the social benefits of scientific research, *The Invisible Man* questions the expectations public opinion has invested in science from the Enlightenment and nineteenth century onwards.
5. http://www.britannica.com/EBchecked/topic/458805/physiocrat (last viewed 23 August 2014).
6. Harcourt goes on to show how this split between nature/reason and society/psychology shapes not only the French but also the American Revolution. He emphasises 'the important role of liberal economic thought in American discourse at the turn of the nineteenth century and the significance not only of Adam Smith, but also that of the Physiocrats' (Harcourt 2011: 210–11).
7. 'Die Natur folgt ruhig und unwiderstehlich ihren Gesetzen, der Mensch wird vernichtet, wo er mit ihnen in Konflikt kommt. Eine Veränderung in den Bestandteilen der Luft, ein Auflodern des tellurischen Feuers, ein Schwanken in dem Gleichgewicht einer Wassermasse und eine Seuche, ein vulkanischer Ausbruch, eine Überschwemmung begraben Tausende. Was ist das Resultat? Eine unbedeutende im großen Ganzen kaum bemerkbare Veränderung der physischen Natur, die fast spurlos vorübergegangen sein würde, wenn nicht Leichen auf ihrem Wege läge' (Büchner 1988: 103).
8. For discussion of a later, early twentieth-century, philosophical critique of the timeless in the thought of Bergson, Hannah Arendt, Husserl and Heidegger see Baars (2012).
9. 'For today's cognitivist analytic philosopher, after the cognitivist turn, philosophy has finally reached the maturity of serious reasoning, leaving

behind metaphysical speculations. For a hermeneutician, analytical philosophy is, on the contrary, the end of philosophy, the final loss of a true philosophic stance, the transformation of philosophy into another positive science' (Žižek 2007: xviii).
10. As Pramod K. Nayar has recently pointed out: 'Driven, monomaniacal and tempestuous, Ahab hates being a disabled captain. Yet, as we see the novel's plot progressing, we understand that Ahab controls everything on the ship. Ahab is an embodiment of the 'reformulation' pattern of the disabled individual's coping with hegemonic views of the male or human body' (Nayar 2014: 105).
11. In this way Judith Butler has analysed the social construction of what may be assumed to be 'natural': gender and sexuality. She does so by referring to Kant's transcendental method (see Butler 2004: 258–77).
12. Significantly, she does so while abstaining from a Kantian prioritisation of the mental over the embodied: 'It must be possible to concede and affirm an array of "materialities" that pertain to the body, that which is signified by the domains of biology, anatomy, physiology, hormonal and chemical composition, illness, age, weight, metabolism, life and death. None of this can be denied. But the undeniability of these "materialities" in no way implies what it means to affirm them, indeed, what interpretive matrices condition, enable and limit that necessary affirmation' (Butler 2004: 151).

4

Contaminating Judgement with its Suspension: Guilt and Punishment in Walter Benjamin, Herman Melville and Henry James

Introduction: Agamben, Benjamin and the contamination of modernity

Natural philosophy or, in other words, traditional science and some strands within literary criticism have been preoccupied with the exploration of orders and patterns – establishing clear but often spurious boundaries between genres such as comedy and tragedy and between life worlds such as society and nature.

Scientists and natural philosophers set out to discover order in nature. According to Bruno Latour, this traditional concern with nature's order informs our modern conception of science. As proof of this persistent privileging of pure categorisations and classifications Latour discusses what he calls a modern division between the assumed perfection of nature and the unpredictability of human society and psychology. Constructions of a virtuous or perfected society – and this equally holds true for socio-economic blueprints derived from either a conservative or revolutionary ambience – took this traditional scientific conception of a natural order as the model for various social theories and practices, from the French revolution's quasi-natural disposition of the sentiment of virtue to the counter-revolutionary categorisation of social hierarchies. Economics is a key social science in this context, because it transposes notions of natural order onto a homogeneous conception of society: one that mirrors the mentally constructed order of nature. Society here turns into a mental model of nature which is posited to be ordered, governmental, or, in contemporary parlance, 'manageable'.

In his recent study *The Kingdom and the Glory*, Giorgio Agamben goes so far to argue that 'modern biopolitics up to the current triumph of economy and government over every other aspect of social life' can be traced to what he calls an 'economic theology, which replaces' political theology's 'transcendence of sovereign power' (i.e. God as sovereign) 'with the idea of an *oikonomia*, conceived as an immanent ordering' (Agamben 2012: 1). The notion 'biopolitics' here describes the imposition of a quasi-scientific order of nature onto the ethical–political core of human sociability. The reference to *Homo Sacer* in the subtitle of *The Kingdom and the Glory* limns the centrality of biopower in this discussion of a theology turned immanent that pervades modern economic discourse and practice, and which Bernard Harcourt has recently analysed as the illusion or myth of 'free markets' (as has been discussed in Chapter 3).

Notions such as modernity or biopower are exposed to contaminations with what their apparent negative is supposed to be. The figure of contamination indeed evokes negativity not in a Hegelian dialectical or plastic way (as recently advocated by the neo-Hegelian philosopher Malabou) where the negative bends or turns into the positive. Rather than a movement from one to the other, here we encounter the co-presence of two or more opposites that contaminate each other. Agamben's recent discussion of economics is deeply indebted to the work of Walter Benjamin who in fact develops a non-Hegelian approach to time and history.

Crucially, Benjamin analyses the dubiousness of purportedly modern understandings of a rational economic order, which under scientific investigation turns out to be more disordered and unscientific than has been acknowledged in some traditional theories and practices. Indeed, Benjamin proposes an alternative image of modernity, which is not hierarchical and that confounds linear or progressive understandings of time. His notion 'Now-time' (*Jetztzeit*) contaminates the past with the present and future: it denotes the co-presence of different temporalities. In the *Arcades Project* he detects in the buildings of modernity what he calls 'images in the collective consciousness in which the new is permeated with the old (Benjamin 1999: 4). These wish images undermine the hierarchical prioritisation of the present over and above the past, because they evidence dissatisfaction with current modes of production and social organisation. Being unsatisfied with the present, they turn to the past, commingling the present as rejection with the past as an opening that could liberate the current state of affairs from past and future injustices.

History thus emerges as the renewing force of the absent, insignificant and forgotten. Modernity describes the birth of what has been suppressed and repressed as scandalous, infectious or contaminating: it instantiates the promotion of the demoted historical past. This attempt to rescue those who have been marginalised and forgotten is affiliated with an idiosyncratic type of theology: one that avoids dogmas and a specific doctrine. As Miguel Vatter has recently argued, Benjamin attempts to free what Agamben would later call 'bare life' from any dogmatic or mentally constructed notions of guilt:

> If life is guilty by nature, then it deserves to be punished, to expiate its guilt. The punishment for disobeying God and eating of the fruit of the tree of knowledge is death. For Benjamin, this conception of a natural life of guilt is entirely 'mythical,' even though it is a mythology that also traverses monotheistic religions, including Judaism. (Vatter 2011: 219)

Benjamin, however, contaminates one aspect of monotheistic religions with its opposite: he argues that the messianic strain in Judaism is not concerned with establishing mythical notions of either guilt or punishment but with overturning such disciplinary mechanisms and procedures.

This holds true also for secular versions of a theological–mythical paradigm: with a despairing gesture, Benjamin saw in the reinforcement of a Kantian divide between freedom (the intellectual/spiritual) and nature (the profane) its messianic overcoming (Mack 2003). To reinforce this dualism between the rational and the natural means to accept a certain level of violence. The violence in question is perpetrated on the demoted body of the profane. This demotion of nature is a crucial theme in Benjamin's book about Baroque tragic drama and in his essays 'Capitalism as Religion' and 'Critique of Violence'. The disgust with nature, the body, and the profane brings about the desire to read the world allegorically. Baroque allegory, in Benjamin's understanding, immanently transcends the immanent to the point of annihilating it. This is exactly what he perceived to be operative in the non-signifying economic transactions that characterise the secular religion of capitalism.

Related to capitalist economics as it emerged within the Christianity of the Reformation and fully developed into the commodification of life at the end of the nineteenth century as analysed in the *Arcades Project*, the reformationist aesthetics of the baroque destroys the profane bodies. This commandment of destroying the profane rules the workings of allegory, just as it seems to motivate the abrupt coming of a redeemed society: 'The human body could be no exception to the commandment which ordered the destruction of the organic so that the true meaning, as it was written and ordained might be picked up from its fragments' (Benjamin 1977: 92).[1] As a self-enclosed, un-contaminated entity, the profane is deprived of meaning.

Such absence of signification engulfs the whole of nature (human nature included) into a maelstrom of guilt. Benjamin foregrounds this point in his essay on Goethe's late novel *Elective Affinities* in such terms:

'With the disappearance of supernatural life in man, his natural life turns into guilt, even without his committing an act contrary to ethics. For now it is in league with mere life, which manifests itself in man as guilt' (Benjamin 1996: 308). Agamben turns Benjamin's notion 'mere life' into his ever so slightly changed coinage 'bare life'. Both expressions, however, refer to life as a pure material, embodied entity uncontaminated by intellectual or spiritual connotations. It is only on the basis of such reduction of life to a zero-point of purity where it is nothing but the biological that the mind emerges in absolute distinction from the body as punitive force. Here the cerebral becomes indistinguishable from politics or power. It exerts violence (what Benjamin calls 'the mythical') by publicly upholding concepts of guilt and punishment which can then be superimposed socially (by the police, by medical authorities and/or courts of law and so forth) on the lives of those who are categorised as being purely alive.

In his 1921 essay 'Capitalism as Religion' Benjamin analyses capitalist economics as such a cerebral–mythical–theological superimposition of guilt onto those who have fallen into debt. *Schuld*, the German word for debt, means both being financially indebted and being legally as well as morally defined as guilty. Benjamin argues that rather than working for a change of heart, Christianity heralds the utter destruction of profane life. Christianity does so when it has become identical with capitalism, declaring the whole of life guilty so that redemption can only be attained in complete despair:

> Capitalism is entirely without precedent, in that it is a religion which offers not the reform of existence but its complete destruction. It is the expansion of despair, until despair becomes a religious state of the world in the hope that this will lead to salvation. God's transcendence is at an end. But he is not dead; he has been incorporated into human existence. (Benjamin 1996: 289)[2]

It is human existence which has been deprived of contamination with the something else of a transcendent, spiritual or intellectual realm. Life in its immanent, purely biological or bare (Agamben)/mere (Benjamin) form is prone to be demoted rather than contaminated by that which is perceived to be its opposite (the life of the mind).

There is a sense in which Benjamin is fascinated by the apocalyptical aspects of the religion of capitalism. He seems to dwell on the *Zertrümering* (complete destruction) unleashed by capitalist economics in a way similar to which the allegorist dwells on the *Trümmer* (ruins) to which profane life has been transformed in Baroque tragic drama.

Are these landscapes of destruction however to be read in a literal sense? Or rather, does Benjamin celebrate this destructive force as what makes incomplete the presumed and presumptuous completion or purity of any kind of work, whether it is that of the profane or that of the spirit/ intellect (i.e. that which the German term *geistig* denotes)? Modernity's destructive force would then be what renders modernity incomplete: it would not necessarily destroy the past which precedes the presence of the modern but it would shatter modernity's pretended position – posing as the temporal endpoint where history's long progress finds its culmination.

Benjamin contaminates the lowly sphere of the profane with the elevations of revelation and redemption. The figure of contamination implicitly operates in Benjamin's work at such crucial moments when it outdoes dualisms between the profane and the redeemed. Benjamin puts this dualism into question. While there is a sense in which one can interpret his thought in terms of a somewhat despairing Kantianism, that is, of Kantianism that despairs of itself, there is also a sense in which he continues a romantic critique – a critique that manifests itself in what Hölderlin perceives as caesura and Benjamin describes as interruption – of Kant's hierarchical divide between freedom and nature. What I have called elsewhere Benjamin's 'transcendental messianism' (Mack 2003: 155–67) outdoes itself if one locates this problematic notion on the ground of an idiosyncratic modernity, one that is not Kantian but Spinozist and romantic. This Spinozist sense of the modern seeks to establish contaminating parallelisms between purported pure concepts and entities (such as mind and body). The modernity of this Spinozism resides in its refusal to assume self-contained forms of identity.[3] On this view, notions such as the profane and the theological lose their semantic stability.

In his 'Theological–Political Fragment', Benjamin seemingly separates the profane from the messianic only to establish their mutual dependence at the end. Politics as the realm of the profane desires a state of happiness but it can reach this state only by way of self-loss.[4] Losing itself, the profane gives way to the reign of the messianic. This is why neither the political nor the theological coincides with itself. Both entities are incomplete and thus contaminate each other. Rather than being autonomous, their seemingly teleological strivings for either profane happiness or messianic redemption diverge from the straight lines of their respective initial constructions and co-inhabit what is, on the surfaces of their appearance, their respective opposites. One path destroys not itself but its reduced, uncontaminated, 'pure' form (as an isolated entity) at the point it enters the pathway of its other.

Is this what Benjamin understands by destruction? If so, his notion of violence is in fact non-violent. It denotes not the annihilation of a given work but its contaminated and contaminating incompletion. In what is pertinent for the discussion of Pasolini's notion of scandal (see Chapter 6), in Nietzschean vein Benjamin argues that 'happiness on earth is encountered only on the way down' (Vatter 2014: 175). The profane finds its fulfilment in states of contamination where it interrupts itself and simultaneously co-inhabits the realm of theology. *Mutatis mutandis*, theologians betray theology when they depict it as autonomous and complete. Theology does not coincide with itself. It requires the profane as its subject matter in a way similar to that in which philology needs a textual basis in order to do its work. Benjamin draws on this non-coincidence of the theological with itself in the N convolute of his *Arcades Project*:

> Bear in mind that commentary on a reality (for it is a question here of commentary, of interpretation in detail) calls for a method completely different from that required by a commentary on a text. In the one case, the scientific mainstay is theological; in the other case, philology. (Benjamin 1999: 460)

This is a rather unsettling argument because it disorders the distinction between the profane and the theological, a distinction on which Benjamin dwells in his theological–political fragment. As 'a commentary on reality', theology depends on the profane in order to do its interpretative work. In order to function it demands of itself a submergence into its opposite, and it has to immerse itself into the profane realm of politics. As Miguel Vatter has shown, Benjamin here refers to Gershom Scholem's notion of 'redemption through sin' (Vatter 2014: 172). Diverging from dialectics, sin, in short the negative, here is not negated but contaminated with its supposed opposite, redemption.

Contaminating economic prudence with mental illness: Melville's Bartleby, the Scrivener and James's The Ambassadors

One could argue that Benjamin was the first thinker who has given us an intriguing account of literature's implicit renunciation of various purification projects which are pseudo-scientific in their reliance on systems of classification and categorisation. Benjamin develops his plea for a suspension of judgements in the face of not so much dialectical or plastic but contaminating, co-focal insights into the apparent incompatible diversity of our lives.

A suspension of judgement is a scientific approach that also informs the analyses of the following two chapters on contamination in the work of Melville, James and Hitchcock. Hitchcock's idiosyncratic notion of suspense indeed derives from holding the audience's convictions about what happens on screen in a suspended position while keeping it in the know. Hitchcock's suspense suspends judgements in the face of knowledge: the spectators are cognisant of crucial pieces of information which elude the protagonists whose actions they are observing.

The same holds true of the relationship between the readers of James's *The Portrait of a Lady* and its main protagonist: we know that Isabel Archer will forfeit her freedom while rushing to marry Mr Osmond, whose aestheticism she imagines will free her from conventional society. As we shall see in the Chapter 4, James's and Hitchcock's practice of suspense slows down and suspends pressures to act and judge. It does so by providing the audience with the knowledge of deleterious actions and judgements of which the main actors in a given work (Isabel Archer in *The Portrait of a Lady* and Scottie in *Vertigo*) are ignorant.

This chapter discusses two novels that set out to persuade us to defer judgements in the face of various uncertainties. It first analyses the reversibility of categories of economic prudence and mental illness in Melville's short novel *Bartleby, the Scrivener* and then explores how such openness to revisions and corrections informs the so far overlooked scientific experiment that Henry James conducts in his impressionist/expressionist novel *The Ambassadors*. Melville's *Bartleby, the Scrivener* radically stages a suspension of judgement confronted with someone whose profession is the law. As Branka Arsić has pointed out, Bartleby's 'I would prefer not to' reverses the priority of the law and its guardian in Kafka's parable 'Before the Law':

> Bartleby seems thus to have reversed Kafka's parable of the law, as if he had managed to go behind the doorkeeper's back, and then to close the open gate, thus keeping the doorkeeper outside of the law. In other words, as if in contrast to Kafka's doorkeeper who claimed that 'this door was open for you,' Bartleby instead says 'this door is closed, and will not be open for you.' By closing the door Bartleby turns the lawyer into the outsider. (Arsić 2007: 20)

According to Arsić, Melville's novella forecloses the narrative scope of Kafka's parable, by closing the gate of the law and thereby excluding anything to do with a legal system. While this is an intriguing reading, it neglects the fact that lawyers (and, as we shall see, economists) still play a significant role in *Bartleby, the Scrivener*. Rather than precluding the law, Melville's short novel confronts notions of guilt and punishment with what they are superimposed upon: the (in Benjamin's words) 'mere life' of the rather innocuous Bartleby. While questioning concepts of a legal order, *Bartleby, the Scrivener* nevertheless presents us with the work of the law, albeit in a rather contaminated context where judgements become suspended rather than executed.

Melville's *Moby Dick* is a key text for a new conception of how literature dismantles illusions of scientific order. Similarly, Henry James's late novels perform a feast of insight into the illusions of perceived modern advancements of order and rationality through the presumed panacea of economic management. Melville's short novel *Bartleby, The Scrivener* (1853) lays the ground for James's engagement with the psychology of disorder which scientific constructions of the certain and the supposedly risk-free tend to neglect. The subtitle of *Bartleby* points to the sphere of high finance: *A Story of Wall Street*. Melville's short novel, however, abstains from displaying economic transactions. The plot of *Bartleby, The Scrivener* is rather uneventful.

In a similar way, James's *The Ambassadors* evokes the economic emporium of Mrs Newsome's New England enterprise only to thwart the expectations it builds. Mrs Newsome sends Lambert Strether from her New England seat of economic power (Woollett) to Paris. In Paris she charges Strether to bring her son Chad back to run the family enterprise. Were he to succeed, Strether would be granted a share of the profits, because he would return as Mrs Newsome's husband. As E. M. Forster has put it: 'Well, whatever it is, Chad Newsome ought to come back and help make it [i.e. economic success at home], and Strether undertakes to fetch him. He has to be rescued from a life which is both immoral and unremunerative' (Forster 1974: 105). In well-established Puritan manner, morality and profit here seem to be indistinguishable.

Strether has therefore much to gain (both morally and financially) from his ambassadorship. Strikingly, he rejects his ambassadorial mission despite the economic personal gain it holds out for him. Chad wants to return to his family's business and to make it more profitable. He sets out to do so with the knowledge about advertisement he has acquired in Europe and which he attempts to introduce to North America. His mother's, Mrs Newsome's, Puritanism in its secular form alludes to traditional notions of both economic and scientific rationality, as made famous in Max Weber's account of the origins of capitalism in his *Protestant Ethics* – a book to which Benjamin implicitly refers in his 'Capitalism as Religion'.

James's novel also associates the character of Mrs Newsome with Puritanism's stringent moralistic ambience. Ironically, the 'new world' of America – to which the name of Chad's mother alludes – is the geographic location of a form of science which appears outmoded from not only the Parisian literary perspective of James's narrator. As has been intimated above, Chad is not so much a literatus but a business innovator, and the innovation he will bring to his American enterprise is the new practice of advertisement which he appraises in a conversation with Strether towards the end of the novel as follows:

> But there was just one thing for which, before they broke off, Chad seemed disposed slightly to bargain. His companion needn't, as he said, tell him, but he might himself mention that he had been getting some news of the art of advertisement. He came out quite suddenly with this announcement, while Strether wondered if his revived interest were what had taken him, with strange consequence, over to London. He appeared at all events to have been looking into the question and had encountered a revelation. Advertising scientifically worked presented itself thus as the great new force. 'It really does the thing, you know.' They were face to face under the street lamp as they had been for the first night, and Strether, no doubt, looked blank. 'Affects, you mean, the sale of the object advertised?'
> 'Yes – but affects it extraordinarily; really beyond what one had supposed. I mean of course when it's done as one makes out that, in our roaring age, it *can* be done.' (James 1964: 339)

Chad here fuses the economic with the scientific. Science promises to enhance profits. The success of the new art of advertisement, which Chad seems to have learned in London, depends on it being 'scientifically worked'. What, however, does it mean to work advertisement in a scientific manner? Chad goes on to clarify what he means by scientific with the term 'the fact of the possible' (James 1964: 340). Money instantiates the factuality of the possible: it promises to render the uncertain certain, the invisible visible – as Chad makes clear when he goes on to say, 'I mean the money in it' (James 1964: 340). Strether's reply 'Oh damn the money in it' (James 1964: 340) encapsulates the rejection of any reduction of the possible to the certain, the measurable.

It is this (Strether's) rejection that harks back to the famous 'I would prefer not to' from Melville's *Bartleby*. Both novels avoid economic transaction by shrinking their respective plots to an impressionist as well as expressionist matter of perception, rather than action.[5] Instead of narrating a certain manifest and linear story, James's *The Ambassadors* adumbrates possibilities of a plot (hence the plural in the title of the novel).[6] Similarly, almost nothing happens in Melville's *Bartleby*, except the arrival and the subsequent removal of a new clerk in the narrator's office, who is in charge of drawing up various deeds. The name the narrator ascribes to his occupation implies movement: 'that of a conveyancer and title hunter, drawer-up of recondite documents of all sorts' (Melville 2001: 9). The novel tells the story of how this legal/economic work undergoes a peculiar change through the arrival of the new clerk Bartleby.

Bartleby disrupts the supposed order of the social sciences (economics and law) not through any disorderly action but by merely being 'motionless' (Melville 2001: 9), by remaining still: by what the narrator calls 'his great stillness' (Melville 2001: 15). Bartleby's strange presence precipitates a heuristic event – a quasi-scientific discovery – on the part of the narrator. The narrator comes to realise that his conception of the world has previously been blinded by taken for granted assumptions, by 'inveteracy' (Melville 2001: 15). Doing away with habituated conceptions of traditional science, the narrator discovers what *Moby Dick* explores in great detail (as has been discussed in Chapter 3): the darkness and uncertainty which traditional scientific quests for the certain and risk-free tend to ignore.

Enlightened by such darkness, the narrator explains: 'Ah, happiness courts the light, so we deem the world gay; but misery hides aloof, so we deem that misery there is none' (Melville 2001: 18). Melville's short novel revolves around the psychological reactions to such insights on the part of the narrator. It is concerned not so much with the figure of Bartleby as with what such unhabituated presence provokes in the internal workings of the mind. It shows how unstable the supposed mental stability of the narrator is when faced with such exposure of a so far neglected aspect of life: 'Revolving all these things, and coupling them with the recently discovered fact that he [i.e. Bartleby] made my office his constant abiding place and hoke, and forgetful of his morbid moodiness; revolving all these things, a prudential feeling began to steal over me' (Melville 2001: 18). Prudence adumbrates far-sighted wisdom and economic calculation. The sagacious and economical narrator attempts to reduce his exposure to risk.

Bartleby provides insight into how such prudent desire to avoid contamination with the economics of loss remains in actual fact blind to the dangers that it does not want to countenance. The narrator shifts from a mode of discovery to one that fears the invisible. The invisible manifests itself in what he and his audience are accustomed not to see, what they avoid acknowledging as existent. The term for such invisibility is 'melancholy', another word for mental illness – a term that Freud used too when he described what we now classify as depression (Ehrenberg 2010: 167).

When Bartleby slightly elaborates on his famous 'I would prefer not to' with 'At present I would prefer not to be a little reasonable' (Melville 2001: 20), fear of mental contamination seizes the mind of the narrator: 'And I trembled to think that my contact with the scrivener had already affected me in a mental way' (Melville 2001: 20). As a result of this anxiety, he decides 'surely I must get rid of a demented man, who already has in some degree turned the tongues, if not the heads of myself and the clerks' (Melville 2001: 21). How can he remove Bartleby's presence?

In what is crucial for the preceding discussion of invisibility, *Bartleby* establishes an implicit contrast between preference and assumption. In order to get rid of his unwelcome employee, the narrator assumes first his departure, and when this does not take place his invisibility, his non-presence: 'Without loudly bidding Bartleby depart – as an inferior genius might have done – I *assumed* the ground that depart he must; and upon the assumption built all I had to say' (Melville 2001: 23). The narrator, however, deludes himself about the non-violent character of assumptions. As in Ellison's *Invisible Man*, the neglect of the other can be deeply hurtful if not lethal (as in the case of Bartleby, who dies of neglect – starvation – in his jail cell).

Melville's short novel shows how assumptions are in fact impositions, while Bartleby's insistence on preference allows for the coexistence of diverse subjectivities. Assumption creates a false sense of scientific objectivity by rendering those invisible who do not fit into what has been axiomatically assumed. The narrator indeed renders Bartleby invisible by assuming his absence: 'In the legitimate carrying out of this assumption, I might enter my office in a great hurry, and pretending not to see Bartleby at all, walk straight against him as if he were air' (Melville 2001: 24). In treating Bartleby 'as if he were air', the narrator falls prey to delusions.

Deluded, the prudent narrator turns out to be deranged rather than Bartleby, whom critics have singled out as mentally ill. In his short novel Melville contaminates medical categorisations of mental illness with what is posited to be their opposite: mental health and economic prudence. A reversal takes place which anticipates the contamination of class hierarchies with madness. *Bartleby, the Scrivener* helps us discover how not only social oppositions but also assumed biological predispositions are subjective constructions of a mind (i.e. that of Melville's narrator who assumes the role of economic prudence).

Melville unsettles what we take to be risk-free or prudent in the economic sphere and shows how social conceptions of the normal also extend to what we have come to consider as a biologically fixed predisposition to mental illness. Melville's Bartleby becomes categorised as mentally ill because he runs counter to societal assumptions of social standing and economic production. Here literature clearly brings together what various scientific purification projects attempt to separate: the sphere of nature and nurture, the natural and the societal. In so contaminating such presumed mutually opposed fields, Melville's short novel makes us realise the unscientific assumption of 'science' when it ignores what does not fit into its notion of certain, risk-free purity – that is to say, those entities that are uncertain, unpredictable, and therefore risky but not to be wished away aspects of our world.

James's *The Ambassadors* and the contamination of boundaries dividing the sciences from the arts

Now we shall see how Henry James further develops Melville's engagement with what we have not been confronted with in standard scientific accounts of gender, class, economics and health. In his 1903 novel *The Ambassadors*, James advances a so far neglected critique of pseudo-scientific assumptions by bringing to the fore the pitfalls of a publicly acclaimed trust in the chimera of economic order. Having intimated some of the discussion that follows, it is worthwhile bearing in mind that the focus of critical discussion (regarding *The Ambassadors*) has so far been on traffic and the network of a growing global information age.[7] The transatlantic trafficking of letters and people is no doubt a major topic in *The Ambassadors*.

What has been overlooked is that the much discussed international theme which constitutes the narrative framework of the novel[8] implicitly refers to the emerging acceleration of global trade in the late nineteenth and early twentieth centuries. In an important and detailed study, the philosopher Robert B. Pippin has highlighted the absence in critical literature of a historical consciousness that partakes of James's international theme as follows: 'But this, this resistance to reading James as having such a significant historical consciousness, is all because the major categories of the International Theme are often treated very much as they appear on the surface of James's narrative, and on the surface they can seem very conventional' (Pippin 2001: 32). The narrators of James's historical consciousness record as well as debate the effects of an accelerating global capitalist economy – which is also an important theme in the preceding discussion of Melville's *Moby Dick* – on social and intellectual life. Pippin maintains that due to the ever increasing intensity as well as predominance of these global financial transactions 'everything of significance in the basic manners of civilized life known heretofore, in the role of history, hierarchy, sensibilities, gender relations, social power, is about to change' (Pippin 2001: 33). Questions of economic rationality certainly lurk in the background of the novel.

Most striking here are the words 'money' and 'Puritanism'. In his notes on the 'Project of the Novel' James depicts the main character of the novel, 'the ambassador' Lambert Strether, as having endured considerable exposure to the Puritanism of New England. Strether's is 'the history of a man no longer in the prime of life, yet still able to live with sufficient intensity to be a source of what may be called excitement to himself, not less to the reader of his record' (James 1964: 367). Strether's excitement is that of consciousness, of reflection and observation.

It is the 'fun' of theory (understood as spectatorship) if you will. Theory, here defined in terms of its Greek or Latin etymology, denotes sight and the act of perceiving or viewing. As a person who views, Strether could be associated with the contemporary (around 1900) ascendency of the modern media cinema, and in a recent article Brenda Austin-Smith has convincingly argued that:

> Strether might be seen as the ideal spectator, the prototype of the person for whom cinema is intended. The possessor of a modern sensibility to seduction by visual impressions, Strether responds with the perfect blend of emotions to what he sees, moving through curiosity, desire, envy, regret, and, finally, detachment as he encounters the scenes and people before him. (Austin-Smith 2012: 40–1)

As a cinematic figure, Strether is also associated with the emergence of modern science which, as Lisa Cartwright has shown, has a close affinity with cinema.[9] Much of what we see while reading *The Ambassadors* becomes mediated through Strether's observations. He is the camera lens that shapes and filters the images projected within the frame of the novel. His perceptions are open and his perspective is detached (or 'objective') like that of the scientist. His detachment brings to the fore the contours of the surface image of the bodies and souls we encounter in *The Ambassadors* but his intensity and sense of excitement also endows these images with an imaginative life which drives and animates the experiments, projections and discoveries of both modern cinema and science. He is a man in his mid-fifties who has left his native New England home for the old European Continent. His fate lies at the heart of the international theme: the ground is not that of stable belonging to one nation and one tradition. As in Melville's *Moby Dick* the ground has become unstable and fluid: land has given way to the shiftiness of the sea. Strether has indeed traversed the sea which separates the new from the old world.

As James, however, makes clear in his letter to T. S. Perry of 20 September 1867, he understands by the term 'America' not the separation but the blurring of distinctions between the old and the new. According to James, America symbolises the liberating and heuristic force of contamination. In his usage America has become a catchword for uncertainty, ambiguity and the dismantling of categories, classifications and national boundaries. Avant-garde science holds out the promise of such contamination, herein departing from the traditional scientific quest for purification, for order and for separate as well as distinct entities. According to James, Americans are ahead of Europeans in having attained the scientific freedom to enquire into truth outside traditional rubrics and boundaries:

> We can deal freely with forms of civilization not our own, can pick and choose and assimilate and in short (aesthetically etc.) can claim our property wherever we find it. To have no national stamp has hitherto been a defect and a drawback, but I think it not unlikely that American writers may yet indicate that a vast intellectual fusion and synthesis of the various National tendencies of the world is the condition of more achievements than any we have ever seen. (James 1986: 1)

Strikingly, here James defines the paradox of a national identity that is transnational and international in aesthetic terms ('aesthetically'). This definition of American identity as the unhindered traversal of all possible national identities performs a form of freedom which we may also experience while engaging with novels and other works of art. More importantly, in the quote above James takes such aesthetic experiences, in which categories turn fluid and national boundaries turn permeable, to be the precondition 'of more achievements' in the larger intellectual-scientific and societal sphere.

Strether's crossing of the Atlantic partakes of this aesthetic experience which goes under the name American. The literary or aesthetic dimension of this undertaking is crucial: through literature the mechanics of travel – acts of traversing the Atlantic and crossing various national boundaries – become part of the traveller's consciousness. The consciousness in question here is, however, no longer that of the tradition. It is no longer assured of its controlling position in the world – a world that has likewise lost stability and no longer resembles the solidity of land but the fluidity of the sea. As James puts it in his project notes, Strether indeed lives an 'incoherent existence, without any of the accompanying entertainment or "fun"' (James 1964: 377). This absence of entertainment highlights another aspect of America which contrasts with its characterisation in literary aesthetic terms. The terms America or Europe (as every other subject matter in James's novels and short stories) become subjected to a multiplicity of perspectives – to open-ended exposure to a variety of sights and significations which outdo the hegemony perpetuated in the purifying system at work in traditional scientific categories. While evoking the illusion of certainty and stability, these pure scientific categories fail to do justice to the open and often contingent constitution of our world.

There is another aspect to Strether's American upbringing: he has been shaped not only by Puritanism but also by the capitalist preoccupation with money and finance. Most importantly, from a literary–aesthetic perspective James takes issue with precisely this economic assessment of what it means to be modern (as encapsulated in Strether's 'Oh damn the money in it') (James 1964: 340). Here James relegates the capitalist dimension of America and modernity at large not to intellectual and scientific advances but to the persistence of Puritan and other European traditions of which doctrinaire religious hostility to the arts and sciences partakes.

In his famous essay 'The Art of Fiction' James indeed defines the freedom of modernity by the intellectual and scientific achievements of literature. The traditional suspicion of the arts, by contrast, is a remnant of a doctrinaire past which rejected the free and open-ended enquiry characteristic of avant-garde science and literature:

> Art, in our Protestant communities, where so many things have got so strangely twisted about, is supposed in certain circles to have some vaguely injurious effect upon those who make it an important consideration, who let it weigh in the balance. It is assumed to be opposed in some mysterious manner to morality, to amusement, to instruction. (James 1986: 168)

From this traditional Protestant perspective – whose tradition goes back to Plato's ban on poets in his ideal *Republic* – literature is more subversive than other arts because it is capable of working most intensely, while invisibly, on the audience's inner life. That is to say, it may have the capacity to transform the reader's consciousness and perception: 'But when it [i.e. art] is introduced into literature it becomes more insidious – there is danger of its hurting you before you know it' (James 1986: 168). The insidious destruction wrought by literature consists in changing consciousness and turning the audience's perception towards the discovery of realities which are new and have yet to be faced up to intellectually-scientifically as well as emotionally.

These changes are to do with modernity's fluidity (the theme of Melville's *Moby Dick*), which requires a new understanding of science, no longer in traditional terms of purity, order and stability. Volatility, fluidity and instability are of course also pertaining to the actual workings of a modern economy of free markets. The traditional Protestant (and Puritan) condemnation of literature amounts to a rejection of complex scientific investigations into what constitutes human knowledge. Modernity's promise of freedom allows for such intellectual journeys and discoveries. In his essay 'The Art of Fiction' James singles out literature as the performance of such modern freedom without which all scientific and moral values would flounder: 'But there will be no intensity at all, and therefore no value unless there is freedom to feel and say' (James 1986: 170). How does literature enact such intellectual-scientific as well as affective freedom? On a formal level it innovates – and to innovate is precisely what James sets out to do when he breaks with the traditional novel in his groundbreaking *The Portrait of a Lady*.

Crucially, not only does innovation in literature change what we understand by a given genre, but it also transforms the way we perceive and act in the world (the insidious work it does to consciousness about which Plato and the Puritans were so concerned). It overturns traditional presumptions of order and other default conceptions of what the world must be like. James defines the social and scientific benefit of art and literature as this work of innovation: 'Art derives a considerable part of its beneficial exercise from flying into the face of presumptions, and some of the most interesting experiments of which it is capable are hidden in the bosom of common things' (James 1986: 175–6). Significantly, James uses a word which encompasses both scientific methods and procedure: 'experiments'.

This scientific, experimental horizon in James's understanding of literature has so far been neglected due to his representation as an aesthete. Indeed for the historians Lorraine Daston and Peter Galison James epitomises the growing divide between arts and sciences at the *fin-de-siècle*. They single out his apparent artistic objections to 'objectivity':

> Conversely, when James himself self-consciously tried to write with 'objectivity,' he described it as a 'special sacrifice' of the novelist's art. The scientists, for their part, returned the favor. For example, in 1866, the Paris Académie des Sciences praised the geologist Aimé Civiale's panoramic photographs of the Alps for their 'faithful representations of the accidents' of the earth's surface, which would be 'deplorable' in art, but which 'on the contrary must be [the goal] towards which the reproductions of scientific objects tends.' The scientific self of the mid-nineteenth century was perceived by contemporaries as diametrically opposed to the artistic self, just as scientific images were routinely contrasted to artistic ones. (Daston and Galison 2007: 37)

Does not James's writing challenge such divisions between the arts and sciences? This chapter, together with the following one, discusses how he contaminates the subjective with the objective, implicitly repudiating the postulate of either 'pure' objectivity (which, as Daston and Galison have clearly shown, public opinion associates with the sciences) or 'pure' subjectivity (associated with the arts).

Rather than subscribe to such common representation of the aesthetic as uncontaminated by science, James argues that both artistic and scientific practices meet on the level of experimentation. Art and literature open up our common, shared world to experiments wherein we may discover new forms of life that we may already inhabit but which we have previously been unconscious of.

This element of conscious (experimental, scientific) discovery in James's literary practice has so far been marginalised and attention has instead been paid to more general discussions about the changed historical setting of capitalist bourgeois modernity – a theme particularly dear to the philosopher Pippin.[10] Pippin importantly emphasises that James perceives in capitalist modernity a destruction of traditional communities and values as well as moral certainties related to such communal life. Pippin argues that James as moralist treats 'not so much the necessities, regularities, deadly conformism and so forth of such a society' as he engages with 'what this new social power has destroyed and how little of what we need it has left in its place' (Pippin 2001: 16). Does James characterise New England's commercialism and Puritanism indeed as new? He traces Puritanism's hostility to art and literature back to traditional Western Christianity (which in turn derives some of its more austere aspects from Platonism and other ancient Greek philosophical schools).

This is not to dismiss or belittle the importance of Pippin's concern with a changed historical context, but to say that James sees within these putatively modern forms of isolation and alienation a radicalisation of inhibitive, consciousness-foreclosing habits which have given rise to all kinds of suspicions and superstitions in premodernity as they do with admittedly much more powerful effect in more advanced, modern times too. Pippin goes on to identify modernity with the historical change of capitalism which renders individuals 'strangers to and suspicious of each other but who nonetheless must find some way of counting on each other, must find some "modern" moral life' (Pippin 2001: 16). Suspicion is of course what drives Mrs Newsome to send her friend Lambert Strether from New England to Paris to report back on the life of her son (Chad) there. The Puritanism of New England does not, however, characterise the newness of America but rather the persistence of old European traditions of which Protestantism and capitalism could be seen to partake.

Breaking with both American and European forms of Puritanism, James's *The Ambassadors* conveys a sense of how Strether becomes acquainted with entertainment, as a spectator rather than an actor. Clearly he inhabits subjectivity and yet his position as outsider also makes for his larger, more objective perspective. *The Ambassadors* indeed contaminates boundaries that are supposed to separate not only Europe from America, but also subjectivity from objectivity, science from art.

Strether – while subjectively engaged – is also at a distancing, more objective remove from what he witnesses in Paris, the location of a certain new freedom and fun of which he has been deprived while spending the prime of his life in the Puritan ambient of the new world:

> He feels tired, in other words, without having a great deal to show for it; disenchanted without having known any great enchantments, enchanters, or, above all, enchantresses; and even before the action in which he is engaged launches him, is vaguely haunted by a feeling of what he has missed, though this is a quantity, and a quality, that he would be rather at a loss to name. (James 1964: 377)

This sense of a loss, of a missed life opens Strether to new ways of living which he encounters in Paris. The new breaks the order of what he has been accustomed to in his old home (America).

The move from New England to Paris has confusing and contaminating ramifications for Strether's moral life. Paris exposes him to a contamination with what is vulgar and in conflict with moral categorisations. Before his move to Paris Strether 'has not been too much mixed up with vulgar things; he has always been occupied and preoccupied, in one way or another, but always in all relations and connections been ridden by his "New England conscience"' (James 1964: 377). This 'New England conscience' indeed instigates his trip to Paris – it is the *raison d'être* for the novel's narration.

The novel, however, questions the rationality of the move – the reason for it is stipulated by the moral, historical and social order to which a New England conscience is beholden – and the ensuing narration. Strether leaves his old unlived life behind while feeling obligated to act as an ambassador to an authority figure in the small New England town Woollett: 'He comes on a kind of moral and sentimental mission, but committed to nothing more than to get hold of Chad tactfully, kindly, to try to fish him out of his deep waters. He is to act only within his full discretion, and he is to report on the situation and enlighten Mrs Newsome's darkness' (James 1964: 382). Here James establishes an interconnection, indeed a chiasmus between darkness and enlightenment. Light here undergoes a visitation or contamination by darkness: like the narrator in the first part of Melville's *Bartleby*, Strether becomes enlightened by the darkness he encounters in Paris.

The question remains, however, whether Mrs Newsome's New England Puritanism allows for the contamination exerted by Strether's ambassadorship. Strether has to report back to Mrs Newsome about the possible moral pitfalls to which her son Chad might be exposed in Paris and to persuade him to return home. He is beholden to Mrs Newsome's Puritan obsession with purity: 'The case has been virtually as simple for them as that. Perdition on one side, salvation on the other' (James 1964: 382). These Puritan certainties collapse for Strether when he receives his 'moral "dishing"' (James 1964: 385). Strether's sense of a moral order collapses when he increasingly senses the validity of Chad's relationship with the much older Madame de Vionnet. His sense of ambassadorship shifts at this point, partly due to Madame de Vionnet's freedom from any sense of guilt about her relationship (outside wedlock) with a young man. From now on Strether sees himself less as a spy who reports to Mrs Newsome about her son's contaminated exposure to Paris, but as someone who himself transmits, telegraphs, as it were, the contamination.

Strether rejects Mrs Newsome's 'idea to spy on Chad's proper freedom' (James 1964: 128). He does not confirm Mrs Newsome's horror of contamination – which here is the contamination of the old (Madame de Vionnet) with the young (Mrs Newsome's son Chad). Strether departs from such horror at contamination, which keeps Mrs Newsome on edge:

> 'And yet Mrs Newsome – it's a thing to remember – *has* imagined, did, that is, imagine, and apparently still does, horrors about what I should have found. I was booked, by her vision – extraordinarily intense, after all – to find them; and that I didn't; that I couldn't, that as she evidently felt, I wouldn't – this evidently didn't at all, as they say, "suit" her book. It was more than she could bear. That was her disappointment.' (James 1964: 299)

Like Bartleby, Strether does not do what is expected of him: he prefers not to condemn or report as horrible what Mrs Newsome wants him to judge as non-acceptable. His subjective-objective spectatorship unsettles prearranged opinions, representations and judgements. In doing so, he overturns a preconceived, axiomatic order of things (which posits Paris as 'impure'). Asked if she wants to find her son Chad the butt of condemnation, Strether makes clear that it would have been the woman whom Mrs Newsome has 'booked' as the source of moral contamination:

> 'You mean to have found Chad himself horrible?'
> 'I was to have found the woman.'
> 'Horrible?'
> 'Found her as she imagined her.' (James 1964: 382)

James transposes Bartleby's refusal to act into the theoretical sphere of seemingly passive observation. Strether's refusal takes place in the sphere of the imagination.

Conclusion: towards a contamination of action with perception

What is crucial for the discussion in the next chapter is that James's late novels (such as *The Ambassadors*) discover perception to be a form of action. Strether's refusal to imagine Chad's relationship with 'the woman' as Mrs Newsome wants him to has clear consequences for the plot of the novel, as it disrupts the implementation (the booking, as it were) of Mrs Newsome's plan.

Strikingly, *The Portrait of a Lady* goes without such refusal or disruption of a prearranged scheme. While trying to avoid confinements, Isabel Archer rushes into a life of action which does not liberate her – as she hopes – but even more deeply ensnarls her into the plot of those whom she admires and yet fails to perceive as who they are: manipulators and schemers (Madame Merle and Mr Osmond). As the following chapter will show, James and Hitchcock in their novels and films engage in aesthetic experiments which help us understand the science of the mind.

Mental activities such as reading, reflecting and thinking are not to be separated from urbane or cosmopolitan ambitions. As the literary critic and neuroscientist Mark Turner has put it:

> The processes of the literary mind are usually considered to be different from and secondary to the processes of the everyday mind. On that assumption, the everyday mind – with its stable concepts and literal reasoning – provides the beginnings for the (optional) literary mind. On the contrary, processes that we have always considered to be literary are the foundation of the everyday mind. Literary processes like blending make the everyday mind possible. (Turner 1996: 115)

Indeed, James contaminates word with world. The compartmentalisation of the literary text from the physical sphere of materialist interests results in an embrace such as Isabel Archer's of tyrannical and reductive manipulators such as George Osmond. Isabel's fate shows how actions that refrain from undergoing various revisions within a mental arena render themselves null and void (are indeed self-destructive). Our active life has to be exposed to mental forces of perception. James makes a strong case for contaminating action with perception and intertwining our embodied with our cerebral life. Only such reciprocal contamination of what traditional scientific and philosophical discourse posits as mutually opposed entities (such as the body and mind) facilitates various corrections and revisions by virtue of which Strether refuses to buy into the plan (the book) of Mrs Newsome.

Notes

1. 'Der menschliche Körper durfte keine Ausnahme von dem Gebot machen, das das organische zerschlagen hieß, um in seinen Scherben die wahre, die fixierte und schriftgemäße Bedeutung aufzulesen' (Benjamin 1974: 145).
2. 'Darin liegt das historisch Unerhörte des Kapitalismus, daß Religion nicht mehr Reform des Seins sondern dessen absolute Zertrümmerung ist. Die Ausweitung der Verzweifelung zu religiösen Weltzustand aus dem die Heilung zu erwarten sei. Gottes Transzendenz ist gefallen. Aber er ist nicht tot, er ist ins Menschenschicksal einbezogen' (Benjamin 1974: 101).
3. In an intriguing discussion of Benjamin's image of Proust, Carol Jacobs has discussed non-identity and non-coincidence as key characteristics of the work of remembrance: 'Spontaneous remembrance at first seems very like that memory that satisfies an elegiac desire for coincidence with past happenings, but it brings us instead to a world of non-identity. As the children play their game, the rolled-up stocking seems, like the *mémoire involuntaire*, to promise access to a plenitude behind it; but what seems to function as container and a sign for fullness is found to have always from the first been a mere stocking, an empty sign. The children's play with the stocking is like a particular gesture of Proust: just as the children cannot satiate their desire to transform the pouch and its contents into the stocking, "so Proust could not get his fill of emptying the dummy, the Self, with a grasp in order over and over to bring in that third thing – the image". The *Attrappe* (which may be translated as "dummy," "imitation," or "trap") for which Proust reaches seems to signify the hidden presence of the self. But the grasp that should render this contents (sic!) present only leads to a voiding of the self. The dummy that seemed to promise the plenitude to self was always a mere image, just as the full pouch of the children was always a mere stocking. The gesture of Proust, like that of the children, is only a game. His insatiable desire is not the longing for the presence of the self, but rather simply to repeat the movement, to transform the dummy over and over into an empty image' (Jacobs 1999: 44–5).
4. Carol Jacobs has noted a similar notion of identity as premised on the loss of selfhood in Benjamin's essay on 'The Task of the Translator': 'The Translatability of the text excludes the realm of man and, with him, the figure to which Benjamin's essay is devoted. The *Aufgabe* of the translator is less his task than his surrender: he is *aufgegeben*, "given up", "abandoned". This is the essay's initial irony' (Jacobs 1999: 87–8).
5. This is not to say that Melville's *Bartleby* is about the fate of the writer/reflective man in a society dominated by commerce, as Leo Marx has claimed: 'It is a commercial society, dominated by a concern with property and finance. Most of the action takes place in Wall Street. But the

designation has a further meaning: as Melville describes the street it literally becomes a walled street. The walls are the controlling symbols of the story, and in fact it may be said that this is a parable of walls, the walls which hem in the meditative artist and for that matter every reflective man' (Marx 2001: 241). Melville's narrator depicts Bartleby not so much as reflective as by being marked by a mental pathology. As we will see, the short novel turns upside down our understanding of what is normal and what is pathological. The issue of the mind and of perception looms large in James's *The Ambassadors* too. As Ian Watt has famously shown, straight from its opening the novel offers 'an immediate immersion in the processes of the hero's mind as he's involved in perplexities which are characteristics of the novel as a whole and which are articulated in a mode of comic development which is essentially that, not only of the following chapter, but of the total structure' (Watt 1960: 274).

6. For a discussion of the avoidance of certainty which is related to the narrative refusal of closure in *Ambassadors* see Bell (1991: 324–77).
7. Perhaps the strongest discussion of the theme of the international network is in chapter 2 of Ellmann (2010).
8. See for example Rivkin (1986) and Goble (2007).
9. See Cartwright (1995).
10. But it is a theme that is also dear to preceding generations of critics that have been preoccupied with historical issues such as commercialism, which is of course an important theme in James's late novels. As Joseph Warren Beach has intriguingly put it: 'For it involves nothing less than the formal opposition of a commercial, utilitarian and narrowly puritan way of living and thinking to that "possible civilization in which the manners, etc., shall be the index, etc.". That is, for Strether it involves his instinct to judge moral situations from the inside by their quality and substance rather than by the labels attached to them by conventional opinion from the outside' (Beach 1918: 7).

Contaminating the Digital: Action and Perception in Henry James and Alfred Hitchcock

'their feeling as their doing'
Henry James, preface to *The Princess Casamassima*

Introduction: acceleration from the Industrial Revolution to the high modernity of our digital culture

Strether is a spectator. As such, he is a theoretical person: according to its Greek etymology, theory is a form of spectatorship. Perception, however, does not exclude praxis. On the contrary, James's writing and thought contaminates the practical with the theoretical. Rather than preventing an active life, Strether's theoretical bent slows down his actions and in doing so renders them more thoughtful. James's back and forth between perception and action, between meaning and deed has a special pertinence for our contemporary digital culture, which accentuates the blurring of the difference between audience and production. As George Dyson has recently argued, Von Neumann invented digital software when he and Turing instigated numbers not only to mean but to do things:

> '"Words" coding the orders are handled in the memory just like numbers,' explained Von Neumann, breaking the distinction between numbers that *mean* things and numbers that *do* things. Software was born. Numerical codes would be granted full control – including the power to modify themselves. (Dyson 2012: 64)

Once the computer was invented in the 1940s, 'numbers would assume a life of their own: numerical organisms were replicated, nourished, and rewarded according to their ability to go out and *do* things: they performed arithmetic, processed words, designed nuclear weapons, and accounted for money in all its forms' (Dyson 2012: 239). Our digital culture places a premium on actions, on *doing*. Actions are, however, more quickly and more efficiently performed by machines than by humans.

Questions of hermeneutics increasingly give way to the startling performance of computer-generated efficiency. Computers read faster than a human could ever read. As Dyson has pointed out, however, 'reading does not imply understanding' (Dyson 2012: 313). Speed does not necessarily coincide with intelligence. Infinite streams of information do not ensure that what is transmitted can also be understood:

> Through large-scale statistical, probabilistic information processing, real progress is being made on some of the hard problems, such as speech recognition, language translation, protein folding, and stock market prediction – even if only for the next millisecond, now enough to complete a trade. How can this be intelligence, since we are just throwing statistical, probabilistic horsepower at a problem, and seeing what sticks, without any underlying understanding? (Dyson 2012: 310–11)

Acceleration has been ever increasing since the Industrial Revolution in the middle of the nineteenth century. Speed elevated doing: the sheer quantity of actions. Henry James and Alfred Hitchcock in different yet related ways show how actions without the perceptive work of understanding can have deleterious – if not lethal – effects.

James's novels and Hitchcock's films work on the way their audience sees the world of action and perception. They do so in order to slow down the way we come to reach a judgement or pursue a certain course of execution. Similarly to Melville's Bartleby, Strether in *The Ambassadors* refuses to come to the conclusions which Mrs Newsome has already commissioned him to endorse. He takes his time, observes Paris for himself and refrains from condemning the relationship between Mrs Newsome's son and a much older Parisian woman. Judgement, condemnation and the concomitant return of her son Chad to the family's business in New England is in 'the books' of Mrs Newsome's plan, which Strether should merely implement as an 'ambassador'. Strether – at least for a while – prefers not to.

As we shall see, the suspension of judgement and action also takes place in Hitchcock's idiosyncratic notion of suspense. Both the writer and the film-maker place a heavy emphasis on deceleration. This may be interpreted as a response to the ever increasing speed of socio-political and economic life in the wake of the rapid technological innovations which have kept proliferating ever since the onset of the Industrial Revolution. Our digital age is an offspring of such innovations.

Slow motion in James's novels and Hitchcock's films contaminates the speed which shapes many aspects of life from the Industrial Revolution to the contemporary digital high point of modernity. Societal pressures in times of acceleration often encourage the endorsement of quick and simple solutions. Jaron Lanier (one of the inventors of virtual reality) has recently admonished the way a digital world governed by algorithms may reinforce the herd mentality of 'group think':

> In each case, human creativity and understanding, especially one's own creativity and understanding, are treated as worthless. Instead one trusts in the crowd, in the big *n*, in the algorithms that remove the risks of creativity in ways too sophisticated for any mere person to understand. (Lanier 2010: 99)

Both James and Hitchcock complicate accelerations of actions as well as judgements by endowing the audience with the suspense of knowledge that the protagonists miss due to their compulsion to move towards and to embrace what turn out to be entrapments.

Contaminating action with observation: Henry James's literary-scientific innovation

What has so far been neglected is that James's *The Portrait of a Lady* and *The Ambassadors* idiosyncratically reveal observation as the kernel of action. *The Ambassadors* effectively collapses the traditional opposition between perception and action. By perceiving the freedom which arises out of Chad's scandalous relationship with a married and much older woman, Strether gains a new sense of an active life outside the restrictions of traditional moral society. James does not problematise this sense of a new, free ranging morality out of the sources of contemplative discovery (i.e. Strether's position of observation). James's literary modernism consists precisely in turning upside down our accustomed usage of concepts such as new versus old, perception as opposed to action. Strether – a product of America's new world – discovers in the old world of Europe (Paris) what his puritanical upbringing previously inhibited him perceiving: the liberating force of the new, the modern and unconventional which transgresses boundaries of age.

In this way, *The Ambassadors* radicalises what James had first spelled out in *The Portrait of a Lady*: the modernist novel's capacity to confound categories and traditional ways of perceiving ethics, science and human knowledge as such. To be more precise, James fully articulates his multi-perspectival approach to literature in the 1908 preface to the novel's New York edition. Strikingly, James wrote this preface after he had already published *The Ambassadors*, which remained, as Michael

Gorra has recently pointed out, his favourite novel: 'The sheets on his desk were from a book he had published in 1881, a quarter of a century ago: *The Portrait of a Lady*, the novel in which, after a period of careful apprenticeship, he had first allowed his imagination full stretch. He didn't think it was his best book – he preferred *The Ambassadors* (1903)' (Gorra 2012: xv). In his 1908 preface to *The Portrait of a Lady* James in fact implicitly refers to *The Ambassadors* when he discusses the house of fiction. This implicit reference concerns a certain contamination of perception with action as highlighted in the characterisation of Strether. James's house of fiction revolves around observation – more precisely, the observational position of the house's many windows.

Critics have, however, neglected the fact that James's famous house of fiction metaphor had repercussions not only for literary studies but also for the development of modern science. The diversity of observational perspectives (windows) wherein James locates the touchstone of our human constitution has important ramifications for a new conception of how we approach scientific enquiry into the workings of both nature and society. It calls into question a view of nature as well as society which is based on notions of purity, order, conformity to universal and systematic laws. As Nancy Cartwright has shown, 'The impressive empirical successes of our best physics theories may argue for the truth of these theories but not for their universality. Indeed the contrary is the case' (Cartwright 1999: 4). The accuracy of our theory is context-specific.

Our scientific observations are contaminated by the context of our actions. The novel's plot *makes us experience perception in terms of action*: Isabel Archer's mode of seeing her environment preconditions the way she acts. In the preface to *The Princess Casamassima* (1886) James describes 'her imagination' as 'positively the deepest depth of her imbroglio' (James 1987: 8). Yet her imagination is not the actual cause of her downfall, because she does not actually realise what she imagines. However, it is her imagination that makes Isabel Archer susceptible to the manipulative fictions of Madame Merle and Mr Osmond. Crucially, she remains blind or imperceptive to these manipulations until it is too late. She is not able to perceive these fictions (Osmond's and Merle's) for what they are.

Due to this fatal flaw of her perceptive capacities she turns these manipulations of reality into a reality that entraps and imprisons her. James's critical focus on the deleterious effects of fancy and fiction (imagination) does not demote the crucial work carried by perception and contemplation. On the contrary, James makes a strong case for blurring the traditional division between the perceptive and the active aspects of our existence. Isabel desires an active, engaged life of freedom capable of realising her imagination. As Gorra has argued, her understanding of freedom is not merely notional or linguistic:

> It isn't just the freedom to name the terms on which she will meet the world. No, she wants the freedom, in Emerson's words, to be self-sufficing, and her ambition will define itself in terms of a radical autonomy, a cultivation of individual identity in which her very sense of self comes to stand as the chief object of her own desire. (Gorra 2012: 52)

The novel reveals this rush to enact one's desire (a form of imaginative action) – which marginalises the slow work of perception – to be working hand in hand with Osmond's oppressive scheme. Lacking enough perceptive capacities, Isabel Archer buys into the manipulations of Osmond's aura. This dear purchase diminishes the scope of her actions and in doing so prevents rather than enhances the realisation of her imagination.

What James has to say about perception and its diverse disorderliness has important implications for how we could revise traditional and modern perceptions of order. We see the world differently and the difference in perception helps create different worlds: 'He and his neighbours are watching the same show, but one seeing more where the other sees less, one seeing black where the other sees white, one seeing big where the other sees small, one seeing coarse where the other sees fine' (James 1995: 7). This quotation opens up a heterogeneous world wherein one thing could be seen in two opposed ways which equally hold true.

Crucially, perception is no longer removed from the world of action as has traditionally been the case in standard oppositions between the contemplative and the active life of politics. The 1908 preface to *The Portrait of a Lady* makes a strong case for the discovery of action within perception. It does so by highlighting not only the literary (as regards the alteration of the established genre of the novel by introducing a non-plot-based element into it), but also the scientific and conceptual innovation of chapter 42 confronting us with an apparent lack of activity. Isabel Archer simply sits by the fire and reflects. James makes it clear that reflection here becomes revealed as an adventure:

> She sits up, by her dying fire, far into the night, under the spell of recognitions on which she finds the last sharpness suddenly wait. It is a representation simply of her motionlessly *seeing*, and the attempt withal to make the mere still lucidity of her act as 'interesting' as the surprise of a caravan or the identification of a pirate. It represents, for that matter, one of the identifications dear to the novelist, and even indispensable to him; but it all goes on without her being approached by another person and without her leaving her chair. It is obviously the best thing in the book, but it is only a supreme illustration of the general plan. (James 1995: 15)

Here the lack of actions paradoxically becomes identified with what happens in adventure stories featuring pirates and the surprise appearance of a caravan. The term surprise evokes its apparent opposite: Hitchcock's innovative redefinition of suspense.

As Paul Marantz Cohen has put it, 'in later films he [i.e. Hitchcock] altered the rules of suspense or rather made a new rule (Hitchcock came to define suspense as the art of letting the audience know what the character didn't), so that the focus fell on character rather than on plot revelation, thus turning the mechanism something closer to literary narrative' (Cohen 1995: 27). Cohen has drawn attention to parallels between James and Hitchcock which have to do with their shared focus on character rather than narrative action: 'James developed from a fairly standard action oriented storyteller, to a psychological novelist, to a novelist for whom the literariness of his medium came to take on a life of its own' (Cohen 1995: 9). James's psychological interest in character has a visual dimension, as the very title of the novel (*Portrait of a Lady*) highlights. A critical concern with epistemology holds together James's and Hitchcock's respective fusions of the pictorial, the psychological and the narrative.

As Susan M. Griffin and Alan Nadel have recently pointed out, both the writer and the film director critique assumptions of omniscience:

> By the same token, because the conventions of mainstream cinematic editing rely on the play of absence as much as they do on creating a window on reality, Hitchcock's exploitation of vacant spaces, false trails, and unseen evidence helps us comprehend James's critique of omniscience. Entailed in such a critique is the construction of the gaze, a device of equal prominence for both James and Hitchcock. (Griffin and Nadel 2012: 20)

The critique of omniscience also concerns the protagonists of a given work. We know well in advance about their delusions of knowledge (such as Isabel Archer's delusions about Madame Merle or Scottie's delusions about Judy/Madeleine in Hitchcock's *Vertigo*) before they do.

According to Hitchcock, suspense anticipates the horror to come. When something actually happens it is no longer surprising: it is like letting the audience know that a bomb has been placed in its midst and that it will explode sooner or later. The suspense of James's *The Portrait of a Lady* operates on a similar level: we know that Ralph Touchett wants to test his cousin in order to see how she will navigate the leeway for action with which his father's inheritance endows her. Money here epitomises the energy providing the material base or engine to carry out what Isabel's imagination impels her to embark upon: an active, cosmopolitan and independent life. According to Ralph Touchett his father's inheritance puts wind into his cousin's sail.

Isabel Archer reconciles herself to her unexpected possession of wealth by conceiving of it as a vehicle for free agency: 'the girl presently made up her mind that to be rich was a virtue because it was to be able to *do*, and that to do could be sweet' (James 1995: 182). Isabel Archer's promise of action, however, never truly materialises: by marrying Gilbert Osmond and thereby letting herself be manipulated by his former lover Madame Merle, she forecloses the horizon of independence and agency. The surprise element folds in upon itself. Ralph Touchett and other characters in the novel might be startled by Isabel's decision to marry Mr Osmond but we, the readers, have already been informed of her fatal misreading of oppression as freedom.

The narrator makes clear that her future husband's abode in Florence resembles a prison, a place of confinement from where it will prove difficult to escape: 'There was something grave and strong in the place; it looked somehow as if, once you were in, you would need an act of energy to get out' (James 1995: 217). The energy which supposedly the money of the inheritance would provide thus turns entropic: it needs to be burned (or spent) to provide the impetus for any attempt to get out of what her wealth in the first place tempted Madame Merle and her former lover to entangle her in (i.e. marriage to an oppressive and misogynist husband).

In contrast to Ralph and other protagonists in the novel, we also know of the heroine having set her heart on going straight into the lion's den – straight into the confinement of marriage to Osmond that is bound to endanger what she holds so dear: independence, freedom, originality and autonomy. We read that 'for Isabel, however, there was of course as yet no thought of getting out [i.e. of Osmond's place described in the previous quotation], but only of advancing' (James 1995: 217–18). We thus already know of Isabel's self-inflicted danger. Rather than surprise us, suspense in James's literary and Hitchcock's cinematic work prepares us for the horror to come.

In the words of Pascal Bonitzer, the 'audience, which is thus no longer able to cling naively to the apparent reality of the image, and knows what is being woven below the surface, has suffered a loss of innocence' (Bonitzer 2010: 19). Suspense contaminates a given entity with its apparent opposite: what appears to be natural turns out to be unnatural, or, in other words, horrible. Hitchcock's cinema lets us perceive the mutual contamination of traditional moral opposites. On the basis of the supposed purity of moral categories, actions may be carried out without hesitation. This is precisely what takes place when Isabel Archer marries Gilbert Osmond, whom she identifies with her moral idea of beauty and truth while not realising that Osmond fabricates an aura of moral autonomy and the aesthetic, which pretentiously and manipulatively devalues any concern for material interests.

Only too late (in chapter 42) perception intervenes to question actions which have already been carried out. As Gorra has pointed out, in chapter 42 the distinction between action and perception becomes blurred: 'These pages do more [i.e. the pages in chapter 42] – they change our very sense of what counts as an event in fiction. Sitting still counts; thinking, doing nothing, not moving. Emotions count, and the activity of perception as well' (Gorra 2012: 236). Gorra goes on to emphasise James's literary innovations in novels such as *What Maisie Knew* (a work which will also be discussed in this chapter) and *The Portrait of a Lady*: 'At once austere and grandiloquent, they are both modern and modernist in the pointillism with which they catch the human mind in the second-by-second act of perception, and modernist too in the symbolic force of their language' (Gorra 2012: 300). How does such innovation of the novel on a formal level intervene in larger scientific and technological facets of our life? While providing a superb literary-historical reading of James's novel, a critic of the stature of Gorra does not attempt to show how literature illuminates larger societal issues which are pertinent to our contemporary context.

Contaminating the literary with the cinematic

In this respect, a comparison between cinema and literature may be worthwhile. Cinema is a more exterior medium than literature. However, as Gilles Deleuze has shown, cinema turns internal with Hitchcock: 'In Hitchcock, actions, affections, perceptions, all is interpretation, from beginning to end' (Deleuze 1997: 204). Deleuze makes it clear that this interpretative bent within Hitchcock's films shifts attention from actions towards intellectual constellations: 'What matters is not who did the action – what Hitchcock calls with contempt the *whodunit* – but neither is it the action itself: it is the set of relations in which action and the one who did it are caught' (Deleuze 1997: 204). These relations constitute what Deleuze calls Hitchcock's 'mental image'. While still working within the precinct of narrative cinema, Hitchcock's mental image gives rise to the thought image (as perfected in the work of Pasolini which will be discussed in the next chapter):

> the mental image would then be less a bringing to completion of the action-image, and of the other images, than a re-examination of their nature and status, moreover, the whole movement-image which would be re-examined

through the rupture of the sensory-motor links in a particular character. What Hitchcock had wanted to avoid, a crisis of the traditional image of the cinema, would nevertheless happen in his wake, and in part as a result of his innovations. (Deleuze 1997: 209)

Hitchcock's innovative employment of suspense calls the traditional movement-image of the cinema into crisis, because it accentuates the audience's knowledge of actions about which the protagonist in a film remains ignorant until it is too late. As has been intimated above, this is precisely the reader's situation faced with the actions of Isabel Archer in James's *The Portrait of a Lady*. Both James and Hitchcock turn narration into a thought experiment. As Deleuze has put it apropos Hitchcock's cinematic legacy: 'The soul of the cinema demands increasing thought, even if thought begins by undoing the system of actions, perceptions and affections on which cinema had fed up to this point' (Deleuze 1997: 210–11). Actions of a given plot morph into the suspense of reflection, perception and thought.

Hitchcock employs techniques of suspense to show on the cinematic screen what escapes our attention when we rush to subscribe to standard categories of good and evil. His films bring to the fore how two seemingly opposed characters are in actual fact contaminations of each other. In *Strangers on a Train* we come to realise how Guy, who seems to embody order, respectability and high achievement, does not simply contrast with Bruno whom he meets by chance on a train ride. By visually connecting via montage parallel images of the law-abiding (superego) Guy and the lascivious, libidinal Bruno (id) Hitchcock's film confronts us with 'the view that ordered life depends on the rigorous and *unnatural* suppression of a powerfully seductive underworld of desire, and we see the reason for the stiff formality of order in the film' (Wood 2009: 178). Robin Wood focuses his analysis on one scene where Bruno contaminates not only his immediate surroundings within the precincts of the film but also implicates the audience in the act of contamination.

This scene takes place at a party given by the father of Guy's mistress (as distinguished from his wife Ann whom Bruno murders fulfilling Guy's secret wishes). The father is a senator – another striking embodiment of order. At this party Bruno asks one of the guests, the elderly Mrs Cunningham, whether he could test on her neck what he takes to be the best technique for murdering someone. What begins as a joke seriously implicates the expectations of the audience, as Wood has put it:

> The scene is a superb example of the Hitchcock spectator trap. First, belief in established order has been undermined in the deflation of the judge [whom Bruno asks what he thinks about murdering a murderer by sentencing the

same to capital punishment]; then the dialogue with Mrs Cunningham and her friend, because of the lightness of tone, gives us licence to accept the notion of common guilt as something of a joke, to connive at in, allowing ourselves to be implicated in the 'game' of murdering Mrs Cunningham, who is anyway a rich, trivial, stupid old woman. Then abruptly the joke rebounds on us – we have nearly been implicated in another murder: swift modulation of tone has seldom been used to such disturbing effect. (Wood 2009: 177)

The film induces the audience to naively cling to what the screen first represents as a joke. We know, however, that there is a parallel image for this apparently light-hearted entertainment: the scene where Bruno strangles Guy's wife in the light-hearted surroundings of a theme park.

Suspense by working with what we already know – the way in which the tongue in cheek strangling at the party re-enacts the scene of lethal murder in the seemingly carefree surroundings of an amusement park – implicates us in what we should not be surprised about and yet are. Hitchcock implicates the audience in the confusion of the lethal and the light-hearted actions taking place on screen. He disorders the distinctive order which separates laughter from seriousness while keeping the audience in the know (we have seen how Bruno has strangled Ann – an action which in the scene with Mrs Cunningham first provokes laughter before it nearly turns lethal).

The disorder we encounter is that of a collapse of categories which divide our lives into neat separations such as good and evil, innocence and guilt. Cinema achieves such contamination through the juxtaposition of images which contaminate each other and thus confuse our experience of order. The encounter between Guy and Bruno in Hitchcock's *Strangers on the Train* stages such an experience.

Another striking case in point is Hitchcock's early American movie *Shadow of a Doubt* which opens with the juxtaposed images of the serial killer, Uncle Charlie, and his niece (also going under the name) Charlie, the apparently innocent daughter of Mr and Mrs Joseph Newton of the small and innocuous Californian town Santa Rosa. In a sequence of opening montage shots we see both in different geographical locations – Uncle Charlie in Philadelphia and his niece in Santa Rosa – simultaneously lying on a bed.

Before we even know that Uncle Charlie is on the run from the police, the contamination of these two bed images calls into question the quiet, relaxed content of what they present. By interlinking the bed of uncle and niece, they evoke the prospect of incest as James McLaughlin has shown: 'The intense togetherness of uncle and niece is registered then in fantasies of incest and identity of name' (McLaughlin 2009: 146). Behind what we take to be innocent and natural dwells a more sinister world which we perceive when the speed of our perceptions slows down.

This is exactly what takes place at the famous opening scene of David Lynch's *Blue Velvet*. At the moment at which the father collapses with a heart attack, the camera movement shifts register and moves into slow motion until it gradually penetrates the surface of the garden onto which the paternal figure falls and the so far unknown kernel of what has taken place comes to the fore: insects devouring each other at a hidden level covered by grass.

James's novels and Hitchcock's as well as Lynch's films explore in their respective fictional work the scientific uncovering of knowledge which is so disturbing that we want to ignore it; and yet it is real, it is, in a positivistic sense, there. As McLaughlin has put it apropos *Shadow of a Doubt*: 'Criminality, Hitchcock insists, hides within domesticity; or, to put it another way, domesticity is merely the most hidden criminality' (McLaughlin 2009: 152). Suspense here works at an epistemological level. It uncovers knowledge which has been hidden by societal concepts of respectability, order, purity, and systematic cohesion.

Isabel Archer holds us in suspense in a similar way: we are aware before she and other characters in the novel are that her quest for freedom will end up entrapping her. By not only providing but also implicating their audience in knowledge, both James and Hitchcock let us experience the active, suspenseful, and riveting aspect of perception – in short, they confront us with theory as activity. Isabel Archer's ideals of freedom and independence end up not only, as at the opening of the novel, defining but, as it turns out in Volume II, confining her. Her active life has been the product of a delusion. In James's novel the work of perception achieves what mere action lacks: the recognition of what has really happened rather than what went on on the surface of narration (or in cinematic terms on the level of what Bonitzer in the quotation above calls 'the image').

The word horror describes this move from surface to actual substance. Towards the end of Volume I Countess Gemini employs the word characterising the furniture of her brother's (Gilbert Osmond's) abode: 'There are some very good seats here, but there are also some horrors' (James 1995: 219). In Volume II, however, Countess Gemini uses the term 'horror' not in the context of the external narrative ambience but rather to describe a loss of innocence which may appear to be inappropriate in the presence of a child (Osmond's Pansy): 'There is no harm in knowing horrors she [i.e. the child Pansy] may be in for' (James 1995: 300). Horror here emerges as the knowledge of what takes place in the novel's narrative. It is the horror of recognition: the new science of various contaminations wherein gaining insight coincides not with knowledge of the systematic but the unsystematic.

James exposes a child to such recognition of the unsystematic in *What Maisie Knew*. The scandal of the horror here is that it avoids moral judgement. This is what enervates the governess Mrs Wix about Maisie's knowledge of her parents' mutual adultery: 'What I did lose patience at this morning was at how it was that without your seeming to condemn – for you didn't, you remember! – you yet did seem to *know*' (James 1985: 214). Mrs Wix defines by the term 'moral sense' (James 1985: 260) a kind of knowledge that is judgemental. Knowledge which does not judge seems to pose a threat, rendering society horrible, unsystematic, disorderly and unnatural. It seems to unleash the animal within the child.

In a similar way, the governess who narrates what she takes to be the unnatural events of *The Turn of the Screw* calls the refusal to acknowledge knowing the ghost the turning point at which the human turns animalistic, at which the child (Miles) morphs into the beast/ghost of the 'unnatural man': 'His [Miles] having lied and been impudent [having knowledge of and yet denying judgement and thus acknowledgement of the ghost] are, I confess, less engaging specimens than I had hoped to have from you of the outbreak in him of the little natural man' (James 1966: 37). The outbreak of the 'little natural man' describes the contamination of the human with the animal, of the child with the dead.

This mixture of disorder and nature marks society at risk of turning animalistic. The epitome of such risk is the child whom a ghost (contamination as such) transmogrifies from innocence to a form of knowledge that goes without the order imposed by moral sense. Rather than label the governess 'mad' as Edmund Wilson and other critics have done,[1] she embodies a form of 'normality' that goes with a dismissal of horrifying knowledge. It is beyond doubt something disturbing that has occurred to the children. It is such knowledge that aggravates the mental state of the governess.

James, as Shoshana Felman has pointed out, abstains from literally pinning down such knowledge: 'The literal is "vulgar" because it *stops* the *movement* constitutive of meaning, because it blocks and interrupts the endless process of metaphorical substitution' (Felman 2003: 153). The knowledge that is so offensive to the governess's sense of respectability is indeed the ambiguous and the contradictory: 'the very scandal of contradictions and ambiguity' (Felman 2003: 160). Felman rightly warns of vulgar psychoanalytical readings that reduce the ambiguity of the text to one meaning.

In contrast to what we know of Isabel's ignorance about Osmond and

Madame Merle, our grasp of knowledge remains suspended in *The Turn of the Screw*. Suspense does not, however, eventuate in self-referentiality as Felman argues when she reduces the text to 'the incessant *sliding* of signification' (Felman 2003: 215). Rather than referring to itself, James's novel sheds light on the societal distortions of knowledge. As Aviva Briefel has recently argued, *The Turn of the Screw* 'confirms that respectability is, in fact, the place in which trouble is likely to occur' (Briefel 2012: 163). Crucially, James as well as Hitchcock frames such societal respectability with cognitive flaws that accompany accelerated actions and judgements. Briefel thus establishes an intriguing correlation between the failures of perception in James's governess and the two main protagonists of Hitchcock's *Vertigo*: 'Marion's cognitive inability links her to Norman, who is also deluded by his construction of Victorian propriety' (Briefel 2012: 172). Propriety keeps us ignorant of knowledge that James's and Hitchcock's respective literary and cinematic figures of contamination illuminate.

Similarly to Isabel Archer's prioritisation of action over reflection in the first part of *The Portrait of a Lady*, a rush to judgement characterises the cognitive inability of the governess in *The Turn of the Screw*. She is convinced that Miles and Flora – the two children under her charge – have already lost the innocence bestowed by nature's presumed order:

> Oh yes we may sit here and look at them, and they may show off to us there to their fill; but even while they pretend to be lost in their fairy tale they're steeped in their vision of the dead restored to them. He's not reading to her,' I declared; 'they're talking of *them* – they're talking horrors! (James 1966: 48)

Horror denotes the point where we recognise the unsystematic in what we previously took to be systematic. At this point order becomes revealed as disorder, nature turns unnatural, and the human morphs into the unruliness of the dreaded beast or animal. James's governess harnesses herself against the 'outbreak of the little natural man' by sheer power of moral will. This will imposes the order of nature against a society at risk of morphing into the beast, the ghost which contaminates the order and innocence of childhood with 'the little natural man':

> Here at present I felt afresh – for I had felt it again and again – how my equilibrium depended on the success of my rigid will, the will to shut my eyes as tight as possible to the truth that what I had to deal with was revolting against nature. I could only get on at all by taking 'nature' into my confidence and my account, by treating my monstrous ordeal as a push in a direction unusual, of course, and unpleasant, but demanding after all, for a fair front, only another turn of the screw of ordinary human virtue. No attempt, none

the less, could well require more tact than just this attempt to supply, one's self, *all* the nature. (James 1966: 80)

While accusing the children under her charge of unacknowledged knowledge of beasts/ghosts, the governess upholds a proud and moralistic refusal of recognition or perception. She posits the order of nature against the disorder of societal-psychological ghosts.

She refuses to live with the apprehensive presence of what she judges to be the unnatural, the beastly or the ghostly (what she calls 'the little natural man' in the previous quotation). Her rigid power of the will which does not recognise any lack of system in the embodied disorder of our world – 'the will to shut my eyes as tight as possible to the truth' – seems to precondition the endurance of moral sense and its judgements. The basis of these judgements is the construction of natural order.

James's expression 'the will to shut my eyes as tight as possible to the truth' should alert us to the science–art opposition and the related objectivity–subjectivity divide prevalent in his as it is in our contemporary public discourse. He clearly critiques in the speech of the governess a wilful repudiation of scientific discovery. Rather than being opposed or disinterested in contemporary scientific debates about objectivity, James's preoccupation with the distorted images produced by the power of the will for order, beauty or aesthetic refinement (Isabel Archer's phantasising about Madame Merle and Gilbert Osmond), purity and systematic coherence has an explicit bearing on the status of science at the *fin-de-siècle*.

As Lorraine Daston and Peter Galison have amply shown, from the mid-nineteenth century onwards objective, scientific operations were increasingly represented in public discourse to be dependent on a paradoxical self-annihilation of the will: 'The divided scientific self, actively willing its own passivity, was only one possible self within the field created by the distinction between objectivity and subjectivity. Its polar opposite, equally stereotyped and normalized, was the artistic self, as militarily subjective as the scientific self was objective' (Daston and Galison 2007: 246). James's *The Turn of the Screw* contaminates such oppositions between subjectivity and objectivity, by highlighting the distortions and paradoxes of a will which preconditions the scientific occlusion of the subject: 'Objectivity and the scientific self that practiced it were intrinsically unstable' (Daston and Galison 2007: 250). The governess of *The Turn of the Screw* refers to the will not only to cover up her instability. Her will mainly serves to suppress any recognition of what might violate preformed conceptions of health, morality and order. Her emphasis on the will is at once eerily resonant of the scientific as well as moralistic insistence on the wilful subjugation of anything subjective – 'Objectivity demanded that the self split into active experimenter and passive observer' (Daston and Galison 2007: 250) – as it accentuates the aesthetic distortions of wilful artistic practice which refuses to engage with any embodied or real issues that may clash with ideal conceptions of beauty and/or moral perfection. For the governess scientific standards of objective truth and moralistic as well as aesthetic ideals coalesce in the concept of nature and its purported order.

The moral, wilful self here is indeed '*all* nature'. Robert Pippin is right to call the reliability of the narrator into question.[2] How can we trust the accuracy of the governess's account if she proudly admits to shutting her eyes tight? Commenting on this passage Pippin, however, disputes the validity of the concept of nature and its related connotation of order and homogeneity: 'She has some sense that there is no nature here, that she is beyond even her own notions of the original stain of sin in human nature (the "little natural man" in Miles), and that whatever has happened cannot be understood in these terms' (Pippin 2001: 121). A suspenseful play with knowledge operates here as it does in our foreknowledge of Isabel's entrapment in *The Portrait of a Lady*: we – the readers – have a clear sense that the nature versus sin (i.e. animal/ghost/beast) opposition is cruel; the governess, however, seems to be convinced of the righteousness of her virtuous turn of the screw.

Part of her cruelty is her commitment to turning the screw – which she mistakes for virtue – and the concomitant refusal to recognise the violence of this conception of nature as order. We know more than her and this creates suspense. It does so by staining the governess who is so obsessed with what she judges to be the sin of those who perceive or know the ghosts. In the governess's view what disorders the supposed order of nature renders us like the 'little natural man' running counter to grand conceptions of homogeneity and order. James's narrative, however, alerts us to the cruelty of such virtue. We know more than the governess who claims to be omniscient and to see the presence of the beastly ghosts. In doing so James's novel trains our capacities of resistance which prevent us from both embracing rash claims to knowledge (the governess in *The Turn of the Screw*) and privileging accelerated actions over the slowing down of speed that is involved in acts of perception and reflection.

An application of Hitchcock's cinematic notion of suspense helps illuminate questions of knowledge, perception and action in James's literary impressionism. Similarly to Hitchcock in his films, James in his novels provides his audience with crucial pieces of information that some of his main protagonists ignore at their peril. This focus on knowledge, perception and reflection inflects the traditional form of both the novel and narrative cinema because it turns epistemological and psychological themes into the main fabric of the plot rather than defining the latter as simply depicting actions. It would, however, be misleading to read this as merely a formal innovation to do with genre. James, as well as Hitchcock, is concerned with the ever increasing speed which technological advances brought about from the Industrial Revolution in the mid-nineteenth century onwards.

By contaminating their respective audiences' view of action with epistemological and psychological issues both *auteurs* interrupt and slow down the plot of either the film or the novel. They indeed make a plea for suspending judgements and actions at a time when technologies of speed are increasingly employed to measure achievements in economics, medicine, education and society at large. This is a process that has been going on since the technological advances of the mid-nineteenth century. Neither James nor Hitchcock dismisses such scientific discoveries which help accelerate the way we act and interact with each other. They are not dismayed about them either. They warn, however, of an uncritical embrace of speed and the concomitant marginalisation of isolated voices that articulate doubt about some aspects of otherwise beneficial developments. The fictions presented in their novels and in their films confront us with a reality we might want to ignore. It is a reality where speed in both cognition and action results in deleterious or lethal consequences. James's and Hitchcock's wariness of the rush to action and judgement is all the more relevant in our digital age where we seem to have become, as Irving Biederman and Edward A. Vessel have put it, 'infoveres' (devourers of information).[3] As the computer scientist Lanier has recently put it: 'Information is alienated experience' (Lanier 2010: 28). Information reduces the complexity of experience to a homogeneous and deceptively clear issue. Scottie in Hitchcock's *Vertigo* takes the information handed down to him by the manipulator Elster and runs with it into disaster.

Critical attention has so far been focused on how *Vertigo* portrays male desire. Indeed this critical preoccupation with phantasy has recently been identified as the generic element which Hitchcock has in common with James. As Eric Savoy has recently put it: 'In the formalist vision of both James and Hitchcock, to desire is to broach the territory of the gothic: that is, to solicit the return of the repressed, to stage the encounter with the traumatic Real, to encounter the void at the centre of subjectivity, to become unhinged' (Savoy 2012: 148). In a rather reductive reading, Savoy establishes an archetypal connection between Hitchcock's male characters (such as Scottie) and those of James's novels. Rather than being a perceptive observer, in this reading (which applies Lacan's notion of the Sinthome to film and literature) Strether becomes as deceived by vertiginous 'captations' of desire and phantasy as Scottie in *Vertigo*, recovering in a psychiatric unit after what he takes to be the suicide of the ghostly Madeleine:

> If, as every theorist of trauma after Freud has emphasized, trauma is characterized by the unconscious repetition of an event that remains unfathomable, then *Vertigo* is an exemplary trauma event. Essentially, it grafts onto the traumatic residue of Scottie's vertigo – the chronic fear of falling – the plot of falling in love with a ghostly illusion. In terms of character alignment, too, Hitchcock's film recalls the quadrilateral emplotment of *The Ambassadors*. Strether falls into the web of deception woven by Chad Newsome and Madame de Vionnet. (Savoy 2012: 153)

Strether clearly takes sides with the contaminating or scandalous (as Pasolini would put it, as will be discussed in Chapter 6) relationship between Mrs Newsome's son and the older Madame de Vionnet. He decides to abandon his preordained role as emissary for Mrs Newsome and her business/family interests in Woollett. He indeed 'takes up the threads of a story that runs counter to Woollett's line' (Savoy 2012: 148), but this is his own thought-through decision and not the work of some manipulation à la Madame Merle/Mr Osmond in *The Portrait of a Lady* or Gavin Elster in Hitchcock's *Vertigo*.

Savoy's reductive psychoanalytical reading has not heeded Shoshana Felman's warning about such literal applications of psychoanalysis to literary works such as *The Turn of the Screw*. An interpretative approach which reduces the content and form of a given work to a prearranged set of issues also informs Laura Mulvey's essay 'Visual Pleasure and Narrative Cinema'. In this article Mulvey has famously indicted Hitchcock's *Vertigo* for foregrounding a male gaze which is active and thereby supposedly contrasts with the passive role allotted by Hitchcock to the female, who is merely a passive object: 'Far from being simply an aside on the perversions of the police, *Vertigo* focuses on the implications of the active/looking, passive/looked at split in terms of sexual difference and the power of the male symbolic encapsulated in the hero' (Mulvey 2000: 492). A rigid opposition between male and female, between action and passivity permeates the discussion of Mulvey's essay.

Recently Marian E. Keane has shown how Mulvey misreads not only Freud's psychoanalysis but also Hitchcock's cinematic techniques. In keeping with the discussion in this chapter, Keane has made amply clear that Hitchcock does not privilege action (associated for Mulvey with the male) over perception/passivity. On the contrary, Scottie's impulsive course of action is clearly troubling, and according to Keane Hitchcock directs the camera to make us sympathise with Judy.

As we have seen in this section, Hitchcock, as well as James, contaminates various actions with the supposed passivity of perception and reflection. In James's *The Portrait of a Lady* a woman has an active role (Isabel). In Hitchcock's *Vertigo* it is a man, Scottie, who is apparently in control of the action. The film makes us discover how the visual pleasure Scottie (James Stewart) takes in his active pursuit of Judy (Kim Novak) turns out to be the work of deception and thus turns the actor into a passive role (as becomes amply clear in Scottie's catatonic state after 'Madeleine's' fall from the Mission Tower). In his critique of Mulvey's essay Charles Barr has astutely brought to the fore how the film subjects Scottie's visual pleasure to both epistemological and psychological scrutiny:

> This pattern is at the root of what is special about *Vertigo*. It draws in, and indulges, the pleasurable gaze with extraordinary fullness, and at the same time foregrounds the mechanisms behind it – first by taking them apart, then by pushing them to an extreme. Indeed, the plot, when fully revealed, will turn out to foreground these mechanisms still more decisively at the level of narrative, hinging as it does on the discovery that the entire scenario of surveillance has been a devious construction, set up by Gavin Elster with the woman's connivance and with Scottie as victim. Kim Novak is not simply, as a first viewing suggests, playing for Hitchcock the role of a woman being voyeuristically observed; she is playing, for Hitchcock, the part of a woman who is playing, for Elster, the part of a woman being voyeuristically observed. Absorbing at first viewing, when we don't know the full plot, these scenes become even more so when overlaid by the bittersweet awareness that, with Scottie, we have been, and are now again allowing ourselves to be, led on, deceived, by a consummate manipulator, complaisant victims of what has all along been – like all cinema – an illusory construction. (Barr 2012: 21)

Suspense revolves around the audience gaining a level of insight which reveals visual pleasure to be the work of manipulation. The emphasis is cognitive. As Barr has shown in the quotation above, Hitchcock employs cinematic techniques of deception in order to undermine the deceptive work of cinema. In a similar way, James writes fiction in order to alert us to the fictive or manipulative environment which we confront in factual or non-fictive settings of our mundane world of work, romance and business. Strikingly, the manipulator Elster in *Vertigo* has financial interests at heart when he kills his wife.[4] The same holds true for Osmond in *The Portrait of a Lady*: his marriage to Isabel Archer turns him from an impoverished bohemian would-be artist to a wealthy socialite.

Crucially, both James's novel and Hitchcock's film reveal unreflective actions, voyeuristic observations and prearranged judgements to be delusions, to be fictions. They are delusory, because they are driven by reductive pieces of information: Madame Merle's about Gilbert Osmond's aesthetic disinterest in conventional worries about finance, and Elster's account of his wife's genetic inheritance from her grandmother of mental illness. Similarly to the governess in *The Turn of the Screw*, Elster imputes to his wife the beastly ghost of mental illness – here, however, it is not a quasi-supernatural cause but a seemingly rational form of haunting: that of genetic inheritance.

Being preoccupied with the sexual politics of desire, critics have ignored how Hitchcock's *Vertigo* critiques simplistic reductions of the cultural to the biological. *Vertigo* indeed narrates how the reduction of a person's identity to biological inheritance – Elster feeds Scottie the lie of how his wife inherited a supposed mental illness from her grandmother – can be used to get away with murdering this person. It is common knowledge that cinematic and literary works are imaginary rather than real. What has so far not been investigated is the way in which these obvious products of the imagination reflect upon how we are sometimes governed by fictions in real life. One obvious example is the way in which we can fall prey to various forms of deception, which is the subject matter of Hitchcock's *Vertigo*.

James's *The Portrait of a Lady* and Hitchcock's *Vertigo* are equally concerned with manipulation and deception. What facilitates the act of being duped is the speed with which the one who is being manipulated accepts the misleading or false information on offer without interrupting this process with time for reflection. Knowledge and reflection are clearly crucial here. What is problematic is the rush to action or judgement: Isabel's distortive judgement of Osmond in *The Portrait of a Lady* and the governess's lethal judgement about the beastly corruption of the children in her charge in *The Turn of the Screw*.

The audience knows about Scottie's lack of knowledge through Judy's flashback which offers the accurate perception about Scottie's fatal rush to action, as Keane has pointed out in her rebuttal of Mulvey's indictment of Hitchcock's film: 'The flashback sequence is inaugurated by a striking turn of Novak's head toward the camera that culminates in her look into the camera. Her look into the camera registers what she knows, and the flashback that follows represents but a piece of that knowledge' (Keane 2009: 237). Hitchcock renders suspense a question of gaining insight or knowledge into what takes place within the plot. He directs the camera to moments of suspense within a psychological or epistemological frame. In *Vertigo* this is not the movement of the action hero but the slow motion of reflective flashbacks, and as Keane has argued: 'At no point in *Vertigo* does Stewart/Scottie possess a knowledge of the camera commensurate with Novak's/Judy's' (Keane 2009: 238). Both James and Hitchcock reverse the traditional prioritisation of action over perception in narratives (in both novels and films). The lead characters of their films and novels are observers (like Strether) and not fast-moving action heroes. By letting the audience know more than the protagonists of the plot, James and Hitchcock make the spectator/reader active participants in an epistemological and psychological quest for complexity.

Beyond thought's purity: contamination in James's *The Portrait of a Lady*

Here we know more than the 'beastly pure mind' of Isabel Archer. In striking contrast to the children in *The Turn of the Screw* the child Pansy denotes innocence untouched by the contamination of ghosts. Isabel is taken in by such displays of innocence at Osmond's abode in Florence. Her disposition lends itself to falling prey to such moral deception. As her friend Henrietta Stackpole unsuccessfully attempts to make her aware, it partakes of her 'dangerous tendencies': 'I mean your exposure on the moral side' (James 1995: 187). She has 'too many graceful illusions' (James 1995: 188). These illusions find their point of reference in the supposed innocence of Osmond's aestheticism. Osmond's child Pansy evidences the innocence in question here. Pansy lives the harmlessness of infantile submission: 'She was evidently impregnated with the idea of submission, which was due to any one who took the tone of authority; and she was the passive observer of the operation of her fate' (James 1995: 202). Her master or father is, however, 'of the world' (James 1995: 202). His interests are political and worldly.

As Lee Edelman has argued, 'the image of the Child invariably shapes the logic within which the political itself must be thought' (Edelman 2004: 2). Osmond's child is indeed the pawn of deception with which he ensnarls the ever so active Isabel Archer. The supposed innocence of both his child and his aesthetic pursuits is a façade that hides his true interests in power and control. Together with Madame Merle he gains power over Isabel's mind through deceptive displays of harmlessness. Isabel's moral exposure to the life of action rather than critical perception preconditions her victimhood. Like Pansy, she is passive even though her goal is an active, free and independent life. Only in chapter 42 does she gain some form of independence. At this crucial point, action and perception are no longer mutually exclusive spheres.

The spell of recognitions haunting Isabel Archer contemplating her life 'by her dying fire' may be surprising to her but not to the readers of the novel. For the readers already know of Madame Merle's manipulative powers. Isabel might have grasped the threat of being at risk of falling into Madame Merle's trap (by marrying the latter's former lover and accomplice Gilbert Osmond): her aunt Mrs Touchett has pointed this out to her before she actually marries Mr Osmond.

As readers, we are privy to a conversation between Madame Merle and Mr Osmond where the former replies to the latter's conscientious question 'Isn't she [i.e. Isabel Archer] meant for something better than that' [i.e. living with him, Gilbert Osmond] by admitting her disinterest in what might be beneficial for others: 'I don't pretend to know what people are meant for' and, worse still, by acknowledging her ruthless and selfish scheme of manipulation: 'I only know what I can do with them' (James 1995: 207). The question of 'doing' has been neglected in discussions of James's *The Portrait of a Lady*. Instead, the focus of attention has been on what Nina Baym has called 'a drama of consciousness', and as Baym, following F. O. Matthiessen and Anthony J. Mazzella, has rightly pointed out there is indeed a striking shift between the 1881 and the 1908 versions of the novel: 'The changes of 1908, transforming the story into a drama of consciousness, overlaid and in places obliterated the coherence of the 1881 version' (Baym 1995: 620). As a consequence of these changes, the action taking place in the 1908 edition 'was the development of her [Isabel Archer's] perception and awareness' (Baym 1995: 620). It is, however, also true that much of what happens takes place not only on the basis of perception and awareness but rather due to a lack of consciousness on the part of Isabel Archer.

The novel is certainly concerned with consciousness but also – and this is the crucial point – with a new understanding of consciousness which cannot be separated from the sphere of action. Isabel, however, compartmentalises thought and deed, perception and action, reading literature or philosophy and embarking on an active life. Right from the beginning she appears as a reader 'trudging over the sandy plains of a history of German Thought' (James 1995: 34). German Thought in the nineteenth century has of course been the vanguard of a philosophy of freedom, autonomy and independence which Isabel is keen to practise in a life of action (see Mack 2003). Despite this implicit connection between the transformational ideas she encounters in her reading and what she attempts to realise in her actual life, Isabel nevertheless repudiates any osmosis between books and reality: 'The poor girl liked to be thought clever, but she hated to be thought bookish; she used to read in secret and, though her memory was excellent, to abstain from showy reference. She had a great desire for knowledge, but she preferred almost any sort of information to the printed page; she had an immense curiosity about life and was constantly staring and wondering' (James 1995: 41). Here we indeed encounter an opposition (as discussed in the previous section) between action in terms of – *avant-là-lettre* digital – 'information' and the contemplation associated with the 'printed page'. It is as though books were to impede access to action: 'Her reputation of reading a great deal hung over her like the cloudy envelope of a goddess in an epic' (James 1995: 41). According to Isabel, books, contemplation and reading seem to impede rather than enhance 'real life'.

Being bookish here seems to be a symptom of being sick, and indeed the mortally ill cousin Ralph Touchett embodies for Isabel the morbid ambience of literature and philosophy.[5] Ralph is indeed an observer and yet, ironically, he also sets in motion the preconditions for Isabel's so longed-for life of action. As she finds out far too slowly and far too late – but as the reader knows from early on – Ralph Touchett persuades his father to make Isabel the inheritor of most of his financial assets. After having inherited £70,000 from Mr Touchett Isabel mistakes wealth to be the springboard for a life of action that should overcome the confinements of bookishness and contemplation.

Ironically, her presumed active life remains incarcerated in visions which turn out to be delusions: 'She lost herself in a maze of visions; the fine things to be done by a rich, independent, generous girl who took a large human view of occasions and obligations were sublime in the mass. Her fortune therefore became to her mind a part of a better self; it gave her importance, gave her even, to her imagination, a certain ideal beauty' (James 1995: 193). The novel reveals Isabel's 'large human view' to be rather narrow. What she takes to be action has been in her mind's eye all along a play of her imagination. The crucial point is her belittling perception without realising that perception preconditions actions. James's novel thus helps us discover how action cannot be segregated, as it has previously been, from perception.

Madame Merle and, in a more innocent, observing way, Ralph Touchett rather than Isabel, are, however, in charge of the doing. Rather than being a heroine of consciousness, Isabel Archer repudiates any form of perception. Her cousin, however, confronts her with perception. Before her marriage, he explicitly warns her that her engagement to Gilbert Osmond would not be one of freedom and independence but one of confinement: 'Because you're going to be put into a cage' (James 1995: 288). Isabel repudiates her cousin's apprehensions of her life and this repudiation enforces a sense of her limited rather than enhanced consciousness. These limitations in consciousness literally prepare for her limited, confined life in her marriage to Mr Osmond.

The presumed life of action eventuates in a state of total passivity. When leaving Osmond's fortress-like palace in Rome to visit her dying cousin Ralph in England she 'envied Ralph his dying' (James 1995: 465). Her shame of being bookish and contemplative ironically leads to her being tired of life:

> She had moments indeed in her journey from Rome which were almost as good as being dead. She sat in her corner, so motionless, so passive, simply with a sense of being carried, so detached from hope and regret, that she recalled to herself one of those Etruscan figures couched upon the receptacle of their ashes. [...] The only thing to regret was that Madame Merle had been so – well, so unimaginable. Just here her intelligence dropped, from literal inability to say what it was Madame Merle had been. (James 1995: 465)

The failure of her decision to marry Osmond is here revealed to be a failure of perception and of consciousness. Hers is a limited imagination, rather than a boundless one. Her action has been shaped by this limited imagination for which only Osmond's show of refinement is imaginable, but Madame Merle's vulgar manipulation remains unimaginable. Significantly, she falls into Merle's trap by crossing over to Osmond's dominion, first by ceding to him in her imagination:

> What had happened [i.e. her falling for Osmond] was something that for a week past her imagination had been going forward to meet; but here, when it came, she stopped – that sublime principle somehow broke down. The working of this young lady's spirit was strange, and I can only give it to you as I see it, not hoping to make it seem altogether natural. Her imagination, as I say, now hung back: there was a last vague space it couldn't cross – a dusky, uncertain tract which looked ambiguous and even slightly treacherous, like a moorland seen in the winter twilight. But she was to cross it yet. (James 1995: 265)

Action – the act of crossing – takes place in the imagination – in the mind – before it actually materialises. What the novel narrates is what its heroine denies from the outset: the interconnection between perception and actions, between reading and life. Towards the end of the novel Isabel's marginalisation of reading intensifies into a state of disinterest and, worse still, incapacity to read: 'Besides, she had never been less interested in literature than to-day, as she found when she occasionally took down from the shelf one of the valuable volumes of which Mrs Touchett had spoken. She was quite unable to read; her attention had never been so little at her command' (James 1995: 482–3). Isabel's inability to read is an inability to perceive passivity in what she takes to be action. It also instantiates her refusal to discover action in what she assumes to be passivity (such as, for instance, reading and reflection).

Conclusion: James, Hitchcock, Benjamin, or the persistence of fiction as 'aura'

For Isabel's imagination Madame Merle has 'a sort of greatness' (James 1995: 166). Her imagination exerts a deleterious spell which turns reality into fiction. It is important to emphasise here that she takes what is fiction to be reality. However, by being taken for real the fictitious or fraudulent indeed shapes our action as it materialises in actuality. Similarly to the way in which Scottie in Hitchcock's *Vertigo* elevates the vulgar con girl Judy into the glamorous Madeleine, James's Isabel Archer extols the scheming and rather worldly characters who manipulate her (i.e. Madame Merle and Gilbert Osmond) into epiphanies of transcendental beauty.

From Isabel's point of view Madame Merle was neither 'affected' nor 'pretentious, since from these vulgar vices no woman could have been more exempt' (James 1995: 167). From this elevated position, Madame Merle manipulates Isabel's mind, describing her American friend who resides in Italy in terms of a blank page – a blank page of emptiness which ideally lends itself to be superabundantly filled by Isabel's phantasies: 'He [i.e. Gilbert Osmond]' s exceedingly clever, a man to be distinguished; but, as I tell you, you exhaust the description when you say he's Mr Osmond who lives *tout bêtement* in Italy. No career, no name, no position, no fortune, no past, no future, no anything' (James 1995: 172). Madame Merle seems to know *avant-là-lettre* the psychoanalysis of desire. She glamorises her companion in terms of what Žižek has recently called 'less than nothing'. Her tactics are Hegelian, dialectical: she depicts Osmond as nothing in order to extol him into the epitome of glamour.

Following Hegel, Žižek has analysed the attractive power of nothingness. Osmond's negativity here gains in positive force:

> At the beginning (even if it is a mythical one), there is no substantial One, but Nothingness itself; every One comes second, emerges through the self-relating of this Nothingness. In other words, Nothing as negation is not primarily the negation of something, of a positive entity, but the negation of itself. (Žižek 2012: 378)

By appearing to negate his substantiality Osmond does not, however, turn the show of ephemeral appearance into an aesthetic programme of the immaterial as he and Madame Merle attempt to make Isabel believe.

When Isabel at last realises that 'Madame Merle's interest was identical with Osmond's' (James 1995: 428) she also recognises the worldly and substance-driven schemes of the two. Madame Merle at one with Gilbert Osmond are indeed the actors who drive Isabel into a life of passivity: 'More clearly than ever before Isabel heard a cold, mocking voice proceed from she knew not where, in the dim void that surrounded her, and declare that this bright, strong, definite, worldly woman, this incarnation of the practical, the personal, the immediate, was a powerful agent in her destiny' (James 1995: 427–8). Isabel, who sets out 'to choose' her 'fate', belatedly (and far too slowly) realises that the activity of choosing has been co-opted not only by Madame Merle but also by her failure of consciousness. Her consciousness has not been perceptive enough to recognise in Osmond's presumed lack of substance the subjectivity of an oppressor who does not so much ignore substantial issues but imposes his own self as the only valid form of all there is to know and feel (i.e. his subjectivity poses as objectivity).[6]

For Isabel's imagination Osmond instantiates Žižek's 'Hegelian motif of "Substance as Subject"' (Žižek 2012: 380). What, however, about a form of subjectivity that assumes the position of substance, of all there is? This is precisely the reality which Isabel's awakened consciousness faces in chapter 42. In chapter 42 Isabel's sight turns into a vision of discovery.

Chapter 40 describes Isabel's process of registering an image that instantaneously vanishes from mental awareness rather than becoming absorbed by the workings of the mind. Here she recognises the connection between Osmond and Madame Merle, and significantly the link is not based on motor-action but on perception – on the gaze which the two share and which binds them together into a unity: 'But the thing made an image, lasting only a moment, like a sudden flicker of light. Their relative positions, their absorbed mutual gaze, struck her as something detected. But it was all over by the time she had fairly seen it' (James 1995: 343). In the last paragraph of chapter 42 her mind turns active in a way we have not witnessed before in this novel and perhaps in any of the novels that preceded it.[7]

It is an internal activity generating so much energy that it achieves the physical effect that the external presence of a fire normally causes: keeping the body warm: 'For herself, she lingered in the soundless saloon long after the fire had gone out. There was no danger of her feeling the cold; she was in a fever. She heard the small hours strike, and then the great ones, but her vigil took no heed of time' (James 1995: 364). Here we witness the collapse of categories which separate the external from the internal, the cerebral from the corporeal.

What, however, causes the fever infusing the body with heat in an otherwise unheated room and makes Isabel lose track of the passing of time? The activity of the mind generates an energy and sense of warmth unrivalled by fire. This mental energy turns the sight of chapter 40 into visions: ' Her mind, assailed by visions, was in a state of extraordinary activity, and her visions might as well come to her there, where she sat up to meet them, as on her pillow, to make a mockery of rest' (James 1995: 364). Sight enlivens into visions. Rest makes a mockery of itself by turning restless.

This move from sight to vision constitutes a shift toward the inner regions of consciousness. It is, however, misleading to characterise consciousness in terms of the immaterial as Anna Despotopoula and Kimberly C. Reed have recently done: 'In other words, the "spirit" in James, in as much as it may be either spectral or human, is always ghostly in the sense that that it is represented as an immaterial consciousness' (Despotopoula and Reed 2011: 5). The form of consciousness may be immaterial but its object of contemplation is nevertheless material. This clearly comes to the fore towards the end of chapter 42 when Isabel's consciousness conjures the material presence of Gilbert Osmond: 'Then it was that her husband's personality, touched as it never had been, stepped forth and stood erect' (James 1995: 362). There is a haptic quality to Isabel's consciousness, as the verb 'touched' highlights. Moreover the sentence closes with the ominous and sexually charged phrase 'stood erect'.

While it may be pertinent to argue that James's concern with consciousness anticipates Freud, neither the writer nor the founder of psychoanalysis retreats from the sphere of matter and embodiment as Anna Despotopoula and Kimberly C. Reed seem to argue: 'And perhaps anticipating Sigmund Freud, James is one of the first writers who acknowledged that we are primarily and most devastatingly haunted from within rather than without' (Despotopoula and Reed 2011: 5). Indeed the novel shows how Isabel Archer becomes entrapped in delusions when she elevates Osmond to transcendental regions beyond substance while refusing to countenance his embodied presence and his material interests. What is crucial here is that it is only when her consciousness moves from the externality of sight to the intellectual gaze of visions that she faces up to the reality of matter.

Whereas Isabel's deceptive play of the imagination creates a world transcending substance, the ghostly play of consciousness – the turn from mere sight to the scientific reach of visions – lets her grasp not only Osmond's sexuality (and his previous affair with Madame Merle) but also his worldly longings and calculations (to do of course with Isabel's substantial inheritance).

Osmond, who first attracted her for his social and sexual innocence (a mere nothing lacking social and bodily substance), here emerges as being 'unable to live without' society:

> he had looked at it [i.e. society] out of his window even when he appeared to be most detached from it. He had his ideal, just as she had tried to have hers; only it was strange that people should seek justice in such different quarters. His ideal was a conception of high prosperity and propriety, of the aristocratic life, which she now saw that he deemed himself always, in essence at least, to have led. (James 1995: 361)

Prosperity refers to the wealth for which he, on Madame Merle's instigation, marries Isabel. Propriety describes the ways in which Osmond tyrannically prescribes his subjectivity as a universal norm of what is appropriate and seemly.

While it is ethically justifiable for him to have his ideal, it is problematic to impose his conception of what is justice onto that of his wife who 'had tried to have hers'. As a tyrant, Isabel's husband denies her independence of mind: 'The real offence, as she ultimately perceived, was having a mind of her own at all. Her mind was to be his – attached to his own like a small garden plot in a deer park' (James 1995: 362). James here and elsewhere conceptualises the mind as being attached to and concerned with matter and embodied life.

Focusing on this innovative interplay between the cerebral and the corporeal, between the material and the immaterial, in his 1908 preface to the New York edition of *The Portrait of a Lady* James highlights chapter 42 as 'obviously the best thing in the book' (James 1995: 15). In making this critical judgement, James clearly emphasises the collapse of traditional distinctions between perception and action as the crowning achievement of his novel. The novel lets us experience reflection as adventure. This coincidence of observation and agency is precisely what Isabel discovers in chapter 42.[8] The 'extraordinary activity of the mind' rivals the claim for the audience's captivated absorption and attention which the genre of the adventure story promises to its readers.

In the preceding chapter (chapter 41) the narrative voice reiterates Isabel's denigration of reflection in terms of suffering and passivity, with which we have become familiar throughout the novel (see discussion above): 'She could never rid herself of the sense that unhappiness was a state of disease – of suffering as opposed to doing. To "do" – it hardly mattered what – would therefore be an escape, perhaps in some degree a remedy' (James 1995: 348). By contaminating perception with action,

James's novel overturns traditional medical associations of suffering and unhappiness with the lack of motor-action, which our contemporary digital culture tends to reinforce.

The 'disease' of reflection turns into an enlivening remedy in chapter 42, where Isabel finally realises that doing without the perception accompanying reading may cause the unhappiness that the escape into action attempted to avoid in the first place. Only then does she recognise that the failure of her action constitutes a misreading of Osmond: 'she had not read him right' (James 1995: 357). A reading sharpened by the 'extraordinary activity of the mind' makes visible the crucial but so far invisible underside of Osmond's glamorous show of doing.

At this point Isabel anticipates a mental sketch of what Walter Benjamin would later in the mid-1930s analyse as the rendition of politics as aesthetics. By marrying Osmond, Isabel Archer risks destroying her independence of mind and her control over her material interests. Benjamin's famous essay 'The Work of Art in the Age of Its Technological Reproducibility' helps illuminate the subordination of aesthetics to serve rather than constitute politics and questions of power. Crucially, Benjamin discusses such subservience of art to power as destruction and self-destruction:

> Humankind, which once, in Homer, was an object of contemplation for Olympian gods, has now become one for itself. Its self-alienation has reached the point where it can experience its own annihilation as supreme aesthetic pleasure. *Such is the aestheticizing of politics, as practiced by fascism. Communism replies by politicizing art.* (Benjamin 2008: 42)

While Osmond is not a fascist, he is certainly a misogynist. He is an instrumentalist who employs aestheticism in order to obfuscate his political interests in gaining power through his marriage to Isabel Archer procuring for him prosperity and propriety.

Making the aesthetic subservient to politics partakes of a political strategy: it anaesthetises, rather than enlivens, the mental activity of those whom power wants to deceive and dominate. James makes clear that Isabel rather than becoming more independent and active has turned passive under the 'spell' of Osmond's aura. 'What, then, is the aura', asks Benjamin and goes on to define it as follows: 'A strange tissue of space and time: the unique apparition of a distance, however near it may be' (Benjamin 2008: 23). The apparition of a seemingly unique distance produces the anesthetising effect of aura.

Too late Isabel realises that she has been the victim of such anesthetisation. She misreads Osmond's show of unique (quasi other-worldly) insubstantiality as an absence of any interest in power and politics. Now she realises that the opposite was the case. Osmond 'was unable to live without' (James 1995: 361) power over society: 'he had looked at it outside his window even when he appeared to be most detached from it' (James 1995: 361). Osmond's narrow, power-driven window on society contrasts with the infinite diversity of windows which, as James makes clear in the 1908 preface to the novel, describes the openness of art: 'The house of fiction has in short not one window, but a million – a number of possible windows not to be reckoned, rather; every one of which has been pierced, or is still pierceable, in its vast front, by the need of the individual vision and by the pressure of the individual will' (James 1995: 357). Art is open-ended and fluid. It encourages a contaminating diversity of views and perspectives.

As Posnock has put it, 'James's heterogeneity translates into something resembling an expressivist pluralism that disperses power and rigid identification with one role or place and replaces them with a dynamic of shifting involvements that resist finitude and definition while breeding possibility and spontaneity' (Posnock 1991: 76). Where the politics of power is conclusive, exclusive and narrows down our perspectives on life, true art is inconclusive, furthering diversity and opening up horizons for both contemplation and action: 'The antidote to the despair of conclusiveness is the inconclusive, or what both Adorno and Henry James call the aesthetic. The surrender of security that Adorno urges upon aesthetics is everywhere the note sounded in James's prefaces' (Posnock 1991: 132). Osmond's politics of power, however, reduces the multiplicity of views to that of one window: his own.

Osmond cannot endure the presence of different perspectives, different minds. This dictatorial mindset preconditions his hatred of his wife and his misogyny.[9] After marrying Osmond, Isabel Archer resembles his façade. According to Ralph, she turns into an advertisement: 'if she wore a mask it completely covered her. There was something fixed and mechanical in the serenity painted on it; it was not an expression, Ralph said – it was a representation, it was an advertisement' (James 1995: 330). As will be discussed in the following chapter, Pasolini's films contaminate such masks, such representations, with the presentation of what he calls an obstacle or scandal (*scandalo*) and what I have theorised in this book under the figure of contamination.

Notes

1. See Wilson (1962: 102) and Renner (1995: 223–41).
2. 'But of course, nature is not a thing that can be "supplied," and the "eyes

shut tight" phrase just about gives completely away the question of the governess's reliability' (Pippin 2001: 121).
3. See Biederman and Vessel (2006: 249–55).
4. See Barr (2012: 63).
5. 'that the finest of pleasures is the rush of action. Living as he [i.e. Ralph Touchett] now lived was like reading a good book in a poor translation' (James 1995: 45).
6. For a detailed discussion of the totalitarian presumptions of a manipulative and deceptive form of 'objectivity' see the discussion of Sylvia Plath's poetry in Mack (2014: 107–39).
7. The reputation of James as formalist has blinded critics to a certain continuity of his conception of art and life. As Ross Posnock has put it, 'James's lived experience of the mimetic continuity of art and life is usually ignored because of his reputation as an archformalist who segregates art from life' (Posnock 1991: 187).
8. As quoted previously in this chapter; see James (1995: 14–15).
9. As quoted previously in the chapter; see James (1995: 362).

Contaminating the Sacred with the Profane: Pier Paolo Pasolini and Biopolitics

Introducing Pasolini and his Hollywood legacy, or the contamination of the mental with the corporeal: Deleuze, Hitchcock, Scorsese

According to Deleuze, Pasolini fully realised Hitchcock's mental image. Here the mind disrupts the distortions (or fictions) governing various forms of representations we confront in everyday life – an important theme in James's novels and in Hitchcock's films, as discussed in the previous chapter. There is no doubt that Pasolini's films have a strong mental or philosophical bent. According to the film director (and former assistant of Pasolini) Bernardo Bertolucci, Pasolini's cinematic style 'can be defined as Romanesque' (Bertolucci 2000: 7): 'His tracking fronts resemble the first tracking shots in the history of cinema. His close-ups resemble the invention of the close-ups' (Bertolucci 2000: 7). Bertolucci distinguishes his own cinematic style from that of Pasolini as follows: 'My style is more impressionistic. I approach things much more gently and don't see them from an entirely frontal position' (Bertolucci 2000: 7). It may be reductive to characterise Pasolini's style of shooting as 'from an entirely frontal position', as Bertolucci seems to be saying here. However frontal shots are characteristic of Pasolini's films. Similarly to film critics such as Naomi Green and Pascal Bonitzer (see Jacobs 2011: 88–121), Bertolucci argues that Pasolini's style is Romanesque or frontal.

However, in his cinematic as well as in his literary work there is also a strong sense of lived embodiment that sits side by side with what Deleuze calls the 'mental image'. Pasolini does not dialectically switch back and forth between the corporeal and the cerebral. Rather, he contaminates the mental sense as conveyed by his close-ups with the bare life of embodied existence. The two entities are not separated in different realms from which they traverse dialectically from one place to another but they simultaneously co-inhabit each other. Roberto Esposito has recently emphasised this element of bare, embodied life which Deleuze's notion of the mental image seems to exclude:

> Although itself the expression of a centuries-old historical development, this 'eager,' 'animal,' 'bodily' life with which the poet identifies in his very flesh, is by now situated on the outer edge of history, in an anthropogenic stratum that is indistinct and chaotic, without any formal characterization – not a 'form of life,' but, in the literal sense of the term, a stripped-down life, coinciding in every way with its bare presence: that life is nothing but a shiver; bodily, collective presence; you feel the absence of all true religion; not life, but survival – maybe happier than life – like a population of animals, in whose arcane orgasm there is no passion other than for their daily functioning: humble fervor which gives a sense of festivity to humble corruption. (Esposito 2012: 202)

As Esposito goes on to elaborate, this bareness of life embraces the presence of death within life: 'Starting from the homage to Gramsci's remains (concluding a cycle of Italian poetry inaugurated by Foscolo's *Sepulchers*), death constitutes the emotional and lexical horizon with a slant destined to traverse and in some way influence Pasolini's entire experience, all the way to his tragic end' (Esposito 2012: 204). Life in its biological pulse has to be simultaneously thought in the frozen stillness of death. The mental – the frontal, arrested image of some of Pasolini's close-ups – contaminates the bare presence of corporeal pulsations. While far from insinuating that Pasolini's murder on the desolate beach of Ostia, on the outskirts of Rome, was a planned self-sacrifice, Esposito interlinks the slaughter of Pasolini's body with the intellectual preoccupation with embodiment in his literary and cinematic *oeuvre* in its entirety:

> Without resorting to the radical hypothesis of a consciously planned sacrifice, there is no doubt that death, taken as a 'frame around the furious gift of life,' represents an essential interpretive key for his entire oeuvre. The author himself, moreover, on several occasions identifies death as the only place from which the meaning of an individual life can be understood, in a remarkable correlation with what Auerbach said about Dante's conception of the 'figure'. (Esposito 2012: 204)

Erich Auerbach's notion of the figure is rhetorical. The figure of contamination, however, encompasses both the embodied and the conceptual. Contamination itself denotes the simultaneity of the corporeal and the cerebral – an alternative to the dialectical changing of places where one entity nevertheless remains distinct and opposed to the other. Pasolini's term 'scandal' (*scandalo*) points to the figure of contamination in so far as it simultaneously comprises the scandalous presence of stripped-down life and the mental image of a form of intellectual-spiritual affront whose extreme may be seen in death itself.

One could say that this co-presence of life's pulse and the freezing of lively states in the mental image is Pasolini's cinematic legacy, which also found its way to some quarters of Hollywood. Martin Scorsese's *Cape Fear* (1991) perhaps best illustrates a meeting of Pasolini and Hitchcock in late twentieth-century Hollywood. This film is obviously indebted to the Hitchcockian use of suspense as the musical score by Bernard Herman makes clear on a formal level. The audience knows more than the protagonists: it is made aware that the psychotic Max Cady will keep haunting the prosperous family of a lawyer who failed in his duties as a defender in a trial that found Cady guilty of rape.

What has eluded critical attention is how Scorsese brings together the art-house film tradition of Pasolini with Hitchcock's Hollywood Studio production. Scorsese himself emphasises the major role Pasolini plays in his work.[1] *Cape Fear* is a case in point, what Deleuze calls a theorematic film: in fact, one based not so much on the previous version of *Cape Fear* but on Pasolini's *Teorema*.[2] In both films, lives arrested in bourgeois conformism encounter the stripped-down life of an outsider who is so alive as to be transgressing the boundaries of regimented conceptions of the human: the psychotic Cade whose body pulses with an energy that bursts the screen of the film,[3] or the boy of *Teorema* whose sexual-mental presence unhinges the entire bourgeois family whom he is visiting – visiting simultaneously in an embodied and in a spiritual sense.

One could discuss *Cape Fear* as a *Teorema*-like observation or theory about what could happen to a normal bourgeois family exposed to an extraordinary, psychotic character. John MacDonald's novel *The Executioner*, on which the two film versions *Cape Fear* are based, establishes an opposition between insider and outsiders, between normal and psychotic, between civilised and savage: 'Cady follows a social and moral code other than that of the Bowdens. Or, indeed, he appears like Lewis Henry Morgan's savage, to adhere to no norms' (Wegner 2009: 89). Pasolini's *Teorema* focuses on such a collapse of bourgeois order and norms, enfolding it into a sociological analysis of anxieties about class, status, propriety and property. Similarly to the mysterious guest of *Teorema*, Cady is a nonconformist. Both are masculine nonconformists. Phillip E. Wegner writes: 'The masculine nonconformist is dangerous precisely because he threatens to disrupt the normal processes by which the social order reproduces itself, processes Lee Edelman names "reproductive futurism"' (Wegner 2009: 89). In *Teorema* as well as in the novel (1957) and the (1962) film versions on which Scorsese's *Cape Fear* is based, a masculine outsider contaminates previously stable notions of class, health and sexuality. Anxieties about outsiders thus inform Pasolini's *Teorema* as they do all three versions of *Cape Fear*.

However, as Wegner has shown, Scorsese's 1991 remake radically departs from the previous version (the 1962 film and the 1957 novel) by presenting Cady as a psychotic outsider who is at the same time uncannily powerful through omniscient and quasi-supernatural insights into the workings of the word and the world: 'However, the most recent *Cape Fear* departs dramatically from both its predecessors in suggesting that Sam's [the lawyer and father of the bourgeois family in Scorsese's *Cape Fear*] reading of the law is the root of the conflict' (Wegner 2009: 108). Comparable to the factory owner and father figure in Pasolini's *Teorema*, the lawyer and patriarch Sam of Scorsese's *Cape Fear* becomes divested of his power and his status. Indeed, Wegner goes on to elaborate that in Scorsese's film Max Cady's reading refers not only to the words on the page but to a sense of almost supernatural power over the world:

> Sam [the lawyer and father of the bourgeois family in Scorsese's *Cape Fear*] becomes the passive looker (through a two-way mirror during the police interrogation; from behind a trash bin during the assault on Cady; and later, through the boat window as his family is abused) and Cady the apparent maker of their world. Cady himself will render explicit the film's equation of the act of reading with power, when he asserts, 'I'm better than you all. I can out-learn you. I can out-read you, I can out-think you, and I can out-philosophize you. And I'm gonna out-last you.' (Wegner 2009: 108)

Similar to the guest in Pasolini's *Teorema*, Cady appears to be the maker of the world, turning upside down a previously seemingly intact sense of order, law, propriety and property. Of course in Pasolini's film the character is not a psychotic but a fusion of the divine and the sexual allure of a boy. In Scorsese it goes without the homosexual connotations of a beautiful boy entering the life of a bourgeois family and turning it upside down. Here it is a quasi-spiritual force nonetheless. In Scorsese's film it is the uncanny presence of the theological which contaminates the psychotic, hyper-alive body of Max Cady quoting the mystic Silesius: 'I am like God and God like me. I am as large as God. He is as small as I. He cannot above me nor I beneath him be. Silesius, 17th century.' The largeness of the evoked spiritual entity only reinforces Robert De Niro's (in the role of Cady in Scorsese's film) larger-than-life physical presence on the screen.

De Niro's hefty muscular and heavily tattooed body confronts the audience at the film's opening scene which closes in a Pasoliniesque frontal shot. Here De Niro literally walks into an arresting and arrested standing camera, bursting the frame of the screen. At the same time as instantiating the bare life of the body, De Niro's Cady is a notably self-conscious psychotic who contaminates the line between health and pathology, between law and transgression. In his final confrontation with the lawyer Sam Bowden, Cady indeed assumes the role of a legal system, saying 'We two lawyers are fighting it out.' This scene indeed highlights a contamination of two spheres which public representation separates into two distinct and opposed entities: violence and law.

By contaminating the violent figure of Cady with that of the purportedly non-violent lawyer, Scorsese demolishes common societal categorisations of legality's opposition to violence. Cady's violence makes visible that of the law, that of the lawyer Sam Bowden.[4] Indeed, towards the end of *Cape Fear* we are shown the frantic enjoyment the lawyer takes in killing Cady who supposedly represents violence as bare life. Cady here 'is the person the violence of the legal system is unleashed on: its immune system consists in perpetuating life through the sacrifice of the living' (Esposito 2012: 33). The logic of this sacrifice is dialectical: the law switches sides with violence in order to protect life.

What, however, if there is not a dialectics but simultaneity of law and violence? Scorsese's *Cape Fear* opens up this question wherein Cady and the lawyer come to be viewed as not distinct selves but as being contaminated and the 'we' highlights this amalgamation: 'We two lawyers are fighting it out.' The 'it' denotes the figure of contamination which Pasolini, following Benjamin, kept insisting on in his scandalous confrontations with the legal system.

Pasolini's context of scandal

'I'll never be able to forget that Italian society condemned me in its courtrooms'

Pasolini, *Il Giorno*, 17 February 1966

As the quote above indicates, Pasolini's life and death were characterised by scandal and outrage. He was summoned to court more than thirty times accused of obscenity, blasphemy and paedophilia. However, despite the intense interest in his personal life, he was never convicted of these offences, yet scandal was nevertheless an important theme in his literary and cinematic work. Indeed, his biographer Enzo Siciliano described it in such terms: 'It is the scandal that bursts forth from confessions, from the projection into words of what our bodies and sensibilities unconsciously contain. This was the scandal that boomeranged on the heart and passion of Pasolini' (Siciliano 1982: 359). Even Pasolini's death was controversial, and his murder on a derelict field on the outskirts of Rome has been the subject matter for debate over the last four decades. It is not therefore surprising that someone so intrigued and connected to sexual controversy chose the topic of incest to play a central role in his work. This chapter will first introduce the reader to Pasolini's ethics and aesthetics of scandal and contamination, through a brief discussion of his early films *Accattone* and *Mamma Roma* (both released in the early 1960s) and his later works *Edipe Re* and *Teorema*.

Pasolini's unarticulated notion of contamination – he does not use this term but the word *scandalo* (scandal) – is at once political and scientific. The term scientific here denotes a broadening of our horizon of knowledge and understanding about cognitive operations that do not fit into accounts of what is considered at a given time as normal and normative. Pasolini's idiosyncratic usage of the word scandal (*scandalo*) precisely describes a departure or divergence from what has become accepted as common knowledge. The discovery of new knowledge about our minds, our feelings, our experiences and our thoughts is scandalous – an affront to the one-size-fits-all slogan of homogeneity. Pasolini does not differentiate between art and science, between interpretation and perception. Strikingly, his approach is backed up by new neuroscientific findings which show that the acquisition of knowledge never goes without interpretation. There is no such thing as immediate or 'pure' empirical perception of facts and data. Bare life is always already contaminated with intellectual questions.

In this context, it is worth introducing Pasolini's controversial approach to cinema – controversial because, taking issue with his non-representational interpretation, Umberto Eco argued that film reproduced semiotic systems which we are already familiar with. According to Pasolini, film presents us with the presence rather than the representation of life on the screen (Vanessa Lemm's term biocentric[5] might best describe what Pasolini, here following Nietzsche and Freud, understands by life – denoting the simultaneity of the biological and the spiritual).

Provoking Eco's critical response, Pasolini sees the filmic medium not in terms of already established semiotics. Rather than representing a sign system, film presents a version of embodied life. This sense of an embodied and simultaneously mental life comes under threat with the increasing virtualisation of life under neo-capitalist consumerism. As Andrea Righi has recently argued, 'Pasolini's most important contribution to the critical understanding of the new modernization takes in fact the form of a linguistic analysis of social processes' (Righi 2011: 82). These new social processes reduce bodies to the zero-point of existence where they are nothing but messages applied to further the consumption of virtual goods. Trying to counter such erasure of the lived in a neo-capitalist information culture, Pasolini locates in cinema ways of contaminating the biological and the intellectual, of co-inhabiting bodies and forms of meaning.

As recent neuroscientific findings have shown, this simultaneity between the embodied and the interpretative constitutes the field of cognition. We co-inhabit the biological and the intellectual not in two separated, compartmentalised structures where we would dialectically switch from one place and one form to another, but these two spheres are in fact not separated at all and instead exist in states of mutual contamination.

According to the philosopher and neuroscientist Daniel C. Dennett, simultaneous and non-linear streams of perception and interpretation constitute cognition:

> What we actually experience is a product of many processes of interpretation – editorial processes, in effect. They take in relatively raw and one-sided representations, and yield collated, revised enhanced representations, and they take place in the streams of activity occurring in various parts of the brain. (Dennett 1993: 112)

There is no central control centre in the brain (the so called 'Cartesian theatre'): 'In other words, discrimination does not lead to a *representation* of the already discriminated feature for the benefit of the audience in the Cartesian Theater – for there is no Cartesian Theater' (Dennett 1993: 113). Pasolini's presentation of scandalous knowledge enriches the multilayered stream of consciousness which constitutes knowledge.

Our acquisition of knowledge resembles 'a narrative stream or sequence, which can be thought of as subject to continual editing by many processes distributed around in the brain, and continuing indefinitely into the future' (Dennett 1993: 113). However, by contaminating our consciousness with what has been deleted from 'multiple "drafts" of narrative fragments' (Dennett 1993: 113), Pasolini illuminates what has been suppressed not so much by the working of our minds but by the rules and commands of a politics which attempts to put an end to the heterogeneity through and by which our brains work (in terms of infinitely multiple drafts of narrative).

This cognitive-scientific questioning of what has become accepted as normative knowledge is also political: it articulates and brings into public discussion voices which have been previously silenced. The 'scandalous' public articulation of what has been marginalised and silenced undermines a politics of homogeneity suppressing knowledge which does not square with what those in power proclaim to be valid.

Foregrounding suppressed knowledge, this chapter will then discuss what I call the cognitive-affective role of the mother, in Pasolini's infamous love poem to his mother, 'Supplica a mia madre', which appears in *Edipe Re*, in his last (posthumously published) novel *Petrolio* and in his play *Affabulazione*. The latter is concerned with a father who becomes his son's lover and is consequently so possessive that he murders the boy. This constitutes a reversal of Oedipus's plot and, as we shall see, Sophocles's ghost is a key character in the play. Thus *Affabulazione* problematises incest with the gay reversal of the Oedipus complex. The crucial point is that the reversal of Oedipus in Pasolini's play *Affabulazione* is Oedipal too, being premised on the desire for power and the power of desire.

Ex negativo, this chapter focuses on the birth of a form of new politics. This novel form of politics interrupts the violence governing the desire for power that has come to coincide with the power of desire. This coincidence of sexuality, domination and violence characterises what Freud discovered when he first discussed the Oedipus complex in his *Traumdeutung* (1899). The work of Pier Paolo Pasolini looms large in reflections about this topic: in different but related ways, his cinematic and literary *oeuvre* pivots around the sexual politics of father–son as well as mother–son relationships. These relationships govern the structure of politics and history. In order to find ways out of this violent arrangement, we therefore need to enquire into the ambiguities of love–hate encounters between fathers and sons. Psychoanalysis and art here meet politics.

Introduction to Pasolini's ethics of subjectivity

The political aspect of mental life and its deceptive representations are themes permeating Pasolini's approach not only towards the father–son relationship but also towards that between mother and son. The assumption of a central, homogeneous, control centre gives rise to deceptive representations which Pasolini attempts to disrupt through his cinematic and poetic presentation of scandalous knowledge. In doing so he adumbrates an understanding of selfhood which is truly diverse and turns false when it appears as homogeneous. As Dennett has argued, the self is indeed a heterogeneous assembly:

> In our brains there is a cobbled-together collection of specialist brain circuits, which, thanks to a family of habits inculcated partly by culture and partly

by individual self-exploration, conspire together to produce a more or less effective, more or less well-designed virtual machine, the *Joycean machine*. By yoking these independently evolved specialist organs together in common causes, and thereby giving their union vastly enhanced powers, this virtual machine, this software of the brain, performs a sort of internal political miracle: It creates a *virtual captain* of the crew, without elevating any one of them to dictatorial power. (Dennett 1993: 228)

Pasolini's cinema of poetry endeavours to disrupt the dictatorial power of one homogeneous voice or narrative which deceptively proclaims to represent the world as it is (an image of itself). This chapter highlights the so far ignored cognitive-scientific basis of Pasolini's political critique of homogeneity. The discussion of this chapter will first focus on mother–son relationships in Pasolini's work. Even though it does not explicitly allude to Oedipus, his early film *Mamma Roma* (1962) has an Oedipal subtext or subplot: the violent, deceitful and exploitative father who – like *Accattone* (1961), his first film produced in the early 1960s – is a pimp; with the important difference, however, that Pasolini turns Accattone into a Christ-like figure due to his social decline and total exclusion.[6]

Accattone performs contamination: the film comingles the profane with the sacred, social abjection with the saintly. At the centre of the film is a fight in the slums of Rome, (*borgate*). The frame of the profane fight scene draws upon sacred allusions: long shots accompanied by Bach's religious music from the St Matthew Passion. The voices of Bach's music sing of eternal peace whereas the reality of the scene in *Accattone* is a seemingly endless fight to drive away the crooked outcast, the loser (in Italian *accattone*), and the mean exploiter and pimp (*pappone*) Vittorio (aka. Accattone). At one point the father of Vittorio's wife even draws a knife, threatening to intervene with deadly force in the hand-to-hand fisting and wrestling.

Accattone's scandal is stylistic: the style of the film contaminates the sacred with the profane. Pasolini's translation of the literary term (derived from a reading of Dante's *Divine Comedy*) 'free indirect discourse' into cinematography describes the simultaneity of two purportedly opposed entities (sacred and vulgar) within the presence of the screen. What brings about this scandalous contamination is the allegorical, highly self-conscious and artistic superimposition of one language (the sacred and highly intelligent, refined music of Bach) onto a radically different one (the profane *parole* of pimps and thieves of the *borgate*). The life of these 'low lives' does not dialectically mutate to its opposite but instead simultaneously inhabits the sacred 'higher' realm of Bach's St Matthew Passion.

As Esposito has recently pointed out, the profane language of pimps and thieves is concrete and present (rather than represented); it confronts us with spiritually and intellectually contaminated 'bare life' becoming increasingly marginalised in the virtualisation that accompanies the high modernity of neo-capitalism: 'All the traumatic transitions that in Pasolini's view had marked Italian society were ultimately attributable to a kind of dematerialization of the bodily dimension which, until a few years previously, had been kept vital or even intact by the lower classes who were not yet affected by consumerism' (Esposito 2012: 208). His subsequent film *Mamma Roma* focuses on the psychological pressures to partake of the disembodied promises held out by careerism and consumerism.

Style in *Accattone* thus becomes a critique of *petit-bourgeois* aspirations in *Mamma Roma*. In Pasolini's words: 'The element that distinguishes this film from *Accatone* is the moral question not to be found in *Accatone*' (Siciliano 1982: 250). Most importantly, the stylistic and the ethical operate on the same level: both are scandalous and diverge radically from the status quo. At the point where it is most disturbing, art embodies as well as enacts difference. As has repeatedly been pointed out, from Enzo Siciliano (1982) to, more recently, Armando Maggi (2009), the word *scandalo* permeates Pasolini's cinematic and literary work in its entirety. What, then, is scandalous? In philosophical terms it is comparable to Benjamin and Scholem's notion of 'redemption through sin' (as discussed in Chapter 4). On a popular, tabloid newspaper level, scandal is what brings about the fall or the vilification of public figures. Indeed, as a celebrity Pasolini was the subject of many scandals which, often instigated by the Italian press, ended up in tedious and hurtful condemnations in over thirty different court hearings.

Pasolini thus came to embody scandal for the Italian and international public at large. It can be said of many authors that they contaminated their literary work with their personal life but this tendency is perhaps most pronounced in Pasolini's case, as Esposito has recently argued:

> Pasolini made his art a sort of living appendix of himself. Not only did he refuse to shield his texts from the emotions, sensations, and excitements that he felt, he literally filled them up with his feelings, sucking his writings into his overflowing, subjective experience. The impression given to the reader is that they couldn't have been written by anyone else – at least not in the form, or to be more precise, in the nonform or antiform that they have. It is as if he had purposely intended, through his own exhibited 'impurity,' to contaminate literature by dragging it into the same maelstrom into which he himself was slipping deeper and deeper. (Esposito 2012: 206)

(This emphasis on subjectivity comes clearly to the fore in section 4's discussion of Pasolini's poem 'Supplica a mia madre'.) According to the statutes of conformist or homogeneous society, scandal is a form of contamination. It must be avoided at all costs, because scandal is what makes one stand out, and makes one different. The cost of such avoidance is of course reality and truth. In reality we are not homogeneous but different: we clearly come from different cultural backgrounds, communicate differently, have different interests and do not all share the same sexual orientation. Pasolini employs the literary device of allegory in order to perform heterogeneity and difference in his cinematic works.

This chapter will show how the ethics of Pasolini's art is scientific – it brings to the fore or makes visible horrendous or scandalous truths of difference. Artistic style and poetic form ethically precondition the acceptance of these different realities which have been repressed, hidden or extinguished by societal forces of homogeneity and conformism. By bringing to light what has been excluded or deleted from the multiple scripts which constitute our consciousness, Pasolini overturns the aesthetic as well as ethical compartmentalisation of the profane and the sacred.

Pasolini's science of difference grows out of the artistic discovery which reveals the sacred and the profane in their mutual contamination.[7] This is precisely what scandal does – it connects the sacred with the profane: 'I am scandalous. I am so to the extent to which I stretch a cord, an umbilical cord, in fact, between the sacred and the profane' (Siciliano 1982: 359). The umbilical cord refers to birth. Pasolini here highlights our non-homogeneous constitution: at birth the profane and the sacred, the corporeal and the mental already contaminate each other.

As the neuroscientist Antonio Damasio has recently argued, the concept of contamination goes hand in hand with the social emotion of disgust: 'Humans can be disgusted not just by seeing spoiled food and the foul smell and taste that accompany it but by a variety of situations in which the purity of objects or behaviour is compromised and there is "contamination"' (Damasio 2010: 117). Our society and culture train and accustom us to feel disgust at what we perceive to be contaminating. The contamination in question precisely concerns the meeting point between purity and danger, selfhood and the other – the latter here appears as a threat.

In terms of visual studies, contamination could be defined in terms of the gaze. Pasolini's aesthetic and ethical notion of scandal makes us see the profane, the threatening other, the abject or poisonous from a new perspective: as being – resembling an umbilical cord – bound up with its seeming opposite, the sacred, the exalted and sound. Introducing us to 'scandal' Pasolini's art opens our horizon towards the discovery of difference. Pasolini's sight of scandal is first of all his selfhood, his autobiographical self.

It is important, however, not to equate the artistic presentation of Pasolini with Pasolini himself (Pasolini in the flesh as it were). The author and director Pasolini often uses his subjectivity for various scientific experiments. He does so from the important poem 'Supplica a mia madre' to his last, posthumously published novel *Petrolio* (1992).

In a letter to his friend, poet Alberto Moravia, Pasolini highlights the novelty of the reader's shocking confrontation with the author's subjectivity. Whereas in traditional novels the author's selfhood recedes, making place for the objectivity of the main characters, Pasolini stages the subjective front and centre:

> In a novel the narrator usually disappears, giving way to a conventional figure who alone can have a real relationship with the reader – real precisely because it's conventional.... [In *Petrolio*] I have spoken to the reader myself, in flesh and bone, as I write you this letter... I have made the novel an object between the reader and me, and I have discussed it (as one can do by oneself when writing). (Pasolini 1997: xi–xii)

Pasolini highlights the contamination of the written text with the presence of bare life: 'I have spoken to the reader myself, in flesh and bone'. Clearly, here Pasolini distances himself from John Keats's 'negative capability'[8] as well as from other poetic and narrative techniques which are premised on the identification with different, 'objective' characters.

Pasolini's innovative scientific, or, in other words, cognitive poetics contrasts with one crucial aspect of Keats's 'negative capability', namely with what Keats has called 'pleasures of not knowing' (Gittings 1979: 262). 'Negative' denotes the not knowing. The capability in question is that of identification. Pasolini's poetic voice, however, knows or wants to know. His cinematic version of Sophocles's *Oedipus Rex* interprets the cause of the tragedy not in a quest for knowledge but in its avoidance through mindless acts which resemble the violence in action movies. Pasolini's Oedipus does not even listen to the Sphinx. Far from solving her riddle, with brute force he pushes her into the abyss.

Knowledge here, however, does not refer to the biographical facts of Pasolini himself. Maggi rightly admonishes some critics not to fall prey to a simple error of narratology:

> Some critics have hailed the novelty of Pasolini's direct voice in his last novel, ignoring or forgetting the distinction between author (the person who has written the book and whose name is printed on the cover) and the

extradiegetic/intradiegetic narrator, that is, the character of the writer who narrates in the 'I' form and, even when he is external to the events, speaks from within the narrative space. (Maggi 2009: 169)

There is still, however, a capability at work in Pasolini's foregrounding of subjectivity: it is the capability to identify with a self that transcends the boundaries of selfhood.

The identification at work here is a knowing or cognisant one which also maps the scientific scope of knowledge beyond the limits which patriarchal society places on matters considered contaminating or scandalous. Rather than revealing private subject matters, Pasolini highlights the self in order to discover universal forms of knowledge whose uncovering has been interdicted by the authority of the father – the figure of the father yet again does not coincide with the father of Pasolini's biography.

Violating the laws of the father (which from a Lacanian perspective are the statutes of society),[9] Pasolini embarks on a scientific or cognitive enquiry into the psycho-physical foundations of his life. His autobiographical self has its foundation in the paradigm established by Freud and Kafka. The precise philological or textual location of Freud's paradigm is not relevant here because, as Nicola Petkovic has pointed out, 'Freud's work exists in bourgeois Europe as a kind of common cultural usage, whether or not that usage refers explicitly to any of Freud's writings' (Petkovic 1997: 42). In this paradigm the father embodies the interdiction of the scientific quest for self-discovery. The father is an allegory for political repression proscribing a cognitive encounter with reality.

The patriarchal figure represses cognition of different realities and he reduces human experience to an instrumental exploitative level. Contrasting with the character of Accattone, in *Mamma Roma* the father figure lacks any contamination with the sacred: his *modus vivendi* is pure instrumentality; he is a pimp, an exploiter of women. The father's exploitative and instrumental role contrasts with the mother who loves her son and does everything for him, only to find out that she has sacrificed their lives to *petit bourgeois* aspirations. She is the victim of deceptions. Pasolini does away with the illusion of love's innocence (most famously in his reputation of his three films comprising the *Trilogy of Life*). Love needs to be exposed to the contamination of knowledge in order to avoid being taken in by deceptions. Pasolini's cognitive rule of contamination, however, allows for the discovery of complex realities.

Crucially, the disclosure of such disavowed actualities falsifies both our fears (of the abject or poisonous) and our hopes (of innocent desire freed from power). The figure of contamination comingles our fears with our hopes. Instead of dialectically moving from one to the other, hope and fear simultaneously coexist. Power, by contrast, depends on dialectics: it includes as distinct entity what it excludes. Quoting Pasolini's line, 'In fact, the only true anarchy is the anarchy of power', Esposito writes: 'The fact that underlying arche – understood in the sense of original domination – there is something that includes its own negation, in other words, that is based on nothingness, demonstrates its power and fragility at the same time' (Esposito 2012: 214). Power posits its own other and includes it into its movements so as to dialectically be able to destroy it. It embraces its own negation in order to erase the negative as part of a dialectical move from one entity to another.

Rather than simultaneously contaminating two supposedly opposed entities, power dialectically spaces out those entities and traverses from one to the other over periods of time. These movements of dialectics seem to be inclusive but, crucially, they exclude what they include. In this way power includes its negation with the aim of excluding it. In the same way, biopolitical dialectics moves to the position of bare life not be contaminated by it but, on the contrary, to exclude it: 'The body defeats poison not by expelling it outside the organism, but by making it somehow part of the body. As we have been saying: the immunitary logic is based more on a non-negation, on the negation of a negation, than on an affirmation' (Esposito 2011: 8). Instead of non-negating the negative, dialectics famously negates the negative. Power enacts this dialectical movement over space and time and does away with what it apparently includes. Rather than affirming difference, power embraces its negations in order to annihilate what differs.

The point of Pasolini's science of difference is precisely to disrupt homogeneity and conformism. The art and ethics of such science consists in what Pasolini calls 'scandal', and his idiosyncratic understanding of scandal amounts to the performance of contamination. Instantiating power/dialectics, the figure of the father attempts to render void the possibility of more than one actuality. The father reduces the past to the present, the virtual to the actual, the exuberant to the profitable, and each entity to that which conforms to its nomenclature.

In this way Pasolini embodies his allegories of power around the figure of the Father. The darkness of his cinematic and literary creations arises from the absence of a clearly delineated alternative to power. Where such an alternative appears as in his light-hearted *Trilogy of Life* (early 1970s) the innocence of desire portrayed in these films (*The Decameron* (1971), *The Canterbury Tales* (1972) and *Arabian Nights* (1974)) turns out to be delusory and deceptive. Hence Pasolini's 'Repudiation of the Trilogy of Life' which finds its cinematic equivalent in the one-dimensional horror of sadistic and criminal domination, torture and murder in his last film *Salò* (1975). *Salò* presents the simultaneity between the contemporary conformism of consumerist and permissive 'freedom' and the systematic genocide of what is perceived to be different in fascist violence.

The *Trilogy of Life*, by contrast, celebrates desire beyond power or domination, and in doing so it has already been co-opted or manipulated by the powers of permissive consumerism. As a result, Pasolini renounces his three highly popular films because of their deceptive and manipulated depiction of desire's innocence. Rather than being innocent, desire has already been controlled by power: 'one must realize how much one has been manipulated by the power structure' (Pasolini 2005: xvii). In Pasolini's work, love is always already contaminated by power and violence. As intimated above, Mamma Roma is obsessed with social advancement – which she attempts to accomplish by working as a prostitute. Her social and economic ambitions ironically prepare for the death of her beloved son. It is advancement towards not well-being but brutality.

Mother-sons: Mamma Roma, 'Supplica a mia madre' and *Edipe Re*

Violence lies at the core of Pasolini's early novels *Vita Violenta* (1959) and *Ragazi di Vita* (Streetboys) (1955). Everyone falls prey to violence. It governs the Oedipal as well as the reversal of the Oedipal. Someone is bound to be killed, whether it is the son or the father, and one parent is bound to be a partner to incest – whether it is homosexual (father–son) or heterosexual (mother–son). Pasolini's Oedipus film emphasises this point.

The concluding part of this chapter will discuss how the alternative to Pasolini's apocalyptical assessment of our private as well as social lives could be called the disruptive (or contaminative) moment. Examples of such a disruptive or contaminative scenario can be found in the ending of almost all of Pasolini's films. In the closing scene of *Mamma Roma* this is exemplified when Anna Magnani's manic stare of recognition prompts the spectator to realise that the view from her middle-class apartment actually coincides with the morbidity of a cemetery – the view of her previous working class flat. The ending of Oedipus also demonstrates this scenario, as it is the absolute exclusion from society that contaminates Oedipus's incest-induced impurity with the purity of the outcast and the blind. Perhaps the prime instance of contamination is in *Teorema* (1968), where the sudden appearance and subsequent absence of the divine boy – whom everyone has fallen in love with – causes complete disintegration. This disintegration is illustrated by the catatonic madness of the daughter, the wild promiscuity of the wife, and by the husband's giving away of cherished possessions, disposing of his factory and his clothes at Milan's train station.

This part of the chapter, however, sets out to discover – mainly via a reading of Pasolini's poem 'Supplica a mia madre' and an analysis of notes from his last novel *Petrolio*, as well as a brief discussion of his film *Edipe Re* (1967) – the ways in which the question of power or desire governs life from its earliest beginnings in the mother–child relationship. Pasolini wrote 'Supplica a mia madre' in the same year in which he filmed *Mamma Roma* (1962). As we have seen, the mother figure is ambiguous, even though she is clearly presented in terms that are likely to win some of the audience's sympathies. Conversely, she represents Pasolini's abhorrent view of the *petite bourgeoisie* as a social group intent upon socio-economic advancement. The film reveals such advancement to result in the catastrophic breakdown of all human relations. Pasolini confronts these false hopes and aspirations with the bitter reality of affect- or desire-ridden politics. As his biographer Enzo Siciliano has astutely put it: 'He was a utopian – but he did not hesitate to rend this utopianism for the inescapable demands of eros. From there sprung his originality – he was not afraid of his own demon' (Siciliano 1982: 389). In his poem 'Supplica a mia madre', he articulates his own demon in a complex and highly original way.

In contrast to other pleas for the survival of a parent, Pasolini's poem does not exclude horrendous aspects of the affective relationship which binds parent and child. Whereas a comparable poem – Dylan Thomas's 'Do not go gentle into that good night' – revolves around humanity's struggle against death ('rage, rage against the dying of the light'), Pasolini's 'Supplica a mia madre' opens and ends with the subjective position of the poet. This is not to play one poem against another. Both poems are major achievements and both are quite related in their concern for the relationship between the fate of the individual (the father in Thomas's poem) and the general prospect of mortality faced by all of us.

The focus of Thomas's famous poem is clearly the confrontation with mortality on a level that includes and yet goes beyond the singular fate of the poet's father. Pasolini's 'Supplica a mia madre' revolves not only about the poet's subjective position but also about power/domination (*schiavitù*) and desire (*amore*). Hence the *orrendo conoscere*: it is indeed a horrendous, terrible subject matter which is of course also that of

Kafka (in his *Letter to my Father*). Similarly to Kafka's *Letter*, Pasolini's poem pivots around power relationships as the foundation of family life.[10]

The poem dramatises its seeming subjectivity and reaches a crisis point with the enjambment:

> ... your love is my slavery:
> My childhood I lived a slave to this lofty
> incurable sense of an immense obligation.
> (il tuo amore è la mia schiavitù:
> ho passato l'infanzia schiavo di questo senso
> alto, irrimediabile, di un impegno immenso.) (Pasolini 1982: 108)

Through its repetition of the *schiav* root, the middle or centre of the poem formally inscribes a sense or feeling of being enslaved. Slavery moves the already hard, difficult (*difficile* 1.1) and anguished situation (*angoscia* 1.6) into a larger socio-political context. The whole poem vibrates in the tension between innocence and corruption, love and domination (*orrendo conoscere* 1.5, *tua grazia ... mia angoscia* 1.6). The halting opening (*È difficile dire*) doubles or mirrors its oxymoronic force towards the opening of its penultimate strophe, when the poet invokes survival after the previous line has already spelled out the end of a certain life or relationship between mother and son: '... now it's over.//We survive ('*ora è finita.//Sopravviviamo*'). This is a most curious survival which takes place after the end, after everything is over. The concept of survival after the end of life is paradoxical and it is of course an important theological *topos* – especially in the New Testament where, according to the Gospel of John, Jesus restores Lazarus of Bethany to life four days after having died.

Pasolini's poem evokes the theological horizon of resurrection while immediately withdrawing from such belief-based context. In keeping with the cognitive approach that permeates the poem in its entirety, the poetic voice characterises the paradox of life after the end as irrational:

> We survive, in the confusion
> of a life reborn outside reason
>
> (Sopravviviamo: ed è la confusione
> di una vita rinata fuori dalla ragione) (Pasolini 1982: 108)

This precarious survival faces yet another end in the last stanza of the poem which only then fulfils what its title promises: it only then turns into a plea and prayer, a 'supplica'. The title already anticipates the invocation of and withdrawal from the theological which the poem as a whole performs. It is a prayer, however, not to a transcendent, theological point of reference but to an immanent one: the mother. It is not until the poem's last two lines where we encounter the main theme of Thomas's poem, 'Do not go gentle into that good night' – the struggle against death, the hope not to die:

> I pray you, oh, I pray: Do not wish [my trans.] to die . . .
> I am here alone, with you, in a future April . . .
>
> (Ti supplico, ah, ti supplico: non voler morire . . .
> Sono qui, solo, con te, in un futuro aprile . . .) (Pasolini 1982: 108)

The poetic voice here too foregrounds selfhood: the mother's life in a future April involves the otherwise isolated self of the poet (*Sono qui, solo, con te*). In Thomas's 'Do not go gentle into that good night', by contrast, we do not find the subjectivity of the speaker foregrounded. On the contrary, the poem invokes general terms which are the subject matter of each strophe, except for the first and last one. The poet refers to 'wise men', then 'good men', then 'wild men' and then 'grave men'. A variety of general types of men should serve as example of how to rage against the dying of the light. In the end, the poem apparently returns from general types of men to the singular figure of the father, but here too the language is broad rather than particular, evoking a range of possible characteristics encompassing the extremities of cursing and blessing.

This is not the place to do justice to Dylan Thomas's complex and most significant poem. 'Do not go gentle into that good night' is evoked here rather than compared with Pasolini's poem about death and life. Striking a related but slightly different note (and tone) from Thomas's, Pasolini's 'Supplica a mia madre' avoids referencing what we may be accustomed with – the traditional forms of cursing and blessing which figure prominently in Thomas's poem. Even before evoking the mortality theme of Thomas's poem, Pasolini introduces us to an end which is not that of the end of life, but the closing of a specific relationship. The poem takes pains to do justice to the specific and the singular. This may be the poem's main theme around which it revolves both in terms of its form and content – and this from the very opening:

> It's so hard to say in a son's words
> What I am so little like in my heart.
>
> (È difficile dire con parole di figlio
> Ciò a cui nel cuore ben poco assomiglio.) (Pasolini 1982: 108)

The poem gives form to the difficulty of finding equivalence in the generality of words for the singularity of events, feelings, happenings both in the subjective and the objective sphere. Its opening almost takes back what it has just begun to unfold: the son's words are not adequate enough to do justice to what is actually taking place in the heart of the self profiled here.

Figlio rhymes with *assomiglio* but the rhyme associates a coincidence called into question by the strophe itself: the son (*figlio*) does not coincide with its representation or likeness (*assomiglio*) established through the generality of words (*parole*).

Representation disrupts itself here. This disruption instantiates the form of the poem, creating a new space wherein we enter a world to which are not accustomed: one in which we are capable of discovering so far invisible or entirely new forms of life. The poem witnesses the discovery of the infinitely contaminated constitution of life, of which the maternal figure is of course the giver or originator. The opening strophe announces and performs this hybridity in its evocation of words which are then almost withheld or withdrawn. Words do not fill the page with wordiness but shrink to little signs or to silences which could do justice to the life of the heart – the subjectivity of the speaker.

In the following strophe the heart no longer belongs to the subject. The mother knows more about the beginnings of affection than the one who carries the heart:

Only you in all the world know what my
heart always held, before any love.

(Tu sei la sola al mondo che sa, del mio cuore,
Ciò che è stato sempre, prima d'ogni altro amore.) (Pasolini 1982: 108)

The son's words are inadequate not least because the subject is always already displaced by what preceded subjectivity. Here the cognitive theme of the poem first introduces the mother (*sa, del mio cuore*) in cognitive terms as a vessel of and for knowledge. The relationship between mother and son covers the intersection of affect and cognition. The poem traces the itinerary of a cognitive trajectory in which the son becomes the discoverer of a terrible recognition:

So I must tell you something terrible to know:
From within your kindness my anguish grew.

(Per questo devo dirti ciò ch'è orrendo conoscere:
È dentro la tua grazia che nasce la mia angoscia.) (Pasolini 1982: 108)

Here we witness a second birth, which is one of cognition. It is the recognition of the hybrid reality of life.

Most importantly, thought and life here contaminate each other. We behold the discovery of a new form of birth in which one phenomenon or characteristic ('*grazia*') simultaneously coexists with that of its supposed opposite ('*angoscia*'). This is exactly what Pasolini understands by scandal: that there are no such things as pure entities but the contamination of such entities with each other. The adjective '*orrendo*' evokes the scandal of this discovery. As Maggi has recently pointed out, Pasolini's central notion of a second birth describes 'the acquisition of a cultural consciousness' (Maggi 2009: 186). Cultural consciousness introduces the subject to the symbolic order.

As Claude Lévi-Strauss has maintained, the prohibition of incest is the foundation of all kinds of symbolic orders which constitute all human societies. Following Lévi-Strauss, Julia Kristeva has argued that the universal prohibition of incest depends on the social conditioning of an affect: that of abjection or disgust when faced with the maternal body. According to Kristeva, affect combines the biological or physical with cognition and science:

> If it be true, as Claude Lévi-Strauss has demonstrated, that the prohibition of incest has the logical import of founding, by means of that very prohibition, the discreteness of interchangeable units, thus establishing social order and the symbolic, I shall maintain that such a logical operation is carried out owing to a subjective benefit derived from it on the level of libidinal economy. (Kristeva 1982: 63)

As Winfried Menninghaus has recently put it, Kristeva's notion of the abject 'is universally and biologically grounded (in the maternal body); likewise, the constitution of the speaking subject through the repudiation of the pre-objectival *corps maternel* and its pleasure belongs, for Kristeva, to the fundamental, unchangeable givens of subject formation and of the symbolic order in general' (Menninghaus 2003: 392). Prohibition of incest is of course normative. No doubt it is a social norm and partakes of the social order. Feeling and intellection are, however, intimately bound up with each other: a feeling of the abject accompanies the normative avoidance of incest.

Pasolini's second birth includes Lévi-Strauss's universal prohibition of incest. The second birth of cognition, however, brings about what I call the disruptive moment of contamination. Pasolini introduces an interruptive or contaminating moment to both Kristeva's and Lévi-Strauss's accounts of the universal homogeneity of prohibiting incest.

This moment is creative and nascent: it validates life from a cognitive perspective, by bringing together dangerous or disgusting elements ('*angoscia*') with beneficial ones ('*grazia*'). Neither one exists without the other. In contrast to Kristeva's account, the mother is here not solely the object of rejection and abjection. Rather Pasolini's science of difference allows for hybridity and fluidity in natural and social entities. His language interrupts itself and in doing so it precludes the consumption of solid and ready-made cognitive statements of truth. Truth here emerges as fractured and highly nuanced. The abject is not so much affiliated with the mother's body (as in Kristeva) but with the symbolic order as a whole. Disgust with the social order, however, does not mean a rejection or repudiation of it. On the contrary, the abject or anxious here includes the peaceful or beautiful: anxiety (*angoscia*) contaminates the peace of grace (*grazia*).

In a repressive and distortive society we have become accustomed to separate or purify entities to one single point of denomination (a striking example is Kristeva's distinct notion of the *abject*). This custom of isolation and compartmentalisation turns our lives into lies. Pasolini's poem attempts to counter such lies of the instrumental, reductive and exploitative by scandalously bringing together what we have been trained to separate. From its opening stanza onwards, 'Supplica a mia madre' takes one step in one direction while simultaneous taking another one into the opposite direction: it evokes words while at the same time highlighting their potential inadequacy. During the course of the poem we discover that the distortion of words resides in their isolation: in the separation of *grazia* from its contaminating opposite *angoscia*, in the separation of the affect (*amore*) from domination (*schiavitù*). The work of art (whether film, the novel or the poem) offers a new space to which we have not become accustomed otherwise: a space in which we discover the hybridity of our world.

Under the figure of contamination, the form of the poem connects what it ostensibly separates. The most glaring point of such separation is the love of bodies without soul:

And I don't want to be alone. I have an infinite
Hunger for love, love of bodies without soul.

(E non voglio esser solo. Ho un'infinita fame
d'amore, dell' amore di corpi senza anima.) (Pasolini 1982: 108)

The hybrid form of the poem, which, as we have seen, instructs us to read words not in isolation, refers the sequestered expression '*senza anima*' back to its deceptive opposite – to:

For the soul is inside you, it is you, but
You're my mother and your love is my slavery

(Perché l'anima è in te, sei tu, ma tu
Sei mia madre e il tuo amore è la mia schiavitù) (Pasolini 1982: 108)

The love for bodies without soul grows out of the attachment to the mother wherein resides the soul (*l'anima è in te, sei tu*). This connection between the chastity of the maternal and promiscuity, which characterises Pasolini's understanding of homosexuality – 'For Pasolini, the male homosexual pursues sexual encounters only with 'real' men, heterosexual men who use the homosexual as woman' (Maggi 2009: 201) – finds a striking point of culmination in the notorious note 55 of his last novel *Petrolio*.

Note 55 describes how a man (Carlo 2) who has been transformed into a woman becomes penetrated by twenty young heterosexual men from Rome's sub-proletariat. Pasolini contaminates promiscuity with its supposed opposite, purity:

> But Carlo's heart was pure, despite the tension of his nerves: a tension due, among other things, to a sexual desire so strong and exclusive as to be, in the end, tragic, or at least to impress itself as such. On the other hand, all twenty of those boys there, standing out against the sky (stupidly crowding on top of a mound, where they could be seen from the street), were poor. (Pasolini 1997: 167)

Carlo 2's humiliating penetration by twenty young men – wherein he is compared to a prostitute who is paid for her services – of course affronts bourgeois values of pride, success and conformity. The field in which it takes place 'evokes [in the context of Pasolini's films and novels] humiliation, suspension of social norms, poverty, and violence' (Maggi 2009: 202). Within this violent suspension of social norms, the maternal manifests itself in the seemingly 'soulless bodies' of the young men:

> He was perhaps barely sixteen and in fact in his eyes sparkled the smile not only of a boy but of a boy who practises the good manners his mother has taught him: a mother from the people, for whom a good upbringing is naturally an instinctive, deep-rooted politeness. This maternal politeness was betrayed in all of Sandro's gestures and movements. It had remained attached to him like a smell. Moreover, his clothes, too, the simple pants and plain shirt, had the appearance of having been bought at some market stall by him and his mother together, with money from the family. (Pasolini 1997: 168)

In loving the 'soulless bodies' of young men the poetic voice honours the soul of the mother. Whereas while still being a heterosexual man,

Carlo 2 violates his mother, grandmother and his sisters in acts of incest, once he has morphed into a woman (or in Pasolini's terminology into a homosexual man) he avoids acts of defilement. 'Carlo 2 brings to the fore (gives life to) a revenant, the image of a maternal home that is gone forever. This home ruled by the mother is natural and divine' (Maggi 2009: 216). Pasolini frames the maternal in terms of the sacred.

One of the most striking instances of such framing emerges at the opening of his film *Edipe Re* where Pasolini stages a mother–baby scene on green grass surrounded by idyllic trees. The camera switches from the baby to the face of the mother and lingers there. We are confronted with an unsettling close-up which traces maternal affects from the peaceful to the foreboding of anguish to come. In *Cinema 1* (1983), Gilles Deleuze characterises close-ups as affection-images. Deleuze goes so far as to claim that on a general and universal level close-ups have to do with nothing else but affects: 'But, in all these cases, the close-up retains the same power to tear the image away from spatio-temporal co-ordinates in order to call forth the pure affect as the expressed' (Deleuze 1997: 99). Deleuze argues that the affection-image removes us from the action-image. Whereas action takes place in time and space, the close-up expresses affect.

Why does Pasolini detach the audience from the sphere of action right at the beginning of the film? Pasolini is of course well known for the contemplative nature of his films. Nevertheless the length (over two minutes) and the position (at the beginning of a movie) of this affect-image highlights its significance. The face of the mother reveals truthful affects, because the foreboding feeling of anguish will prove to be true in acts of violence and incest. The baby we see will literally violate his mother.

With a Kafkaesque sensibility Pasolini thus combines the affective with the truth or factuality of the action-image. As Deleuze has pointed out, Kafka was the first to connect two types of modern technologies of transport:

> Kafka distinguished two equally modern technological pedigrees: on the one hand the means of communication-translation, which ensure our insertion and our conquests in space and time (boat, car, train, aeroplane . . .); and on the other hand the means of communication-expression which summon up phantoms on our route and turn us off course towards affects which are unco-ordinated, outside co-ordinates (letters, the telephone, the radio, all imaginable 'gramophones' and cinematographs . . .). (Deleuze 1997: 102–3)

Ironically, in the close-up of the mother at the opening of *Edipe Re* communication-translation does not summon up phantoms but the action to come.

Hence its central position at the beginning of the movie. Here the affect-image in a sense anticipates the action-image. How does it do so? Similar to the operation of the poem 'Supplica a mia madre', Pasolini's work in its entirety explores affects not to detach us from factual reality but, on the contrary, to make us recognise truths that we would otherwise not be able to uncover.

Feelings partake of cognitive processes. As Damasio states, 'emotion and core consciousness are clearly associated' (Damasio 2000: 169). The close-up of the mother's face in the opening section of *Edipe Re* depicts consciousness. We do not hear and read words but are faced with an image which in turn re-enacts the workings of the mind. Damasio has shown that *'core consciousness occurs when the brain's representation devices generate an imaged, non-verbal account of how the organism's own state is affected by the organism's processing of an object, and when this process enhances the image of the causative object, thus placing it saliently in a spatial and temporal context* [italicised in the original quote]' (Damasio 2000: 169). Crucially what we see in the affect-image of the mother's close-up is not the spatial and temporal context – as discussed above, this would be an action-image – but how her facial expressions anticipate (as affective states) the violence and anguish to come in the action scenes of Oedipus's fratricide and incest.

Whereas the mother's affective work at the same time brings truth to the fore, her son Oedipus spaces out and separates emotions from cognitions, moving from one to the other. However, the maternal sphere is simultaneously emotive and truthful. The son, by contrast, violates the mother by dialectically moving from affect to action. His action includes both affect and cognition in order to expel these two entities which the mother contaminates by binding them together at one and the same time.

In striking contrast to Sophocles, Pasolini's Oedipus does not solve the riddle of the Sphinx. Instead of solving a cognitive problem, Oedipus here simply shouts and pushes the Sphinx into the abyss. Before dying, the Sphinx quickly admonishes Oedipus to search for knowledge in his interior sphere rather than blindly rushing from affect into action. Oedipus, the adult son, has abandoned the contemplative sphere which his mother inhabits in the close-up discussed above. The maternal is the sacred where we encounter the affective as at once a cognitive force, illuminating truths hidden by conventions. The action scenes of *Edipe Re* show the work of affects which are no longer contemplated or thought through. They are blind acts of violence or incest.

In his poem 'Supplica a mia madre', Pasolini associates the maternal with both the affective and the cognitive – with the emotions of the soul. Like anguish or the abject, the soul, however, is not a pure entity. Pasolini's cinematic and poetic and novelistic forms uncover purity as scientific illusion which turns out to be pseudo-scientific.

Impurity is a fallacious concept too. At the point of Oedipus's recognition of his impure actions, he blinds himself and becomes an outcast of his native city. As outcast Oedipus, however, is no longer one-dimensionally impure. On the contrary, Pasolini has the blind Oedipus with his young partner Angelo wander dissatisfied through both modern Italian bourgeois and working class society. He only reaches peace when he finds himself on the spot on which the close-up of the maternal face took place at the opening section of the film. Oedipus the impure contaminates the purity of Oedipus the seer (blind like the seer Tiresias) and outcast. In the poem 'Supplica a mia madre', apparently soulless bodies are contaminated with the soul. *Edipe Re* ends where it began: on the green and tree-lined idyllic spot of the mother's affect-image. The form of the poem as well as the film allow for the flowing together of otherwise compartmentalised spheres of purity and impurity, of falsehood and truth.

In doing so, Pasolini's cinematic and poetic work changes the meaning of words as we encounter them in their instrumentalist and reductive isolation. Far from saying that the love for bodies without souls is soulless, 'Supplica a mia madre' connects this affect with the attachment to the soul which is the mother. The flow of the poem's form thus disrupts the order of separated entities which is the work of reduction. The confusion outside or beyond the realm of reason may not be irrational. It could give rise to a new constellation. As Armando Maggi has recently postulated, Pasolini diagnosed modernity in terms of confusion and mental illness (schizophrenia):

> His interviewer Jean Duflot remarks that, according to Herbert Marcuse, our modern values require a new language. Nowadays, it is impossible to conceive of a morality based on the concept of beauty. Pasolini responds by saying that this is because 'we are entering the moment of variants', by which he means a time of variations and confusion, a sort of modern tower of Babel whose builders await divine punishment. (Maggi 2009: 159)

The image of the tower of Babel evokes the sin of hubris and its consequent divine punishment. This moralistic aspect is, however, absent from Pasolini's diagnosis of modernity. As Maggi points out later on, 'the "form" invoked by Pasolini is a statement, a "something" that exposes itself as neither good nor bad , neither progressive or regressive, but only existent' (Maggi 2009: 159). The notion of confusion refers back to 'Supplica a mia madre', but also alludes to Pasolini's film *Edipe*

Re and his last novel *Petrolio*. The two latter works profile the scandal of incest which Pasolini's poem of 1962 evokes but eventually avoids – hovering ambiguously in the confusing hybridity of soulless bodies and the soul of the mother. Crucially, neither the main protagonist of *Edipe Re* nor Carlo 2 of *Petrolio* find a defining moment of identity in the act of incest, because Pasolini's aesthetics and ethics has done away with points of beginning and end which would define a distinct identity or entity.

Pasolini's last novel creates a new form that has overcome the compartmentalisation or isolation of specific subjects and substances. The novel unfolds not so much the vertical line of a building such as the tower of Babel but the horizontal growth of infinite birth: 'The concept of giving birth to a form is crucial for a correct understanding of *Petrolio*. The "initial form of thought" is a thought that is in a perennial state of birth' (Maggi 2009: 160). Strikingly, the novel begins with the repudiation of a beginning: 'This novel does not begin' (Pasolini 1997: 3). Having neither beginning nor end, Pasolini's last novel grows laterally rather in terms of linearity. It practises as form what Gilles Deleuze and Félix Guattari have confined to a thought-image: that of the rhizome which is non-hierarchical and allows for multiplicity and diversity.

Multiple narrators compose *Petrolio* and its main character is not even a single subject, but splits into two: Carlo 1 and Carlo 2. Carlo 1 desires power and wealth by trying to climb the hierarchical ladder of the state-owned Italian petroleum company Eni. Power is, however, not pure but corrupted. Corruption does its work through Carlo 1 and Eni's as well as various political parties' affiliation with the Mafia. The other side of impurity is the splitting of Carlo 1 (who as Eni executive belongs to the ruling class) into Carlo 2 (who is a middle-class heterosexual engineer). Carlo 2 is driven by incestuous desires: he has sexual intercourse with his mother, grandmother and his sisters. The identity of the man Carlo 1 and Carlo 2 completely breaks down when they both undergo a sex-change from male to female.

The stories of Carlo 1 and Carlo 2 are, however, not the subject matter of the novel, as Pasolini repeatedly emphasises:

> Well, these printed but illegible pages are intended to announce my decision in a way that is extreme – but is then established symbolically for the rest of the book; that is, not to write a story but to construct a form (as will become clearer later on): a form consisting simply of 'something written'. I do not deny that certainly the best thing would be to invent an alphabet, perhaps of ideographs or hieroglyphics, and to print the entire book that way. (Pasolini 1997: 129)

Pasolini goes on to refer to Henri Michaux's *Idéogrammes en Chine* (1975) – a book constituting 'the patient invention of non-alphabetic signs' (Pasolini 1997: 129). Rather than working with non-alphabetic signs, Pasolini reconstructs modern allegories which are illegible, which refuse to turn into linear and understandable narrative. The form which Pasolini creates not only in *Petrolio*, but also in various films (*Accattone* to *Edipe Re* to *Teorema* and *Salò o le 120 giorante di Sodoma*) is that of allegory – an allegory bursting with a multiplicity of meanings so as to render 'meaning' or 'narrative' into multiple and contaminating constellations. Pasolini's notion of allegory comes close to Walter Benjamin's. The relationship between Pasolini and Benjamin has, however, not yet been investigated. Regardless of whether Pasolini was deeply familiar with Benjamin's work, their mutual emphasis on a modern form of allegory is crucial for a better understanding of their critique of regressive or brutalising elements within modernity, of which incest is a most striking example. Central to both Benjamin's and Pasolini's interpretations of allegory is the element of interruption.

Allegory is modernity's interruption of itself. A break of course constitutes the definition of the modern: the departure from the past, from tradition or the beginning of the new (modernity is *Neuzeit* in German). Why does the break with the past require a second break – a breaking away from itself? This is due to the failure of the modern project to implement what it had promised: a plural world beyond pressures to embrace homogeneity and other forms of violence.[11]

From Pasolini's perspective incest instantiates the homogeneous operations of power: for him, incest increases rather than abates in the wake of neo-capitalism. He argues that the modern urgently needs renewal – a renewal that returns to premodern forms of cognition such as allegory. The birth of the modern requires a second cognitive birth which returns to the intellectual-spiritual realm of the contemplative mother which predominates the opening sequence of *Edipe Re*. Pasolini describes this renewal out of the past as follows: 'Even if I had not determined it, willed it, this writing necessarily had to be a "new game" – even if not, perhaps, lexically and formally; everything in it, in fact, is heavy allegory, almost medieval (that is, illegible)' (Pasolini 1997: 37). According to both Pasolini and Benjamin modernity's second, more thoughtful birth coincides with the renaissance of a modern and premodern hybrid of contemplation: allegory.

Conclusion: Walter Benjamin's allegory and Pasolini's *Affabulazione*

In order to address the question of how the politics, and by implication the history, with which we are familiar is closely bound up with sexuality, I shall briefly discuss a play which Pasolini wrote while working on his film *Edipe Re*. Pasolini's *Affabulazione* (*Fabrications*) stages incest as a neo-capitalist form of globalisation. Here incest is no longer heterosexual but has turned homosexual. As in almost all of Pasolini's works, the play *Affabulazione* revolves around family life. The setting is the home of a wealthy Milanese industrialist. We do not know his first name or his surname. He simply appears as 'Father', his wife as 'Mother' and his son as 'Son'. The absence of specific names turns the characters into representatives of their roles. They act out a specific role. In this way they are allegories. As allegories, the actors purport to represent some form of truth in a symbolic way.

Walter Benjamin has established a salient account of allegory which relates the term to the radically secularised world of bourgeois modernity. Benjamin developed his understanding of allegory in his *Trauerspiel* book. Here he analyses how the Baroque mourning play depicts secularisation in a highly aestheticised manner in order to debunk both the attraction of this world and the status of those who wield power over the world, of those who are privileged to enjoy such attractions. The desire to escape from this world is motivated by the confrontation with a radically this-worldly, secularised society.

The disgust with the profane – evoked by its radical aestheticisation – brings about the will to read the world allegorically. As a secularised literary device Benjamin's modern and postmodern allegory may have become stripped of its theological context but it nevertheless relates to theology, whose content it empties of spiritual as well as intellectual meaning. According to Benjamin, allegorical readings destroy profane bodies, reassembling them in the body politic of a messianic age. Secular forms of destruction rule the workings of allegory. Signs are now valid without carrying any spiritual or intellectual significance. The prospect of transcendent redemption has disappeared but what remains is the now secularised version of guilt – Augustine's original sin – that encompasses nature and our embodied life on an all-encompassing scale.

This contempt with nature, with the body, with the profane, furthers the desire to read the world allegorically. Allegory performs the destruction of the natural and the corporeal. According to Benjamin it is the literary trope for the destruction of an immanence that cannot be salvaged by a now defunct transcendence. The command to destroy the profane motivates allegorical readings of the world (here these readings of course go without any reference to a spiritual realm).

According to Benjamin, this allegorical destruction of the body gains in force with the progress of capitalism. Benjamin does not abandon the theological. Indeed the profane re-discovers and thereby re-establishes its spiritual or intellectual significance at the point where it burst into fragments, into shards which could form the basis of a new life and a new form of politics. Creative and destructive aspects of the arts are the basis for this novel polis.[12] Intellectual critique is therefore always already part of the constructive work towards a less violent body politic.[13]

In order to gain a new perspective on politics – which is central to a discussion of Pasolini's art that does justice to its political potential – a brief consideration of Raymond Geuss's social thought may be pertinent. Geuss has recently suggested that we 'would be well advised to take as basic' concepts for politics not – as has been philosophy's predilection from Plato to Rawls and Habermas – 'belief' or 'opinion' but 'action': 'Political judgments are not made individually one by one, but always stand as parts of larger sets of beliefs and judgments, and a political judgment is always embedded in a context of *action*' (Geuss 2010: 5). As we have seen in the above discussion of Pasolini's film *Edipe Re*, cinema can be at once contemplative (affect-image) and active (action-image). Affect here partakes of cognition. The affect-ridden actions of the incestuous politician Oedipus, have, by contrast, severed any connection with contemplation or cognition.

Pasolini's cinematic and literary work is indeed pertinent here: it performs a fierce animadversion with the norms of the status quo. His work reads norms allegorically until they burst into pieces, into fragments where they can be reassembled in new configurations that may be the basis for a new form of politics. Pasolini undermines heterosexual normativity by contaminating these norms with the incestuous. His heterosexual men betray the maternal by violating it in incest (Oedipus, Carlo 2). The allegory of the father in his play *Affabulazione* goes one step further: by reading the heterosexual father in terms of a homosexual abuser and, worse still, murderer of his son.

Allegory here interrupts the workings of signification. Patriarchal power so insistently reinforces its rights to ownership that it makes impossible what sanctions its existence: heterosexual partnerships. The father drives his son's girlfriend away by accusing her of having stolen what properly belongs to him, the father:

Father
Well tell me then, if you're as brave as you seem
Are you satisfied with that part of my son's body
You've stolen from us? (Pasolini 2010: 34)

Power in the form of neo-capitalist rights to ownership creates a biopolitics which unceasingly fabricates new forms of violation. Fabrications act as if they were reality and indeed within the confines of the play they do turn out to be real: they happen. In the latter part of the play the father fabricates an image of the son as one attempting to set sight on the patriarch's genitals. A complete reversal has taken place. The father here projects himself to be his own son who is keen on his father's penis:

Kill me, kill the child
that wants to see your prick (Pasolini 2010: 56)

Rather than contemplating his son's life, the father imposes his affect-ridden fabrication onto the body of his offspring. When the ghost of Sophocles appears to intervene in the play he admonishes the father to make use of his contemplative and cognitive capacities:

But you, instead of contemplating him
are chasing after him to grab hold of him.
Ah that old, dreadful habit of possession! (Pasolini 2010: 65)

In a long monologue before he kills his son, the father allegorically reveals the history of violence to coincide with the action/affect-driven rule of patriarchy. The opening of *Edipe Re* stages an alternative to such mythic as well as modern violence in the affective-cognitive close-up of the maternal:

Thousands of sons are murdered by their fathers,
while just occasionally a father's killed by his son
– this can't be denied. But how does
the murder of sons by fathers come about?
By means of prisons, trenches, concentration camps
cities bombed to bits. And how,
on the other hand, does the murder of fathers
by sons occur? By means of the growth
of an innocent body, which is just there,
a newcomer in the old city, the city of the old,
and which finally asks nothing but
to be admitted. (Pasolini 2010: 89)

The allegorical reflection of the incestuous father illuminates violence as the rivalry between youth and age. The desire for power, and with it possession, amounts to sexual rivalry between old and young. The reversal of the Oedipus complex, as Laius complex, extends the sphere of incest from heterosexuality to homosexuality. Pasolini reveals both forms of incest to be driven by affect- as well as action-ridden urges to possess and dominate; similar to his last film *Salò* in which homosexual as well as heterosexual practices have been corrupted to exertions of power over life.

Pasolini thus foregrounds his contemplative techniques (such as his usage of allegory or his cinematography of close-ups) to make us see ways out of such circles of incest/violence – alternatives wherein we contaminate cognition and affect. Here the figure of contamination could give rise to a thoughtful form of politics that avoids exertions of power over life. The following chapter analyses ways in which we can overcome a dialectics of inclusion and exclusion that has governed biopolitics not only in traditional humanism but also in some contemporary versions of posthumanism. Uncritical approaches to posthumanist issues (such as cloning) may merely reproduce the dialectics of inclusion and exclusion if they do not sufficiently address the Cartesian understanding of the mind as controlling the bare life of the body. Posthumanism may then be at risk of replicating past types of bio-political power under new technological apparel.

Notes

1. As Stephen Holden (1993) has put it: 'Of all the films in the series that exerted an impact on Mr Scorsese, the two that have had the most sweeping influence, he said, are John Cassavetes's "Shadows" (1960), which opens the series today, and Pier Paolo Pasolini's "Accatone!" (1961). He studied both films when he was a film student at New York University.'
2. This is of course not to deny that Scorsese's *Cape Fear* is a remake of its earlier version. However, as Phillip E. Wegner has recently pointed out, the earlier film is itself a remake of John D. MacDonald's novel (1957), *The Executioner*: 'the mid-Century Cold War and gender anxieties evident in MacDonald's novel; the nightmares of racial conflict allegorically staged in the first film; and finally, in Scorsese's 1991 remake, the explosive re-emergence – as these earlier fears seem to have been put to bed (an illusion, as I will show later) – of anxieties about new forms of class conflict. In each case, this complex of fears results in violence against a variety of what Evan Watkins calls "throwaway" bodies – those of women, poor whites, African Americans, immigrants, and working people – precisely out of a paranoid anxiety contained in them' (Wegner 2009: 88).
3. As Wegner has pointed out, this scene 'has become the stuff of countless film and television parodies, by his [i.e. Cady's] aggressive march, on his release, directly into the lens of the camera' (Wegner 2009: 86).

4. As Wegner has put it, 'Late in the film, Cady tells Sam, "Now you and I will truly be the same." The irony is that they always already were the same, Sam's violence perhaps more covert, but having no less devastating consequences for his victims' (Wegner 2009: 114–15).
5. Vanessa Lemm has recently described this term as follows: 'This biocentric notion of culture in Nietzsche, as reconstructed in *Nietzsche's Animal Philosophy*, is different from previous materialist and spiritualist interpretations of his philosophy of culture, because it avoids the biologism of the first and the anthropomorphism of the second. Rejecting a biologistic interpretation of life, I consider Nietzsche's thesis to be that every organic cell has spirit' (Lemm 2009: 2).
6. For a discussion of this point see Siciliano (1982: 247).
7. So far scholars of Pasolini's work have confined the notion of contamination to the aesthetic sphere only where it concerns the mediation and interaction between different cultures and historical moments. See Rumble (1997).
8. For a discussion of Keats's term 'negative capability' see Gittings (1979: 262–71).
9. Commenting on Freud's Oedipus complex Lacan establishes the law of the father as follows: 'Why does this minimal schema of human experience which Freud gave us in the Oedipus complex retain its irreducible and yet enigmatic value for us? And why privilege the Oedipus complex? Why does Freud always want to find it everywhere, with such insistence? Why do we have here a knot that seems so essential to him that he is unable to abandon it in the slightest particular observation – unless it's because the notion of father, closely related to the fear of God, gives him the most palpable element in experience of what I've called the quilting point between the signifier and signified' (Lacan 2000: 268).
10. For a detailed discussion of Kafka's avoidance of becoming a father in terms of an avoidance of power see Elias Canetti (1989).
11. For a discussion of modernity as promise of diversity see Mack (2010).
12. The term polis is appropriate here because Benjamin's politics of art sharply contrasts with Plato's exclusion of the arts from his conception of an ideal republic.
13. For a discussion of the innovations that are part of the work of critique see Mack (2014).

7

Contaminating Posthumanism

Introduction: posthumanism, biopolitics and the figure of contamination

This chapter will analyse the ways in which we can see both posthumanism and bio-political theory in the new context of contamination. Both theoretical approaches are capable of contaminating what have traditionally been posited as opposites: human and animal, nature and society, mind and body, natural and human history. The bio-political concern with life has an emancipatory potential. As Miguel Vatter has recently put it: 'The constitution of a life-world makes possible "man" as a species because from the start it identifies human life as a form of animal life that additionally has the capacity of being-political or being-rational' (Vatter 2008: 48). This new understanding of biopolitics liberates embodied life from the traditional sovereign rule of the cerebral (going under various names such as law, medicine, economics and politics). Instead of subordinating one to the other – mind to body or body to mind – a parallelism between the two comes into the purview of scientific and philosophical discourse, a Spinozan parallelism which, according to contemporary neuroscientist Antonio Damasio, has always constituted our life in an embodied, natural environment. As we will see, like bio-political theory, posthumanism emerges from mid-twentieth-century schools of thought such as poststructuralism, deconstruction, feminism and subaltern studies. What these schools have in common is a hermeneutics of suspicion as regards claims to universalism.

Contamination as both an idea and a way of life, however, allows us to conceive of the common or the universal not in the traditional terms of inclusion or exclusion but as the interdependence of what has so far been seen as incompatible. Firstly we will see how posthumanism shares with bio-political theory a critical concern with what traditional forms of philosophy, science, economics and politics have excluded from a supposedly inclusive conception of life. However, the main part of this chapter discusses how we can come to understand both posthumanism and a critical engagement with biopolitics as transgressing twentieth-century forms of theory at the point at which a new universal emerges under the sign of contamination. Contamination is truly universal because it has outdone the binaries of inclusion and exclusion with which subaltern studies, feminism and deconstruction have rightly taken issue.

Posthumanism critically reflects on the unacknowledged practices of exclusion which have informed and inflected the history of humanism. The work of posthumanism is thus one of critique. It takes issue with standards of normality, gender-, ethnic- and species-cohesions, as well as with other forms of homogeneity. Pramod K. Nayar has recently defined critical posthumanism as follows:

> Critical posthumanism, as we shall come to call this philosophical and political theme in literature, popular culture and theory, is the *radical decentring of the traditional sovereign, coherent and autonomous human in order to demonstrate how the human is always already evolving with, constituted by and constitutive of multiple forms of life and machines*. Literary texts that have since the Renaissance always shown us how humans behave, react and interact – indeed it has been said that literature 'invented' the human – have now begun to show that the human is what it is *because* it includes the non-human. (Nayar 2014: 2)

Rather than abandoning or avoiding the term humanity,[1] however, posthumanism expands our understanding of what is human into areas which have traditionally been deemed to be the opposite of our constitution – namely, other species, such as animals or plants, and technological apparatuses such as machines. Posthumanism contaminates the human with what has traditionally been seen as its opposite: the animal and the machine.

By contaminating assumed binaries with each other, posthumanism may prove capable of achieving a so far elusive form of universalism that allows for the mutual contamination of different entities. The term 'posthumanism', however, may be quite misleading because it may suggest a teleological or progressive movement that has done away with or, in other words, has overcome the human. This form of temporal abandonment of what preceded it – signalled by the prefix 'post' – would, however, reiterate past exclusions in a new context in which whatever goes under the sign of 'human' denotes the inferior or excluded. As Cary Wolfe has recently put it, 'the point is not to reject humanism *tout court* – indeed, there are many values and aspirations to admire in humanism – but rather to show how those aspirations are undercut by the philosophical and ethical frameworks used to conceptualize them' (Wolfe 2010: xvi). As we will see through a close reading of Kazuo Ishiguro's novel *Never Let Me Go*, the point of posthumanist writing and thought is to contaminate what has traditionally been defined as the non-human (the animal or the cyborg) with the human (or vice versa, to contaminate the animal with the human). The figure of contamination as it has been developed in this book thus changes the way we perceive ourselves and our environment.

From its inceptions, posthumanist writing and thought has contaminated the organic with the inorganic and in this respect it shares, on a structural level, a bio-political concern with the relationship between form and mere life, between the cerebral and the corporeal, between mind and biology. In perhaps the first posthumanist manifesto (1990), Donna Haraway combines the technological with the organic when she focuses on the hybrid nature of the cyborg: 'A cyborg is a cybernetic organism, a hybrid of machine and organism, a creature of social reality as well as a creature of fiction' (Haraway 2001: 465). The collapse of the distinction between the inorganic machine-like and the organic (the animal) accentuates a blurring of the traditional opposition between social reality and fiction:

> Late twentieth-century machines have made thoroughly ambiguous the difference between natural and artificial, mind and body, self-developing and externally designed, and many other distinctions that used to apply to organisms and machines. Our machines are disturbingly lively, and we ourselves frighteningly inert. (Haraway 2001: 468)

Humans create or fabricate fictions and machines. Once these inorganic productions turn organic, the distinction between literature and social reality collapses. Then fictions and machines have a life of their own and interact with social reality.

This is not entirely new.[2] Literature has previously shown how the fictitious can exert a powerful and lively – if deleterious – hold over social reality. A striking example is of course Henry James's *The Portrait of a Lady*, in which the heroine Isabel Archer takes the aesthetic deceptions of Madame Merle and Mr Osmond for real, realising only too late what socio-political and economic interests art here serves to cover up. Isabel Archer's imagination makes her fall prey to the all too real materialistic interests of Madame Merle and Mr Osmond. James's novel depicts how our lives are ambiguously shaped by narratives, by the fabricated or artificial, by fictions which are capable of forming our social reality with unintended consequences.

Neither the blurring of the line that divides the imagined or fictitious from social reality – think of the ambiguity of the ghost in Shakespeare's *Hamlet* – nor the inclusion of machines into human society are new. It is important to keep in mind that humans have always been interacting with machines – such as prostheses (witness captain Ahab in Melville's *Moby Dick*) – and with other species such as animals. Following Jean-Luc Nancy, Roberto Esposito has argued that 'what we should be talking about is the supplemental, or technical, character of the body itself' (Esposito 2011: 150).[3] Uncritical or non-reflective humanism has, however, tended to define machines and animals in terms of what the human is not.

At this point posthumanism critically intervenes and argues for what Nayar has recently called 'multispecies citizenship that involves *all* forms of life' (Nayar 2014: 155). This 'species cosmopolitanism is an openness toward the Other but also an opening up to uncertainty and possibilities of the not-yet' (Nayar 2014: 155). Nayar's term 'species cosmopolitanism' counters various strategies of exclusion that he sees operating in the entire history of humanism, even in humanism's more self-reflective and critical strands:

> [. . .] critical posthumanism proposes that the category of the human was constructed by expelling the animal, the plant and the machine. In other words, where critical humanism unravelled the exclusionary nature of the allegedly sovereign human, critical posthumanism proposes that the sovereign human is in fact a hybrid, constituted by the very forms of life that were excluded to define the limits and identity of the human. (Nayar 2014: 30)

The quotation, however, raises the question whether critical humanism does not already acknowledge the hybridity and the fluid identity of the human when it undermines notions of sovereignty, disregarding whether they are supposedly human or supposedly non-human. Machines can be violent too, as can clearly be seen in their employment in military activities (a striking example is of course the use of drones for bombing missions). We might therefore ask whether critical posthumanism may be inclined to abstain from the work of critique when it thoughtlessly welcomes machines.

Here the idea and praxis of contamination may prove beneficial. How so? Contamination allows for a blurring of distinct entities. As result of such blurring, we can no longer employ the term machine to demote the human, as is sometimes done when robots are appraised for their economic and ethical efficiency over and above the vulnerability and inefficiency of the human. Robots are positively opposed to humans due to their non-emotive, 'cool' or rational behaviour and their inexhaustibility and their independence of embodied needs.

Rather than pitching the machine against the human (or, vice versa, the human against the machine), contamination outdoes such oppositions which perpetuate traditional bio-political forms of exclusion and inclusion as analysed by Foucault and Agamben (see discussion below). Thinking and acting within the force field of contamination makes us realise that the distinction between machines and humanity is spurious, because both entities have been mutually implicated with each other: humans after all invent and programme machines.

As Haraway has pointed out, machines such as robots or cyborgs have been first developed not in the interest of species cosmopolitanism but intra-species warfare: 'The main trouble with cyborgs, of course, is that they are the illegitimate offspring of militarism and patriarchal capitalism, not to mention socialism' (Haraway 2001: 467). Haraway, however, goes on to belittle this militaristic aspect of a posthumanist infatuation with machines, writing: 'But illegitimate offspring are often exceedingly unfaithful to their origins. Their fathers, after all, are inessential' (Haraway 2001: 467). In contemporary literature and theory, however, the distinction between the organic and inorganic has become increasingly important to the establishment of the posthumanist field of animal studies.

Whereas Haraway's 1990 *A Cyborg Manifesto* partakes of a postmodernist and poststructuralist linguistic turn, contemporary animal studies are part of a countermovement: the post-linguistic turn.[4] In her recent study *Animal Capital: Rendering Life in Biopolitical Times*, Nicole Shukin has analysed the way in which poststructuralist theory, from Deleuze to Derrida (to Lippit, who follows Derrida), operates in a disembodied, symbolic environment which is akin to the high modernity of our current capitalist forms of exchange:

> Rather than idealizing the alterity of animal affect, as Deleuze, Derrida, and Lippit are variously prone to do, one of the questions this book poses is How does animal affect function as a technology of capital? The Deleuzian and Derridean figures of animality I have traced unravel the presumption that Homo sapiens is an all-powerful presence and self-same subject. Yet in liberating animality from the metaphysical strictures of Western thought and reenvisioning animals as pure intensities and undying specters, these poststructuralist discourses may inadvertently resonate with market forces likewise intent on freeing animal life into a multiplicity of potential exchange values. (Shukin 2009: 42)

Haraway's approach of the 1990s is clearly affiliated with a poststructuralist exclusion of embodied, 'natural' life. According to Haraway's 1990 *A Cyborg Manifesto*, social reality is not a natural given but subject to political-linguistic construction.

In the wake of a recent post-linguistic turn, however, contemporary writing and thought increasingly deviates from postmodernism's 'general emphasis on the textuality of our environments, to the neglect of material realities' (Boxall 2013: 15). Literary as well as philosophical attention has shifted from the supposed self-referentiality of texts to the material interconnections of our lives.

It might, however, be rather one-sided to neglect or marginalise poststructuralism's preoccupation with language. Rather than being either linguistic or embodied, our world contaminates the symbolic with the corporeal, the societal with the natural. The figure of contamination makes us wary of discarding the linguistic for the post-linguistic turn. As with the machine, the animal and the human, oppositions between the symbolic and embodied are fictions that precondition societal acts of exclusion. Rather than being one instead of another our life is always already contaminated, blurring and meshing various opposites. The idea and praxis of contamination alerts us not to exclude one school of thought in favour of another.

In this way, deconstruction has taught us that our perception of material reality remains mired within various textual practices and linguistic systems. To be oblivious of this postmodern insight into the artificiality of what appears to be innocuously 'there' risks embracing a rather distorted view of our society and our environment wherein we uncritically endorse new technological developments as if they were not part of socio-linguistic constructions and political agendas. While in many ways contemporary posthumanism has initiated a post-linguistic turn, the question of the human and the question of language still, however, haunt our approach to human knowledge and ethics.

Posthumanism has thus to take into account linguistic constructions when it seriously engages with the ethics of material, embodied experiences that go beyond what has traditionally been considered human (i.e. animals, clones and cyborgs). The question of how to include aspects of our world which traditional humanism excluded from its linguistic construction of what supposedly constitutes humanity is at once a political and ethical issue. This contamination of the ethical and the political first emerges while being articulated (i.e. on a linguistic level). We simply cannot ignore or belittle the role of language in inter- or intra-species politics and ethics. Indeed language is often employed as a criterion for exclusion.

In this way, animals have often been marginalised or excluded with reference to their supposed lack of linguistic capacities. In Giorgio Agamben's words: 'Just as, in the words of Foucault, man "is an animal whose politics places his existence as living being in question," so also is he *the living being whose language places his life in question*' (Agamben 2010: 69). Both Foucault and Agamben include the notion of the animal in their understanding of humanity. Humanity is, however, a linguistic and political animal. In order to engage with the politics and ethics of posthumanism we therefore ignore the preceding linguistic turn at our peril.

Within the contemporary post-linguistic turn, Haraway's postmodern 1990 appraisal of cyborgs has been subjected to critical analysis in some recent approaches to posthumanism. As Stefan Herbrechter has argued, Haraway's combination of the organic and the inorganic in her notion of the cyborg repeats the humanistic mind–body division in which the embodied becomes subservient to the controlling agency of cerebral work. As Herbrechter has put it in his critique of Haraway's cyborgs manifesto:

> Cyborgization is, therefore, not merely a hybridization of the organic and the mechanical, but the grafting of an informational and digital (i.e. virtual and virtualizing), coded and simulated (i.e. no longer relying on representation) reality onto human embodiment. And this new hybrid reality already functions according to the rules and codings of an artificial intelligence. The idea of embodiment, in turn, however, runs the danger of, in fact, contributing – as a quasi-extension and continuation of the long history of Christian and Cartesian duality between mind and body – to the notion of the body as the location of animality or organicity, while the neuro-informatic combination of consciousness and simulation technology is seen as liberation or 'purification' of the eternal mind from its bodily demise. This dualism allows for new forms of ideological dematerialization (as can be seen in the *Matrix* trilogy), which might make an intensified biotechnological exploitation of the 'animal' body (whether in human or nonhuman animals) more likely. (Herbrechter 2013: 188)

This return of the traditional Christian and, in its modern scientific form, Cartesian mind–body duality within a posthumanist social reality – shaped as it is by digital and genetic technologies – constitutes the so far underappreciated critical kernel of Ishiguro's novel *Never Let Me Go*.

Contaminating the linguistic with the embodied: Ishiguro's *Never Let Me Go*

There is no doubt that *Never Let Me Go* does not dispute the rights of clones to equal rights. However, this is not the moot point of the novel. Ishiguro narrates the novel from the personal plural perspective of the clones. This means that we experience the clones as humans. The socio-political order of the novel, however, categorises the clones as non-humans. The novel thus lets us experience (from the first person plural perspective of the clones) the injustice of unequal rights. Indeed, as Nancy Fraser has shown, *Never Let Me Go* reveals the humaneness of those whom we choose to label 'non-human':

> Unlike Plato, Ishiguro makes no attempt to represent a just social order, but instead offers a chilling picture of one that the reader comes to view as deeply unjust. This already makes a profound point: justice is never actually experienced directly. By contrast, we do experience injustice, and it is only through this that we form an idea of justice. Only by pondering the character of what we consider unjust do we begin to get a sense of what would count as an alternative. (Fraser 2012: 43)

What is crucial is that the clones are (of course unjustly) represented by their guardians as mere bodies which lack thought, consciousness and feelings. The guardians categorise the clones as non-humans and yet the novel shows them to be part of humanity. It is this tension between representation or categorisation and actual reality which constitutes the theoretical framework of the novel: 'The clones can be exempted from moral consideration because they are categorically different from the originals' (Fraser 2012: 44). Ishiguro's *Never Let Me Go* contaminates the symbolic with its supposed opposite: embodied life. In a related way it presents us with the contamination of binaries which prepare for the political division between the organic and the inorganic (and the human and the animal in a different context). Similarly to the replicants in Ridley Scott's film *Blade Runner* or the cloned child in Steven Spielberg's *Artificial Intelligence*, the clones in Ishiguro's *Never Let Me Go* are capable of the same emotions and the same forms of behaviour characterising humans. These films as well as Ishiguro's novel persuade us to change the way we think about distinct and opposed entities: as no longer distinct in opposition but as mutually implicated with each other. The figure of contamination describes this force of mutual implication and interdependence.

As Fraser has shown, the injustice of socio-political representation in Ishiguro's novel goes so far as to encompass the self-perception of the clones: 'Clearly, injustice is a matter of objective victimization, a structural relation in which some exploit others and deny them moral standing as subjects of justice. But the harm is compounded when the exploited lack the means to interpret their situation as unjust' (Fraser 2012: 45). Fraser concludes her argument about the injustice depicted in Ishiguro's novel by making a plea for the inclusion of those who are excluded from equal rights, status and respect:[5] 'We should examine the public sphere for biases that impede equal access to political voice, and figure out how to overcome them, by broadening the terms available for naming social problems and disputing their causes' (Fraser 2012: 51). Her concern is both with structural and interpretive injustices. The figure of contamination reverses unjust structures of interpretation precisely by prioritising what has been rejected, marginalised, or excluded as the abject, deficient, abnormal – in short as the contaminated.

Contamination fuses the singular with the plural and thus practises a universalism that is non-exclusive. Significantly, Ishiguro's novel is composed in a first-person plural narration – from the perspective of the clones. The narration establishes this point of view in terms of a mirror that de-familiarises us from accustomed forms of representation. The narration projects mirror images that turn freakish or monstrous. The monstrosity in question is the realisation of a difference superimposed by linguistic devices to do with representation and categorisation. For the clones, accustomed forms of representation produce not identity but alienation. What they see in the mirror does not validate their selfhood but, on the contrary, renders it disturbing, monstrous, freakish:

> So you're waiting, even if you don't quite know it, waiting for the moment when you realise that you are really different to them [i.e. the guardians and 'proper' humans in general]; that there are people out there, like Madame [i.e. one of the guardians], who don't hate you or wish you any harm, but who nonetheless shudder at the very thought of you – of how you were brought into this world and why – and who dread the idea of your hand brushing against theirs. The first time you glimpse yourself through the eyes of a person like that, it's a cold moment. It's like walking past a mirror you've walked past every day of your life, and suddenly it shows you something else, something troubling and strange. (Ishiguro 2005: 33)

Critics have so far ignored how this crucial passage harks back and subverts Lacan's 1936 lecture on the mirror stage. According to Derrida (2008: 114), Lacan introduces the mirror stage to establish his humanist credentials by differentiating between a young chimpanzee's and a child's first encounter with its mirror image. Lacan emphasises how in the case of the chimpanzee the mirroring act exhausts itself 'once the image has been mastered and found empty' (Lacan 1977: 1). The human child, by contrast, fully absorbs the illusion of the act of mirroring: 'he [i.e. the human child] experiences in play the relation between the movements assumed in the image and the reflected environment, and between this virtual complex and the reality it duplicates – the child's own body, and the persons and things, around him' (Lacan 1977: 1) The child takes the virtual or symbolic mirror image to be real.

This is exactly what the clones do in *Never Let Me Go* too. In the quotation above they do not master and disregard the mirror image for what it is – as is the case with Lacan's chimpanzees – namely as an insubstantial illusion, a sign but not the thing as such. As Derrida has recently argued, by depriving animals of the mirror stage, Lacan denies them access to language and to the symbolic. For Derrida, Lacan's thesis about the mirror stage has clear implications for animals and other non-humans: 'the animal has neither the unconscious nor language, it does not have the other, it has no relation to the other as such, except by an effect of the human order, by contagion, appropriation, domestication' (Derrida 2009: 114). The passage through the mirror stage initiates the child into the order of the symbolic, which prepares for human responsiveness – the openness to the other which Lacan categorically rules out for the non-human.

Ishiguro's clones, however, have gone through the mirror stage in exactly the same ways as other humans have. They are subjects of images and signs. It is precisely at this point that they are vulnerable to feelings of discrimination and inadequacy. Having been told that they are different, that they have come into the world as cloned materials rather than human persons, they suddenly see their mirror image no longer in terms of reassurance but as 'something troubling and strange'. It is this symbolic estrangement that prepares for the acceptance of their real, material inferiority as mere embodiment or (as we shall see) 'bare life': 'And it's curious, when we were older and the guardians were giving us those talks [about the prearranged purpose of their life as mere materials for organ donation] nothing came as a complete surprise. It *was* like we'd heard everything somewhere before' (Ishiguro 2005: 75). Paradoxically, it is through language, through their exposure to categorisation and representation that the clones accept their exclusion from humanity as distinguished by linguistic and other signifying practices which go beyond the merely embodied sphere of 'bare life'. Linguistic and other cerebral operations are violent if they are used to demote life. Ishiguro's novel takes issue with a political regiment that through the mental constructions of representation or categorisation governs life from a position outside the merely embodied: i.e. within the symbolic sphere of sign-systems.

Against this background one could argue that *Never Let Me Go* affirms mere life in a way that chimes with Agamben's and Esposito's respective approaches to bio-political theory. As Vatter has pointed out:

In both Agamben and Esposito, therefore, the power over life has its source outside of life. It is as if there is something irreducibly affirmative about the concept of life, of 'biopower,' that never lets itself be placed at the service of the power over life, which is also the power of death ('thanatopolitics'). (Vatter 2011: 218)

Indeed we could say that the clones in Ishiguro's novel are subjected to the power over life at the point where the political regiment represents the purpose of their existence as organ donors who can be left to die once their organs have fully matured. Maturation of life here coincides with cessation of life (i.e. the lethal effect of a body deprived of organs which have been donated for the non-cloned population). The sociolinguistic reality within the precincts of Ishiguro's novel demotes and thereby reduces those who are called 'clones' to bodily organs which can be of instrumental use to humans – the latter are defined as humans on the basis of their exclusive possession of signifying practices which in turn serve to evidence mental life.

By questioning this discriminatory and exclusivist divide between body and mind – which is Cartesian and humanist but one that is nevertheless capable of returning in the posthumanist age of genetic engineering – Ishiguro's novel prepares for contemporary theoretical approaches in the field of both biopolitics and posthumanism. These theoretical approaches are self-reflective about the way in which new technologies may merely aggravate rather than help alleviate traditional forms of discrimination and exclusion. In order to overcome such accustomed structures of ostracisation, we need to reflect on the history of the mind–body division which keeps informing our approach both to new technologies and to what is perceived as the non-human. Ishiguro's novel thematises the bio-political kernel of posthumanism with its focus on one form of life (i.e. that of the clones), which becomes represented as being deprived of mental capacities.

Within in the political regiment of the novel the clones are representative of life that goes without creativity, contemplation and thought. *Never Let Me Go* confronts us with the violence accompanying a radical division between life and thought, body and mind, nature and society. In doing so it sensitises us to contaminate these supposedly separate entities. From a bio-political perspective Vatter has done so when he argues that 'philosophy becomes truly political when it provides a conception of life (*zoé*) that is immediately theoretical and contemplative. Philosophy is political, or political philosophy exists, only where biology is philosophical' (Vatter 2011: 218). Another complementary way to call representation's mentally constructed power over life into question is to abandon the Cartesian prioritisation of the mind over the body. This is precisely Cary Wolfe's new approach to posthumanism:

> To return, then, to the question of posthumanism, the perspective I attempt to formulate here – far from surpassing or rejecting the human – actually enables us to describe the human and its characteristic modes of communication, interaction, meaning, social significations, and affective investments with *greater* specificity once we have removed meaning from the ontologically closed domain of consciousness, reason, reflection, and so on. It forces us to rethink our taken-for-granted modes of human experience, including the normal perceptual modes and affective states of *Homo sapiens* itself, by recontextualizing them in terms of their entire sensorium of other living beings and their own autopoietic ways of 'bringing forth a world' – ways that are, since we ourselves are human *animals*, part of the evolutionary history and behavioural and psychological repertoire of the human itself. (Wolfe 2010: xxv)

Literature and the arts have a crucial role to play when it comes to a critical engagement with new technologies and issues of life and death.[6] As we shall see in an analysis of Ishiguro's *Never Let Me Go*, this is a moot point not only as regards a theoretical broadening of our approach towards what constitutes a distinct species (such as the plant, the animal and the human) but also for practical questions of bioethics, whether they concern what is seen to be human or what is seen to be non-human.

Whether some theoretical approaches (such as Wolfe's) like it or not (such as N. K. Hayles's), the notion of the human will continue to loom large in our ordinary lives, shaped as they are by the politics of life. Posthumanism introduces new possibilities of being human. As Rosi Braidotti has recently put it:

> Concrete, actualized praxis is the best way to deal with the virtual possibilities that are opening up under our very eyes, as a result of our collectively sustained social and scientific advances. Human embodiment and subjectivity are currently undergoing a profound mutation. Like all people living in an age of transition, we are not always lucid or clear about where we are going, or even capable of explaining what exactly is happening to and around us. (Braidotti 2013: 196)

Ishiguro's novel foregrounds precisely this lack of distinction in biopolitics between what is human and what is not. Like the replicants in *Blade Runner*, Ishiguro's clones are alive and suffer regardless of whether they are categorised as being incapable of human feelings. The film as well as the novel challenges us to countenance the violence inherent in aspects of our cerebral activities – such as categorisation. Humanism has elevated the mind into a controlling position over merely material life. Uncritical humanism has habituated us to see mere matter as being stuck in the lowly sphere of embodiment. What it has thereby neglected are the violence and the distortion to which mental life can give rise. A case in point is the linguistic or symbolic construction of difference which posthumanism rightly takes issue with.

Difference, however, is not in itself problematic. What we need to be cautious about are representations which demote what is different to a matter of 'mere' life that goes without creativity, contemplation and other intellectual capacities. Such distortive mimesis of the 'merely alive' paves the way for a politics of violence and death. The category 'merely alive' represents an aspect of life which is deficient or inferior in mental life. Ishiguro makes us question such dichotomies of the merely corporeal and the cerebral, by contaminating our perception with that of the others, the clones who according to the political regiment of his novel are confined to being alive in a body deprived of a mind.

The crucial issue is therefore not so much the question of how to define the human or the non-human but how the various socio-linguistic constructions of politics affect life. As Derrida has shown, the rationalist humanist tradition of Descartes's *cogito ergo sum* (and, as we have seen, which Lacan belongs to) has been premised on the demotion, denigration and exclusion of mere life or 'bare life': 'Descartes proposes abstracting from his "I am," if I can put it this way, everything that recalls life' (Derrida 2008: 72). The central focus of Ishiguro's *Never Let Me Go* is life subjected to the language games that exert power over life. In this linguistic theatre life turns into a copy of a given political norm. Everything that does not conform to this norm has to be excluded from the sphere of the living. The purported rendering knowledgeable so far arcane processes of life so that life itself can become a subject of certainty and predictability – in short a subject of rule and subjected to rule – eventuates into the equation of the biological with the politically normative. As Michel Foucault has succinctly put it, 'a normalized society is the historical outcome of a technology of power centered on life' (Foucault 1979: 144). The normalised society of biopolitics is particularly disturbing if the knowledge on which it is founded is not that of science but that of the pseudo-science and pseudo-theology of racism.[7] Here the focus is on life too: on what distinguishes a racial definition of human life from what racism excludes from belonging to humanity (i.e. groups against which it discriminates).

Critical humanism focuses on intra-species strategies of exclusion and discrimination – in short it questions various forms of racism and sexism. Ishiguro's novel *Never Let Me Go* engages with a posthumanist problematic that has grown out of the scientific discovery of cloning. So far animals – the famous sheep Dolly – but not humans have been cloned. The novel imagines a future which takes place in a post-World War II past. This extraordinary cohabitation of the past with the future highlights the persistence of traditional forms of exclusion premised on the mind–body divide.

In the past future of Ishiguro's novel humans will have been cloned. Strikingly, the novel gives us a sense that clones are human and it is precisely the political denial of their humanity that turns them into 'mere bodies' which can be used and abused – into what Giorgio Agamben has called 'bare life'. As Agamben has argued, 'bare life' can legally be killed: the clones in *Never Let Me Go* are left to die (deprived of their biological substance) once they have donated their fully developed organs. Agamben emphasises that the main argument of his famous book *Homo Sacer: Sovereign Power and Bare Life* analyses the blurring of the distinction between life (the organic) and the juridical (inorganic) mechanism of discrimination and judgement, writing:

> The present enquiry concerns precisely this hidden point of intersection between the juridico-institutional and the biopolitical models of power. What this work has had to record among its likely conclusions is precisely that the two analyses cannot be separated, and that the inclusion of bare life in the political realm constitutes the original – if concealed – nucleus of sovereign power. *It can even be said that the production of a biopolitical body is the original activity of sovereign power.* (Agamben 1995: 6)

Life has become a question of power, turning into mere embodiment or mere matter which can be used for so-called higher ends as determined by juridical processes.

This is precisely the subject matter of Ishiguro's *Never Let Me Go*. The clones are socio-politically categorised in terms of lacking the mental life of humans. Their bodies are represented as uncontaminated by the life of the mind. This abrogation of mind-centred humanity renders them non-human and thereby mere bodies that are deprived of the souls and minds by which traditional humanism defines humanity's distinction over and above the animal and the machine. Critics who see parallels between Agamben's notion of 'bare life' and the status of the clones in Ishiguro's novel nevertheless avoid establishing a crucial connection to the traditional mind–body divide which makes for the fusion of past and future in *Never Let Me Go*.[8]

Agamben's notion of 'bare life' refers back to the important Greek terms *bios* and *zoé*. *Bios* denotes a distinct or idiosyncratic way of life – that of a particular group or a particular person. It is a unique journey of life and our word biography derives from this semantic field. *Zoé*, on the other hand, expresses 'the simple fact of living common to all human beings (animals, men, or gods)' (Agamben 1995: 1). Significantly, our word for the study of animals, zoology, derives from *zoé*. According to Agamben's analysis, traditional humanist political theory and practice has been constituted by this distinction between merely embodied 'bare life' (*zoé*) and mentally endowed life (*bios*):

> The fundamental categorical pair of Western politics is not that of friend/enemy but that of bare life/political existence, *zoé/bios*, exclusion/inclusion. There is politics because man is the living being who, in language, separates and opposes himself to his own bare life and, at the same time, maintains himself in relation to that bare life in an inclusive exclusion. (Agamben 1995: 8)

According to Agamben politics (and thereby biopolitics) operates in and through language. It is mired in the illusive insubstantiality of Lacan's mirror stage which, as we have seen, Lacan uses to distinguish the human from the animal (his example of the chimpanzees who do not buy into the symbolic illusion of the mirror image). This insubstantiality of sign systems (images as Lacan calls them) prioritises the mental over and above the merely embodied (the latter is what Agamben calls 'bare life').

Agamben, however, refers to the mind–body problem within humanism while not mentioning it. His notion of the political denotes the intellectual/mental aspect by which humanism has defined humanity's distinctiveness. This is *bios*. The living, embodied part of humanity cannot be denied but it has become an issue evoking shame. Bare life (*zoé*) gives rise to shame because it betrays humanity's possible animal nature. It is therefore included in order to be excluded or, as Agamben has put it, 'at once excluding bare life from and capturing it within the political order' (Agamben 1995: 9). This paradoxical, theoretical movement of an inclusion that excludes what it purportedly includes is lethal in socio-political praxis.

In this bio-political scenario Agamben speaks of 'the originary exception in which human life is included in the political order in being exposed to an unconditional capacity to be killed' (Agamben 1995: 85). Strikingly, Agamben speaks of human life here while at the same time saying that the boundary between the human and the non-human has become indistinct in the founding movement of a bio-political city: 'Not the act of tracing boundaries, but their cancellation or negation is the constitutive act of the city' (Agamben 1995: 85). The preconditions for violence and murder are societal representations or categorisations which are employed to reduce life to the homogeneous phenomenon of bare life: the mechanical functions common to all biological systems which this socio-political system represents as being cut off from, as being uncontaminated by the life of the mind.

Racism and other forms of discrimination depict the life of the other as 'pure' body that proves resistant for any contamination by intellect or spirit (the German word *Geist* connotes this indistinction between the intellectual and the spiritual). The figure of the animal has come to represent the purity of the biological uncontaminated by the mind. As Nicole Shukin has recently put it apropos the treatment of Iraqi prisoners in Abu Ghraib:

> Trophy photos of U.S. military personnel terrorizing Iraqi prisoners in Abu Ghraib prison in 2004 showed, among other things, a naked Iraqi man on all fours, with a leash around his neck, and prisoners cowering before German shepherd dogs. Cruelly, the dog is made to function as a racist prosthetic of the U.S. military's power to animalize 'the other,' a power that applies in the first instance to the animal itself. The biopolitical production of the bare life of the animal other subtends, then, the biopolitical production of the bare life of the racialized other. (Shukin 2009: 10)

Once the distinction of the human *bios* has been reduced to the generality of the animal or the genetic (*zoé*) – as is the case with the clones in Ishiguro's *Never Let Me Go* – life, on a theoretical as well as practical level, can be legally killed. If we are no longer valued for our mental contribution to humanity (either as individuals or as groups) we are expandable and thus superfluous: mere bodies to be used for the greater mental/spiritual good which defines humanity in a non-critical, traditional humanist framework. This is precisely the topic of Ishiguro's *Never Let Me Go*. The setting of this novel is a posthumanist future. Crucially it is a posthumanist future that is still governed by both the rejection of the figure of contamination and the embrace of a traditional mind–body divide – long-established by uncritical humanism which reaches back to Plato, Christianity and the scientific paradigms of Cartesian thought.

Biopolitics of memes

In *Never Let Me Go*, the clones exist to satisfy a health market – a non-cloned population that consumes their vital organs. Liberalism coincides with an immanent or bio-political control of freedom: 'The new governmental reason needs freedom therefore, the new art of government consumes freedom. It consumes freedom, which means it has to produce it' (Foucault 2008: 63). In Ishiguro's *Never Let Me Go*, the production of free consumer goods clearly coincides with the creation of clones whose very existence depends on the consumption of their vital organs by the larger population. The clones are not physically forced to do what they have to do. Rather their life freely turns into a copy of what has been preordained for them: not to procreate as well as not to age and instead to die prematurely due to the donation process.

The life of clones is subjected to the power of political and legal institutions. By questioning the working of biopolitics, Ishiguro's novel assists us in analysing how philosophy and literature engage in the ethical work of uncovering the illusions and distortions within some aspects of post-Darwinian biopolitics. This chapter (and the book as a whole) aims to fill an important gap within contemporary bioethics.

As Cary Wolfe has recently pointed out, bioethics has become an uncritical support mechanism for the exertion of power over life: 'Indeed, contemporary bioethics is best understood, perhaps not as an ethics at all, in the sense that someone like Derrida will use the word, but rather as a textbook example of what Michel Foucault has analysed as the rise of "biopower" during the modern period' (Wolfe 2010: 51). Wolfe's analysis has clearly shown it in such terms:

> Bioethics as it is currently institutionalized represents something like the apotheosis of this medico-administrative edifice and its dense imbrication in contemporary apparatuses and institutions of state and economic power, serving, as it were, as its self-designated conscience. (Wolfe 2010: 53)

One of the arguments developed in this book *Contaminations* questions our current conflation of ethics with the interests of institutional administration and economic power. It does so by bringing to the fore the fabrication (rather than the actual existence) of a dualism between mind and body (order and disorder and so forth). It is a fabricated dualism that confounds the ethical credentials of contemporary bioethics at the point at which the latter becomes indistinguishable from the exertion of power over life. At the same time, the figure of contamination as defined here emerges as an alternative to notions which posit divisions between 'pure' entities such as the one separating mind from body, natural history from human history or *bios* from *zoé*.

The term biopolitics has rather sinister or lethal connotations.[9] Foucault, who coined the word, employed it in order to analyse modernity's attempt to control the body via various forms of power.[10] In biopolitics the body has become one with politics. Here our life only has any worth or meaning when we embody the ideological norms and commandments that certain forms of politics impose on us. Bio-political forms of control may be assisted by physical force and violence, or they may operate in a more subtle manner. The more elaborate forms of biopolitics do their work not so much in violent ways. Instead they try to establish a type of mental control through a sophisticated political or managerial usage of representation. The precondition for bio-political violence is the representation of a certain group of people as being purely biological or animalistic, as being solely defined by *zoé*.

Representations here have the function of *memes*, which replicate standard types of behaviour within a given community. Evolutionary biologist Richard Dawkins and neuroscientific philosopher Daniel C. Dennett define the term memes as follows: 'the units are the smallest elements that replicate themselves with reliability and fecundity. Dawkins coins a term for such units: memes' (Dennett 1993: 201). Memes are the cultural equivalent – what Lacan would call linguistic/symbolic – of genes. Strikingly Dennett uses the term in a celebratory manner, arguing that memes adumbrate human immortality: 'As with genes, immortality is more a matter of replication than of the longevity of individual vehicles. The preservation of Platonic memes, via series of copies of copies, is a particular case in point' (Dennett 1993: 205). The ethics of literature questions the violence that can accompany the replication of various symbolic orders which have consequences for embodied life. The clones of Ishiguro's *Never Let Me Go* allow us to experience what it is like to be subjected to the symbolic order of bare life. They are objectified and used in a system of representation and replication, thus bringing to light the potential violence of memes and the mimetic.

What is important to note is that it is not life which is problematic here but its representation as uncontaminated by a soul or intellect or spirit. In order to counteract past and future discriminations against those who happen to get classified and represented as merely alive, it is ethically incumbent upon us to contaminate *bios* with *zoé* and thereby to undermine traditional divisions between the two terms (replicating the split between body and mind). As Vatter has put it: 'if biopolitics can be transformed into thanatopolitics, this may derive from the fact that the life here produced, namely, a *zoé* entirely separate from a *bios*, is a life destined to die, a life that has death inscribed into it from the very beginning' (Vatter 2011: 218). The future of posthumanism is at risk of repeating the violence of the past when it structurally adheres to notions of a pure mind or pure spirit separating *zoé* from *bios*. In *Never Let Me Go* the clones are indeed removed from the so-called proper human population. By avoiding the figure of contamination, posthumanist futures may thus replicate the violence in traditional (and, according to Latour, modern) purification projects.

Significantly, the setting of Ishiguro's novel about cloning simultaneously features a science fiction-like future – where humans are subjects of cloning – and the traditional humanist context of an educational institute in post-World War II Britain. The political scenario is thus not that of totalitarianism but of liberal democracy. The British government has ordered the cloning of citizens with the aim of enhancing the health of the population. The agenda is thus in keeping with the benign form of biopolitics as appraised in Rose's *The Politics of Life Itself*. Rose argues that such an innovative and harmless type of biopolitics promotes hope rather than fatalism or despair: 'Crucially, it is a biopolitics in which references to the biological do not signal fatalism but are part of the economy of hope' (Rose 2007: 167). In Ishiguro's *Never Let Me Go* we encounter an economy of hope but it only applies to those who are in receipt of organ donations rather than those who are excluded from full participation in such a society focused on the management of health. The clones participate in a rather one-sided way in such an 'economy of hope'. They are born not to give birth, in return, but to serve as donors for the non-cloned and procreative part of the population.

Here we witness the complete separation between birth and age, because the clones exist solely for the purpose of aging and dying prematurely. Theirs is an ever shrinking world: due to the single-minded and socio-political purpose of their life – that of donating organs for the non-cloned part of the population – their life is foreshortened. They thus embody traditional humanism's avoidance of any form of contamination between *zoé* and *bios* within a posthumanist setting. They are included in order to be set apart, and they are incapable of procreation and their world is a closed and continually declining one. While describing an imaginary community that is circumscribed by the stereotypical perimeters of death – death which, as Vatter has argued, is 'bare life' uncontaminated by anything intellectual or spiritual – the novel's hidden heart is that of birth. The title of the novel *Never Let Me Go* is a quotation from a pop song which profoundly captivates its narrator, Kathy H. 'What was so special about this song?', she queries and goes on to say that it was what she read into it that made the song special for her:

Well the thing was, I didn't use to listen properly to the words; I just waited for that bit that went: 'Baby, baby, never let me go . . .' And what I imagined was a woman who's been told she couldn't have babies, who really, really wanted them all her life. Then there's a sort of miracle and she has a baby, and she holds this baby very close to her and walks around singing: 'Baby, never let me go . . .' partly because she is so happy, but also because she is so afraid something will happen, that the baby will get ill or be taken away from her. Even at the time, I realized this couldn't be right, that this interpretation didn't fit with the rest of the lyrics. But that was not an issue for me. (Ishiguro 2005: 64)

As we will find out a couple of pages later on, the issue is that, like all clones, Kathy cannot have babies. Remembering her fascination with the lines of the song, she recalls: 'By then [the time of her captivation by the song], of course, we all knew something I hadn't known back then, which was that none of us could have babies' (Ishiguro 2005: 66). The significance of the song for her is that of a delusion that keeps her going. She thinks the song represents the miracle of birth for someone who – similar to her – has been excluded from procreation. She has been excluded from childbirth because her life has been categorised as *zoé* uncontaminated by *bios*. Her existence represents use-value only.

Ishiguro's novel depicts the way in which we submit to social and political forms of control without being physically forced to do so. The clinging to delusions, to various fictions and to a belief that the fictitious will turn real in a miracle-like fashion make us avoid reality. *Never Let Me Go* shows how we are enthralled by ideational and self-replicating fictions when we uncritically subscribe to the influence of memes. In other words, Ishiguro's novel alerts us to the potentially deleterious consequences of self-replication patterns within a given society. The pattern in question here revolves around the rejection of the idea and praxis of contamination in a traditional humanist society and a possible future posthumanist one. By refusing to allow for a contamination between body and mind, between *zoé* and *bios*, politics demotes embodied life (i.e. the clones whose organs are used as resource for the rest of society) under that of a higher entity that goes by the name 'soul' or 'mind' (and of which the clones are represented to be deprived). As Derrida has shown, this idea has been the self-replicating foundation of traditional humanism from Plato via Christianity to Descartes and Lacan.

The cloned protagonists of *Never Let Me Go* willingly do what is expected of them because they avoid both recognising and believing in the reality of their lives' preordained purpose. Instead they fabricate fictions and trust in miracles. The imposition of a preordained sociopolitical model upon the life of the cloned community characterises the plot of the novel. As teenagers, the cloned are not allowed to be young. They are forbidden to plan their own life itineraries. They are interdicted to interact with the world on their own terms – leaving for America, working in a supermarket or being film stars, for example. Miss Lucy – one of the educators or guardians at the Hailsham boarding school for the cloned – attempts to be clear about what cannot be fully spelled out and acknowledged:

> The problem, as I see it, is that you've been told and not told. You have been told, but none of you really understands, and I dare say, some people are quite happy to leave it that way. But I'm not. If you are going to have decent lives, then you've got to know and know properly. None of you will go to America, none of you will be film stars. And none of you will be working in supermarkets as I heard some of you planning the other day. Your lives are set out for you. You will become adults, then before you're old, before you're even middle-aged, you'll start to donate your vital organs. That's what each of you was created to do. You're not like the actors you watch on your videos, you're not even like me. You were brought into this world for a purpose, and your futures, all of them, have been decided. (Ishiguro 2005: 73)

Miss Lucy's message is that of the *meme*: it does not so much explicitly impose but it spreads a preordained life from which there seems to be no way out. The aim of her message is mimetic: it tries to represent the future of the community of cloned teenagers. The representation makes claims to be accurate but the phrasing is highly euphemistic and distorts the bleak reality of the life that has been prearranged for the clones. The euphemism mainly consists in depicting their biography as being free from aging. They will never reach old age. This bleak prospect euphemistically turns into its opposite. Instead of being subject to the forces of aging, the clones – so the euphemistic account goes – will live decent lives. The hope of decency depends on their willingness to copy what the preordained representation of their life tells them to do: namely to find their sole purpose and fulfilment in the donation of their 'vital organs' for the non-cloned community.

Decency here denotes the voluntary embrace of life as copy, as a clone. If nothing else, the word 'vital' betrays the euphemism. How can someone have a 'decent life' with the near or preordained prospect of missing one's vitality? More importantly, life that is that of a representation is static and lacks the unpredictability that comes with growth. Growth is another word for aging. By being deprived of growth, the clones are already at their endpoint, close to death. They live within the deadly arena of a *zoé* which is uncontaminated by *bios* (as analysed by Vatter).

Strikingly, Miss Lucy's revelation about their prefabricated biography does not strike the students of Hailsham as new or surprising (see Ishiguro 2005: 75). This testifies to the power of the *meme*: it spreads in such subtle ways that those it affects are not even aware of it. The content of the flat mimesis which advertises its message in *meme*-like fashion is that of a fiction which nevertheless determines socio-political life: the Britain depicted in *Never Let Me Go* is indeed divided into the sphere of the human non-clone population and those who are considered to be clones and thus non-humans. The name of the boarding school for the clones is telling: Hailsham literally means the counterfeit or fraud (sham) of glory or acclaim (Hail).

Part of the hoax at Hailsham is the guardians' focus on the creativity of the students (i.e. the clones). The students have to paint and to write poetry. The product of their creative efforts is then collected by the guardians of Hailsham. The students read much into such apparent appreciation of their creativity. They see in it the attempt of a romantic or lamp-like insight into the workings of their inner life. As we find out at the end of the novel such interest is actually driven by a political agenda, as one retired former guardian makes clear:

> You said it was because your art would reveal what you were like. What you were like inside. That's what you said, wasn't it? Well, you weren't far from wrong about that. We took away your art because we thought it would reveal your souls. Or to put it more finely, we did it to *prove you had souls at all*. (Ishiguro 2005: 238)

Proof of the clones' inner life would support the claim that they are humans. This means that the touchstone of our humanity is that of a unique or idiosyncratic core which is denoted by the term *bios* (sometimes called 'soul' or 'inner life' or someone's distinctive biography).

The clones, by contrast, represent *zoé* separated from *bios*: they are defined not as singularities, but as mere copies lacking psychic complexity. Creativity here turns into a benchmark which tests whether one resides either on the side of *bios* or that of *zoé*. The parameters of this test are crucially premised on the rejection of any contaminating principle whereby *zoé* might fuse with *bios*. The outcome of the test is as such already established: those who are categorised as purely residing within *zoé* are categorically precluded from being creative, because creativity would presuppose contamination with *bios*. The presupposed lack of artistic capacities serves as evidence of going without a mental life (and thereby failing to be a language-endowed agent who has gone through Lacan's mirror stage). Indeed creativity here becomes reduced to an instrumental device by means of which society differentiates between *bios* and *zoé*.

Art and literature, however, promise to disrupt the workings of flat mimesis. Having seen evidence that those under their charge are indeed creative, the well-meaning guardians could now go to their superiors and dispute that the clones are mere copies, mere representations of someone else: 'Look at this art! How dare you claim these children are anything less than fully human?' (Ishiguro 2005: 239) – they could exclaim.

Yet the power of socio-political representations seems to be insuperable. The guardian could not change the public image of the clones. The politics of representation does away with the suggestion that those who are categorised as belonging solely to *zoé* – in this case those represented to be clones – are humans: 'But I have to tell you, my dear, it wasn't something commonly held when we first set out all those years ago. And though we have come a long way since then, it's still not a notion universally held, even today' (Ishiguro 2005: 66). Here, clearly literature does not have the ability to disrupt mimesis's power over life. This is so because creativity is seen not as a disruptive political force but rather as yet another mimetic or representational device. The public perception of the arts remains that of mimesis and representation: they merely copy the world rather interacting with it.

The poetry and the paintings of the students at Hailsham are nothing more than a lamp-like copying of the otherwise invisible regions of their inner life. The arts are segregated and separated from the medical and political management that governs society. This is why creativity cannot disrupt the power over life that condemns Hailsham's students to live solely for the purpose of organ donations. As one retired guardian makes clear, a deferral of their bleak fate would not have been granted under any past or current circumstances: 'But this dream of yours, this dream of being able to *defer* [i.e. being able to defer the donations of their vital organs]. Such a thing would always have been beyond us to grant, even at the height of our influence' (Ishiguro 2005: 238). The guardians – even the best-intentioned ones – are also shaped by the public representation of their students as clones. Their response therefore mirrors that of their society at large.

It is one of disgust and revulsion – despite their protestation of empathy and admiration of a mimetic kind of creativity. Even the best inclined of the guardians admits: 'We're *all* afraid of you. I myself had to fight back my dread of you all almost every day I was at Hailsham. There were times I'd look down at you all from my study window and I'd feel such revulsion' (Ishiguro 2005: 246). Ishiguro's *Never Let Me Go* focuses on the all-pervasive power of public representations that reject the possibility of contamination, thus dividing society into the included and the excluded, into *bios* and *zoé*. This division characterises mimesis's power over life in its totalitarian as well as in its more subtle medical and free market version as depicted in Ishiguro's presentation of an imaginary post-World War II Britain where clones serve to increase the health of the nation.

Serving the health of the nation is of course a euphemism for the power and violence exerted over those who provide the service. As we have seen, the 'persistence of this euphemistic language' (Currie 2009: 100) that pervades the novel is only one aspect of a larger critique of mimesis. The title *Never Let Me Go* refers to the capacity for birth or creativity as a potential disruption of representations that have come to shape various uncontaminated forms of mind and body; of *zoé* and *bios*. Were the clones allowed both to procreate and to age, they would have outdone their public representation as that of clones that represent bare life and are thus mere material or corporeal copies (*zoé*) rather than distinct and mentally animated individuals (*bios*). The clones, as well as their guardians and their society at large, are held captive by the perimeters of what they have come to represent. This is why they cannot find a way out of victimisation. A non-mimetic-natal form of creativity would have disrupted mimesis's lethal power over life. Birth as the creation of something new would have unsettled their public representation as 'purely' *zoé*, as clones.

Notes

1. As Kari Weil has recently argued: 'we should understand posthumanism not as the death of humanism, but as a necessary rethinking of humanist frameworks, including rethinking what thought is, what agency and autonomy are in order to further humanism's noble aims' (Weil 2012: 149).
2. As N. Katherine Hayles has put it in a discussion of the blurring between fiction and social reality in Borges's famous short story 'Tlön, Uqbar, Orbis Tertius': 'Text metamorphoses into context, context into text, text into context, in a Strange Loop that makes the distinction between "fiction" and "reality" an undecidable question' (Hayles 1984: 146).
3. Esposito (2011: 150). See also Nancy (2008: 107).
4. In this way Kari Weil has recently argued that 'theory's turn to animals grows out of, on the one hand, a weariness with post-structuralism's linguistic turn and a resulting search for a postlinguistic and perhaps posthuman sublime and, on the other hand, an often conflicting turn to ethics that raises the question of human responsibility to the animal-other' (Weil 2012: xx).
5. Fraser elaborates: 'as sweat shop labour, as breeders, as disposable workers; as providers of organs, babies and sex; as performers of menial service, as cleaners and disposers of waste; as raw material to be used up, ground down and spat out, when the system has got from them all it wants' (Fraser 2012: 49).
6. As Herbrechter has put it: 'It is the task of the posthumanities of the future to guarantee that the question of the human will not become the exclusive domain of the bio- and life sciences – a development which might in fact merely represent a replacement of a transcendental *humanist* definition of the human with an equally transcendent scientist *posthumanist* one' (Herbrechter 2013: 169).

7. For a detailed discussion of how racism pseudo-science is founded on a pseudo-theological paradigm see Mack (2003).
8. Concurring with Shameem Black's comparison between Agamben's notion of 'bare life' and that of the clones (see Black 2009: 785–807), Nayar argues that 'the clones in Ishiguro's are what Giorgio Agamben identifies as *Homo sacers*: they are bodies and lives that may be terminated (by humans through legally and socially accepted procedures, in hospitals, in 1990s London, according to the novel) without attracting punishment, but they may not be sacrificed' (Nayar 2014: 61). Clearly, the novel is set not in the recent past of the 1990s but a past future when human cloning would have become a socio-politically acceptable scientific practice; moreover a future that constitutes a continuation of past models of thought which demote embodied life (i.e. those of the clones).
9. As Cary Wolfe has rightly pointed out, recent discussion of biopolitics as 'neutral' or innocuous management of life wilfully ignores this lethal aspect which Agamben's analysis highlights. See Wolfe's critique of Rose (2007) in Wolfe (2013: 50–1).
10. For a detailed discussion of the history and meaning of the term biopolitics see Esposito (2008).

Bibliography

Adorno, T. W. (1997), *Beethoven: The Philosophy of Music*, ed. R. Tiedemann, trans. E. Jephcott, Stanford: Stanford University Press.
Agamben, G. (2012), *The Kingdom and the Glory: For a Theological Genealogy of Economy and Government (Homo Sacer II, 2)*, trans. L. Chiesa and M. Mandarini, Stanford: Stanford University Press.
Agamben, G. (2010), *The Sacraments of Language: An Archaeology of the Oath (Homer Sacer II, 3)*, trans. A. Kotsko, Cambridge: Polity.
Agamben, G. (2004), *The Open: Man and Animal*, trans. K. Attell, Stanford: Stanford University Press.
Agamben, G. (1995), *Homo Sacer: Sovereign Power and Bare Life*, trans. D. Heller-Roazen, Stanford: Stanford University Press.
Arendt, H. [1958] (1998), *The Human Condition*, 2nd edn with an introduction by M. Canovan, Chicago: University of Chicago Press.
Arendt, H. [1963] (1973), *On Revolution*, London: Penguin.
Arsić, B. (2007), *Passive Constitutions or 7½ Times Bartleby*, Stanford: Stanford University Press.
Austin-Smith, B. (2012), 'Secrets, Lies, and "Virtuous Attachments": *The Ambassadors* and *The 39 Steps*', in S. M. Griffin and A. Nadel (eds), *The Men Who Knew Too Much: Henry James and Alfred Hitchcock*, Oxford: Oxford University Press, pp. 35–47.
Baars, J. (2012), *Aging and the Art of Living*, Baltimore: Johns Hopkins University Press.
Barad, K. (2007), *Meeting the Universe Halfway: Quantum Physics and the Entanglement of Matter and Meaning*, London: Duke University Press.
Barr, C. (2012), *Vertigo*, 2nd edn, London: Palgrave Macmillan.
Baym, N. (1995), 'Revision and Thematic Change in *The Portrait of a Lady*', in H. James, *The Portrait of a Lady*, London: Norton Critical Edition, pp. 620–34.
Beach, J. W. (1918), *The Method of Henry James*, New Haven: Yale University Press.
Beer, G. (2000), *Darwin's Plot: Evolutionary Narrative in Darwin, George Eliot and Nineteenth-Century Fiction*, Cambridge: Cambridge University Press.
Bell, M. (1991), *Meaning in Henry James*, Cambridge, MA: Harvard University Press.

Benhabib, S. (2003), *The Reluctant Modernism of Hannah Arendt*, New York: Rowman & Littlefield.
Benjamin, W. (2008), 'The Work of Art in the Age of its Technological Reproducibility', in W. Benjamin, *The Work of Art in the Age of its Technological Reproducibility and Other Writings on Media*, ed. M. W. Jennings, B. Doherty and T. Y. Levin, trans. E. Jephcott, R. Livingstone and H. Eiland, Cambridge, MA: Harvard University Press, pp. 19–55.
Benjamin, W. (1999), *The Arcades Project*, trans. H. Eiland and K. McLaughlin, Cambridge, MA: Harvard University Press.
Benjamin, W. (1996), *Selected Writings: 1913–1926*, Vol. 1, ed. M. Bullock and M. W. Jennings, Cambridge, MA: Belknap Press.
Benjamin, W. (1977), *The Origin of the German Baroque Tragic Drama*, trans. J. Osborne, London: NLB.
Benjamin, W. (1974), *Gesammelte Schriften*, Vol. 4, ed. R. Tiedemann and H. Schweppenhäuser, Frankfurt am Main: Suhrkamp.
Berlant, L. (1991), *The Anatomy of National Fantasy: Hawthorne, Utopia, and Everyday Life*, Chicago: University of Chicago Press.
Bertolucci, B. (2000), *Bernardo Bertolucci: Interviews*, ed. F. S. Gerard, T. Jefferson Kline and B. Sklarew, Jackson: University of Mississippi Press.
Biederman, I. and E. A. Vessel (2006), 'Perceptual Pleasure and the Brain', *American Scientist* 94: 249–55.
Black, S. (2009), 'Ishiguro's Inhuman Aesthetics', *Modern Fiction Studies* 55: 785–807
Blumenberg, H. (1974), *Säkularisierung und Selbstbehauptung*, Frankfurt: Surhrkamp.
Bonitzer, P. (2010), 'Hitchcockian Suspense', in S. Žižek (ed.), *Everything You Always Wanted to Know About Lacan . . . But Were Afraid to Ask Hitchcock*, London: Verso, pp. 15–30.
Boxall, P. (2013), *Twenty-First-Century Fiction: A Critical Introduction*, Cambridge: Cambridge University Press.
Braidotti, R. (2013), *The Posthuman*, Cambridge: Polity.
Briefel, A. (2012), 'Specters of Respectability: Victorian Horrors in *The Turn of the Screw* and *Psycho*', in S. M. Griffin and A. Nadel (eds), *The Men Who Knew Too Much*, Oxford: Oxford University Press, pp. 159–73.
Bryant, J. (1998), '*Moby Dick* as Revolution', in R. S. Levine, *The Cambridge Companion to Hermann Melville*, Cambridge: Cambridge University Press, pp. 65–90.
Buber, M. (1979), *Ich und Du*, Heidelberg: Lambert Schneider.
Buber, M. (1970), *I and Thou*, trans. W. Kaufmann, New York: Simon & Schuster.
Büchner, G. (1993), *Complete Plays, Lenz and Other Writings*, trans. with an introduction and notes by J. Reddick, London: Penguin.
Büchner, G. (1988), *Werke und Briefe*, ed. K. Pörnbacher, G. Schaub, H.-J. Simm and E. Ziegler, Munich: Deutscher Taschenbuch Verlag.
Burn, S. J. (2008), *Jonathan Franzen at the end of Postmodernism*, London: Continuum.
Butler, J. (2004), *The Judith Butler Reader*, ed. J. Butler and S. Salih, Oxford: Blackwell.

Canetti, E. (1989), *Kafka's Other Trial: The Letters to Felice*, New York: Schocken Books.
Cartwright, L. (1995), *Screening the Body: Tracing the Visual Cultures of Biomedicine*, Minneapolis: University of Minnesota Press.
Cartwright, N. (1999), *The Dappled World: A Study of the Boundaries of Science*, Cambridge: Cambridge University Press.
Chakrabarty, D. (2009), 'The Climate of History: Four Theses', *Critical Inquiry* 35: 197–222.
Clack, B. (2008), 'After Freud: Phantasy and Imagination in the Philosophy of Religion', *Philosophy Compass* 3: 203–21.
Cohen, P. M. (1995), *Alfred Hitchcock: The Legacy of Victorianism*, Lexington: The University Press of Kentucky.
Connor, S. (2006), *Fly*, London: Reaction Books.
Currie, M. (2009), 'Controlling Time: *Never Let Me Go*', in S. Matthews and S. Groes (eds), *Kazuo Ishiguro: Contemporary Critical Perspectives*, London: Continuum, pp. 91–103.
Damasio, A. (2010), *Self Comes to Mind: Constructing the Conscious Brain*, London: Vintage.
Damasio, A. (2003), *Looking for Spinoza: Joy, Sorrow, and the Feeling Brain*, London: Harvest Books/Harcourt Inc.
Damasio, A. (2000), *The Feeling of what Happens: Body, Emotion and the Making of Consciousness*, London: Vintage.
Daston, L. and P. Galison (2007), *Objectivity*, New York: Zone Books.
Deleuze, G. (1997), *Cinema 1: The Movement Image*, trans. H. Tomlinson and B. Haberjam, London: Continuum.
Dennett, D. C. (1993), *Consciousness Explained*, London: Penguin.
Derrida, J. (2009), *The Beast and the Sovereign*, Vol. 1, ed. M. Lisse, M.-L. Mallet and G. Michaud, trans. G. Bennington, Chicago: University of Chicago Press.
Derrida, J. (2008), *The Animal That Therefore I Am*, ed. M.-L. Mallet, trans. D. Wills, New York: Fordham University Press.
Despotopoula, A. and K. C. Reed (2011), 'Introduction: "I see Ghosts everywhere"', in A. Despotopoula and K. C. Reed (eds), *Henry James and the Supernatural*, New York: Palgrave-Macmillan, pp. 1–11.
Dongen, J. van (2010), *Einstein's Unification*, Cambridge: Cambridge University Press.
Dyson, G. (2012), *Turing's Cathedral: The Origins of the Digital Universe*, London: Allen Lane.
Edelman, L. (2004), *No Future: Queer Theory and the Death Drive*, Durham, NC: Duke University Press.
Ehrenberg, A. (2010), *The Weariness of the Self: Diagnosing the History of Depression in the Contemporary Age*, trans. E. Caouette, D. Homel, J. Homel and D. Winkler, Montreal: McGill University Press.
Einstein, A. (1950), 'On the generalized theory of gravitation', *Scientific American* 182: 13–17.
Elden, S. (2006), *Speaking against Numbers: Heidegger, Language and the Politics of Calculation*, Edinburgh: Edinburgh University Press.
Ellison, R. [1952] (2001), *Invisible Man*, with an introduction by J. Callahan, London: Penguin.

Ellmann, M. (2010), *The Nets of Modernism: Henry James, Virginia Woolf, James Joyce and Sigmund Freud*, Cambridge: Cambridge University Press.
Esposito, R. (2012), *Living Thought: The Origins and Actuality of Italian Philosophy*, Palo Alto: Stanford University Press.
Esposito, R. (2011), *Immunitas: The Protection and Negation of Life*, trans. Z. Hanafi, Cambridge: Polity Press.
Esposito, R. (2008), *Bios: Biopolitics and Philosophy*, trans. and with an introduction by T. Campbell, Minneapolis: University of Minnesota Press.
Felman, S. (2003), *Writing and Madness (Literature/Philosophy/Psychoanalysis)*, trans. M. N. Evans and the author with the assistance of B. Massumi, Palo Alto: Stanford University Press.
Forster, E. M. (1974), *Aspects of the Novel*, London: Edward Arnold.
Foucault, M. (2008), *The Birth of Biopolitics: Lectures at the Collège de France 1978–1979*, ed. M. Snellart, trans. G. Burchell, Basingstoke: Palgrave Macmillan.
Foucault, M. (1979), *The Will to Knowledge: The History of Sexuality: Vol. 1*, trans. R. Hurley, London: Penguin.
Franzen, J. (2013), *The Kraus Project*, London: Fourth Estate.
Franzen, J. (2012), *Farther Away*, London: Fourth Estate.
Franzen, J. (2010), *Freedom*, London: Fourth Estate.
Fraser, N. (2012), 'On Justice: Lessons from Plato, Rawls and Ishiguro', *New Left Review* 74: 41–51.
Freed, M. M. (2011), *Robert Musil and the NonModern*, London: Bloomsbury.
Freud, S. (1975), *Studienausgabe*, Volumes 1–10, ed. A. Mitcherlich, A. Richards and J. Strachey, Frankfurt am Main: Fischer.
Freud, S. (1964), *The Future of an Illusion*, trans. W. D. Robson-Scott, New York: Doubleday.
Geuss, R. (2010), *Politics and the Imagination*, Princeton: Princeton University Press.
Giles, P. (2011), *The Global Remapping of American Literature*, Princeton: Princeton University Press.
Gittings, R. (1979), *John Keats*, London: Penguin.
Goble M. (2007), 'Wired Love: Pleasure at a distance in Henry James and Others', *English Literary History* 74(2): 397–427.
Gorra, M. (2012), *Portrait of a Novel: Henry James and the Making of an American Masterpiece*, London: Norton.
Graedel, T. E. and P. J. Crutzen (1997), *Atmosphere, Climate, and Change*, New York: Scientific American Library.
Griffin, S. M. and A. Nadel (eds) (2012), *The Men Who Knew Too Much: Henry James and Alfred Hitchcock*, Oxford: Oxford University Press.
Haraway, D. (2008), *When Species Meet*, Minneapolis: University of Minnesota Press.
Haraway, D. (2001), 'A Manifesto for Cyborgs: Science, Technology and Socialist Feminism in the 1980s', in P. Rice and P. Waugh, *Modern Literary Theory*, London: Bloomsbury, pp. 465–83.
Harcourt, B. E. (2011), *The Illusion of Free Markets: Punishment and the Myth of Natural Order*, Cambridge, MA: Harvard University Press.
Hawthorne, N. (1970), *The Scarlet Letter*, with an introduction by N. Baym and notes by T. E. Connolly, London: Penguin.

Hayles, N. K. (1984), *The Cosmic Web: Scientific Field Models and Literary Strategies in the Twentieth Century*, Ithaca, NY: Cornell University Press.
Heine, H. (1986), *Religion and Philosophy in Germany*, trans. J. Snodgrass, Albany: State University of New York Press.
Heine, H. (1968), *Schriften über Deutschland*, ed. H. Schanze, Frankfurt am Main: Insel.
Herbrechter, S. (2013), *Posthumanism: A Critical Analysis*, London: Bloomsbury.
Herman, D. (2013), *Storytelling and the Sciences of the Mind*, Cambridge, MA: The Massachusetts Institute of Technology Press.
Holden, S. (1993), 'The Movies that inspired Martin Scorsese', *New York Times*, 21 May 1993.
Ishiguro, K. (2005), *Never Let Me Go*, London: Faber and Faber.
Jacobs, C. (1999), *In the language of Walter Benjamin*, Baltimore: Johns Hopkins University Press.
Jacobs, S. (2011), *Framing Pictures: Film and the Visual Arts*, Edinburgh: Edinburgh University Press.
James, H. (1995), *The Portrait of a Lady*, 2nd edn, ed. R. D. Bamberg, London: Norton.
James, H. (1987), *The Princess Casamassima*, ed. with an introduction by D. Brewer, London: Penguin.
James, H. (1986), *The Art of Criticism: Henry James on the Theory and Practice of Fiction*, ed. W. Weeder and S. M. Griffin, Chicago: University of Chicago Press.
James, H. (1985), *What Maisie Knew*, ed. with an introduction and notes by P. Theroux, London: Penguin.
James, H. (1966), *The Turn of the Screw*, ed. R. Kimbrough, London: Norton.
James, H. (1964), *The Ambassadors*, ed. S. P. Rosenbaum, London: Norton.
James, S. J. (2011), 'H. G. Wells's *The Time Machine* and the End of Literature', in N. Saul and S. J. James (eds), *Evolution of Literature: Legacies of Darwin in European Cultures*, New York: Editions Rodopi, pp. 113–23.
Kandel, E. R. (2012), *The Age of Insight: The Quest to Understand the Unconscious in Art, Mind, and Brain: From Vienna 1900 to the Present*, New York: Random House.
Kandel, E. R. (2006), *In Search of Memory: The Emergence of a New Science of the Mind*, New York: Norton.
Keane, M. E. (2009), 'A Closer Look at Scopophilia: Mulvey, Hitchcock, and Vertigo', in M. Deutelbaum and L. Poague, *A Hitchcock Reader*, 2nd edn, Oxford: Wiley-Blackwell, pp. 234–49.
Kirschner, S. (1996), *The Religious and Romantic Origins of Psychoanalysis: Individuation and Integration in Post-Freudian Theory*, Cambridge: Cambridge University Press.
Kristeva, J. (1982), *Powers of Horror: An Essay on Abjection*, trans. L. S. Roudiez, New York: Columbia University Press.
Lacan, J. (2000), *The Psychoses: The Seminars of Jacques Lacan, Book III 1955–56*, ed. J.-A. Miller, trans. R. Grigg, London: Routledge.
Lacan J. (1977), *Écrits: A Selection*, New York: Norton.
Lanier, J. (2010), *You are Not a Gadget*, London: Penguin.

Latour, B. (1993), *We Have Never Been Modern*, trans. C. Porter, Cambridge, MA: Harvard University Press.
Lehrer, J. (2007), *Proust was a Neuroscientist*, London: Canongate.
Lemm, V. (2009), *Nietzsche's Animal Philosophy: Culture, Politics, and the Animality of the Human Being*, New York: Fordham University Press.
Levenson, M. (2011), *Modernism*, New Haven: Yale University Press.
Lippit, A. M. (2005), *Atomic Light (Shadow Optics)*, Minneapolis: University of Minnesota Press.
Löwith, K. (1949), *Meaning in History*, Chicago: University of Chicago Press.
Luhmann, N. (1986), *Love as Passion: The codification of intimacy*, trans. J. Gaines and D. L. Jones, Cambridge: Polity Press.
MacIntyre, A. (1999), *Dependent Rational Animals: Why Humans Need the Virtues*, Chicago: Open Court.
Mack, M. (2014), *Philosophy and Literature in Times of Crisis: Challenging our Infatuation with Numbers*, New York: Bloomsbury.
Mack, M. (2012), *How Literature Changes the Way we Think*, London: Bloomsbury.
Mack, M. (2010), *Spinoza and the Specters of Modernity: The Hidden Enlightenment of Diversity from Spinoza to Freud*, New York: Bloomsbury.
Mack, M. (2009), 'The Holocaust and Hannah Arendt's philosophical critique of philosophy: *Eichmann in Jerusalem*', *New German Critique* 36: 35–60.
Mack, M. (2003), *German Idealism and the Jew: The Inner Anti-Semitism of Philosophy and German Jewish Responses*, Chicago: University of Chicago Press.
McLaughlin, J. (2009), 'All in the Family: Alfred Hitchcock's *Shadow of a Doubt*', in M. Deutelbaum and L. Poague (eds), *A Hitchcock Reader*, 2nd edn, Oxford: Wiley-Blackwell, pp. 145–55.
McLean, S. (2009), *The Early Fictions of H. G. Wells: Fantasies of Science*, London: Palgrave.
Maggi, A. (2009), *The Resurrection of the Body: Pier Paolo Pasolini*, Chicago: University of Chicago Press.
Malabou, C. (2012), *The New Wounded: From Neuroscience to Brain Damage*, New York: Fordham University.
Marx, L. (2001), 'Melville's Parables of the Walls', in Dan McCall (ed.), *Melville's Short Novels*, New York: Norton, pp. 239–56.
Mayr, E. (2002), 'Foreword', in L. Margulis and D. Sagan, *Acquiring Genomes: A Theory of the Origins of Species*, New York: Basic Books, pp. xi–xiv.
Melville, H. [1851] (2001), *Melville's Short Novels*, ed. D. McCall, New York: Norton.
Melville, H. [1851] (1992), *Moby Dick; or, The Whale*, introduced by A, Delbanco, ed. T. Quirk, London: Penguin.
Mendes-Flohr, P. (2010), 'Reflections on the Ethical and Political Dialectics of Commitment', *Criterion* 3: 11–13.
Menninghaus, W. (2003), *Disgust: Theory and History of a Strong Sensation*, trans. H. Eiland and J. Golb, Albany: State University of New York Press.
Morton, T. (2013), *Hyperobjects: Philosophy and Ecology after the End of the World*, Minneapolis: University of Minnesota Press.
Morton, T. (2007), *Ecology without Nature: Rethinking Environmental Aesthetics*, Cambridge, MA: Harvard University Press.

Müller, J.-W. (2003), *A Dangerous Mind: Carl Schmitt in Post-War European Thought*, New Haven: Yale University Press.
Mulvey, L. (2000), 'Visual Pleasure and Narrative Cinema', in R. Stam and T. Miller, *Film and Theory: An Anthology*, Oxford: Blackwell, pp. 481–94.
Nancy, J.-L. (2008), *Corpus*, trans. R. A. Rand, New York: Fordham University Press.
Nayar, P. K. (2014), *Posthumanism*, London: Polity.
Nelson, C. (2013), 'Life, liberty, happiness and Jonathan Franzen's *Freedom*', *Australasian Journal of American Studies* 32: 1–12.
Olson, C. (1967), *Call me Ishmael: A Study of Melville*, London: Jonathan Cape.
Pasolini, P. P. (2010), *Fabrication (Affabulazione)*, trans. J. McKendrick, London: Oberon Books.
Pasolini, P. P. (2005), *Heretical Empiricism*, trans. B. Lawton and L. K. Barnett, Washington, DC: New Academic Publishing.
Pasolini, P. P. (1997), *Petrolio*, trans. A. Goldstein, New York: Pantheon Books.
Pasolini, P. P. (1982), *Poems*, selected and trans. N. MacAffe with L. Martinengo, New York: Farrar, Straus and Giroux.
Peretz, E. (2003), *Literature, Disaster, and the Enigma of Power: A Reading of Moby Dick*, Palo Alto: Stanford University Press.
Petkovic, N. (1997), 'Re-writing the Myth, Rereading the Life: The Universalizing Game in Pier Paolo Pasolini's *Edipe Re*', *American Imago* 54(1): 39–68.
Pfister, O. (1963), *Psychoanalysis and Faith: The Letters of Sigmund Freud and Oskar Pfister*, ed. H. Meng and E. L. Freud, trans. E. L. Mosbacher, New York: Basic Books.
Pippin, R. B. (2001), *Henry James and Modern Moral Life*, Cambridge: Cambridge University Press.
Posnock, R. (2010), Color and Culture: Black Writers and the Making of the Modern Intellectual, Cambridge, MA: Harvard University Press.
Posnock, R. (1991), *The Trial of Curiosity: Henry James, William James, and the Challenge of Modernity*, Cambridge: Cambridge University Press.
Reddy, W. A. (2001), *The Navigation of Feeling: A Framework for the History of Emotions*, Cambridge: Cambridge University Press.
Renner, S. (1995), '"Red hair, very red, close-curling": Sexual Hysteria, Physiognomical Bogeyman, and the "Ghosts" in *The Turn of the Screw*', in P. G. Beidler (ed.), *The Turn of the Screw*, Boston: Bedford/St Martin's Press, pp. 223–41.
Righi, A. (2011), *Biopolitics and Social Change in Italy: From Gramsci to Pasolini to Negri*, London: Palgrave Macmillan.
Rivkin, J. (1986), 'The Logic of Delegation in *The Ambassadors*', *PMLA* 101(5): 819–931.
Robespierre, M. [1791] (2007), 'On the Silver Mark, 1791', in M. Robespierre, *Virtue and Terror*, introduced by S. Žižek; texts selected and ed. J. Ducange; trans. J. Howe, London: Verso, pp. 5–19.
Robin, L. and W. Steffen (2007), 'History for the Anthropocene', *History Compass* 5: 1694–1719.
Rose, N. (2007), *The Politics of Life Itself: Biomedicine, Power, and Subjectivity in the Twenty-First Century*, Princeton: Princeton University Press.
Roth, P. (1961), *Reading Myself and Others*, New York: Vintage Books.

Rumble, P. A. (1997), *Allegories of Contamination: Pier Paolo Pasolini's Trilogy of Life*, Toronto: University of Toronto Press.
Santner, E. L. (2001), *On the Psychotheology of Everyday Life: Reflections on Freud and Rosenzweig*, Chicago: University of Chicago Press.
Savoy, E. (2012), 'The Touch of the Real: Circumscribing *Vertigo*', in Griffin and Nadel (eds), *The Men Who Knew Too Much*, Oxford: Oxford University Press, pp. 142–58.
Scheingold, S. A. (2010), *Political Novel: Re-imagining the Twentieth Century*, London: Bloomsbury.
Schmitt, C. [1922] (1990), *Politische Theologie: Vier Kapitel zur Lehre von der Souveränität*, Berlin: Duncker & Humblot.
Sharp, H. (2011), *Spinoza and the Politics of Renaturalization*, Chicago: University of Chicago Press.
Shukin, N. (2009), *Animal Capital: Rendering Life in Biopolitical Times*, Minneapolis: University of Minnesota Press.
Shuttleworth, S. (2010), *The Mind of the Child: Child Development in Literature, Science and Medicine, 1840–1900*, Oxford: Oxford University Press.
Siciliano, E. (1982), *Pasolini: A Biography*, trans. from the Italian by J. Shepley, New York: Random House.
Tanenhaus, T. (2010), 'Peace and War', *The New York Times*, 19 August 2010.
Thomsen, M. R. (2013), *The New Human in Literature: Posthuman Visions of Changes in Body, Mind and Society after 1900*, New York: Bloomsbury.
Turner, M. (1996), *The Literary Mind: The Origins of Thought and Language*, Oxford: Oxford University Press.
Vatter, M. (2014), *The Republic of the Living: Biopolitics and the Critique of Civil Society*, New York: Fordham University Press.
Vatter, M. (2011), 'Eternal Life and Biopower', *The New Centennial Review*, 10(3): 217–50.
Vatter, M. (2008), 'In Odradek's World: Bare Life and Historical Materialism in Agamben and Benjamin', *Diacritics* 38: 45–70.
Vatter, M. (2006), 'Natality and Biopolitics in Hannag Arendt', *Revista De Ciencia Politica* 26: 137–59.
Watt, I. (1960), 'The Paragraph of *The Ambassadors*: An Explication', *Essays in Criticism* X: 250–74.
Wegner, P. E. (2009), *Life Between Two Deaths, 1989–2001: US Culture in the Long Nineties*, London: Duke University Press.
Weil, K. (2012), *Thinking with Animals: Why Animal Studies Now?*, New York: Columbia University Press.
Wells, H. G. [1895] (2005a), *The Time Machine*, ed. P. Parrinder with an introduction by M. Warner, London: Penguin.
Wells, H. G. [1897] (2005b), *The Invisible Man*, ed. P. Parrinder with an introduction by C. Priest and notes by A. Sawyer, London: Penguin.
Williamson, J. (1973), *H. G. Wells: Critic of Progress*, Baltimore: The Mirage Press.
Wilson, E. (1962), *The Triple Thinkers*, London: Penguin.
Wolfe, C. (2013), *Before the Law: Humans and other Animals in a Biopolitical Frame*, Chicago: University of Chicago Press.

Wolfe, C. (2010), *What is Posthumanism?*, Minneapolis: University of Minnesota Press.

Wood, R. (2009), 'Strangers on a Train', in M. Deutelbaum and L. Poague (eds), *A Hitchcock Reader*, 2nd edn, Oxford: Wiley-Blackwell, pp. 172–81.

Yovel, Y. (1992), *Spinoza and other Heretics, Volume 2: The Adventures of Immanence*, Princeton: Princeton University Press.

Žižek, S. (2012), *Less than Nothing: Hegel and the Shadow of Dialectical Materialism*, London: Verso.

Žižek, S. (2009), *The Plague of Fantasies*, new edn, London: Verso.

Žižek, S. (2007), 'Introduction: Robespierre or the "Divine Violence" of Terror', in M. Robespierre, *Virtue and Terror*, introduced by S. Žižek; texts selected and ed. J. Ducange, trans. J. Howe, London: Verso, pp. vii–xxxix.

Index

Adorno, Theodor W., 97, 157
Agamben, Giorgio
   'bare life', 46, 59, 200–1
   and Benjamin, 110
   biopolitical paradigm, 6
   and Foucault, 195–7
   Homo Sacer, 108, 204–6
   The Kingdom and the Glory, 107–8
Anthropocene, 10–11, 16, 23
Arendt, Hannah, 70–1, 80, 85, 86, 87, 94, 97, 104
   on contamination of the worldly and the other-worldly, 61, 64, 65–9
   on French Revolution, 86–7, 94, 97
   her critique of modern science, 1–2
   literature and her critique of modern science, 70–1
   on loss of worldliness, 104
   and H. G. Wells, 80, 85
   The Human Condition, 55
Arsić, Branka, 113
Auerbach, Erich, 160

Barad, Karen, 3–4, 8
Barr, Charles, 146
Beer, Gillian, 32
Benjamin, Walter
   on allegory, 185–7
   on 'dialectics at a standstill', 108
   on legal system, 163
   on modernity, 64, 67
   on the negative, 9
   on 'redemption through sin', 168
   Arcades Project, 109, 112
   'Capitalism as Religion', 110
   'Theological-Political Fragment', 111
   'The Work of Art in the Age of Its Technological Reproducibility', 156

Bertolucci, Bernardo, 159
biopolitics, 107–8, 192, 201–9
   bare life, 30–46, 85–7, 109–10, 163–4, 203–6
Blumenberg, Hans, 62–6, 67–8, 69
Bonitzer, Pascal, 135
Braidotti, Rosi, 8–9, 202
Bryant, John, 98
Buber, Martin, 18–19
Büchner, Georg, *Danton's Death*, 92

Chakrabarty, Dipesh, 10–12, 15–16
climate change, 7, 9, 10–13, 14, 17, 23
Cohen, Paul Marantz, 134
Conor, S., 4
Crutzem, Paul J., 10

Damasio, Antonio, 24–5, 30–1, 47, 169, 182, 191
Datson, Lorraine and Galison, Peter
   on divide between the arts and the sciences, 122
   on Einstein's Relativity Theory, 51–2
   on objectivity, 50, 57, 59, 142
deconstruction, 2, 65, 196
Deleuze, Giles
   on affection image, 181, 184
   on cinema's 'mental image', 136–7, 159–61
Dennett, Daniel C., 165, 166–7, 208
Derrida, Jacques, 195
   on Adorno, 97
   on the animal, 89, 90, 91, 96, 98
   on the animal and Kant, 97
   on the animal and Lacan, 200
   and autoimmunity, 8
   and deconstruction, 2, 65
   on Descartes, 203
   on humanism, 210

Derrida, Jacques (*cont.*)
  on Lacan, 199
  on sovereignty, 93
  and trace, 1, 64, 66
Descartes, René, 20, 23, 26, 27, 34, 50, 66, 68, 71, 89, 90, 97, 98, 99, 210
  and *cogito*, 2, 26–7, 34, 63, 203
dialectics, 1–2, 4, 5, 6
  and negation/negativity, 1, 2, 4, 6, 9–10, 12–13, 14, 16, 19, 28, 35, 108, 112, 152, 172
Dwight, Timothy, 103
Dyson, George, 129–30

Eco, Umberto, 164
Einstein, Albert, 5, 51–2, 55, 56, 83
  and contamination of objectivity, 52
  and contamination of positivism, 53–4
Eliot, George, *Middlemarch*, 55, 58
Ellison, Ralph, 86
  and art, 82–3
  on Henry James, 82
  Invisible Man, 81: and contamination, 82; and Enlightenment, 83–4; and French Revolution, 84, 92; and mind-body, 89; and socio-economics, 88, 90; and visibility, 81–2, 84, 92, 89–90, 94, 117
Ellmann, Maud, 66
Entanglement, 3–4
Esposito, Roberto, 6, 8, 30, 200
  on bare life, 160, 168
  on body, 194
  on dialectics and immunity, 6–7
  on power, 172

Felman, Shoshana, 140
Ferrara, Abel, 9
Forster, E. M., 114
Foucault, Michel
  on animality in the human, 197
  on biopolitics, 195, 203
  on biopolitics and liberalism, 206–7
  on biopower, 207
Franzen, Jonathan, 15
  The Corrections, 14, 17
  Freedom, 13–19, 20
Freed, Mark, 2
Freud, Sigmund, 24, 164, 171
  and contamination, 26, 29, 30, 31–2, 35, 36, 39, 41, 42, 43–4, 45–6
  and drives, 24, 29, 34, 35, 39, 41, 42–3, 44
  and Jewish thinkers, 35
  on Kant, 31, 33, 40, 42
  and Lacan, 29
  and materiality, 26, 30, 31, 40
  and neuroscience, 25, 26, 27, 45–6
  and 'new science' *see* psychoanalysis
  and Oedipus complex, 43, 166
  on philosophy and methodology, 44
  and political philosophy, 30, 46
  and psychic life, 28–9, 30, 31, 40, 42, 43–5
  and psychoanalysis, 25, 30–1, 32–4, 37, 40, 41, 44, 45–6, 73, 145, 154
  and religion, 37–8, 39–40, 41–3, 44–5

global warming, 10, 11, 13, 15
Gorra, Michael, 136

Haraway, Donna, 4–5, 193, 195–6
Harcourt, Bernard, 88–9, 90, 92, 102
Hawthorne, Nathaniel, 55, 93, 101–2, 103
  The Scarlet Letter, 21, 61, 78, 104–5
Hayles, N. Katherine, 56, 202
Hegel, G. W. F., 8, 12, 26, 34, 152
  and dialectics, 1–2, 6, 12, 35, 66, 108, 152
Heidegger, Martin, 66–7, 85, 99
Heine, Heinrich, 36–7
Hitchcock, Alfred, 21, 113, 126, 131, 161
  and audience, 137–8, 144, 146, 147–8
  and contamination, 135, 141, 144
  and deception, 146–7
  and knowledge, 134, 139, 141, 144, 147
  and mental image, 136–7, 159
  and the real, 147
  and suspense, 130, 134–5, 137, 139, 143
  Shadow of a Doubt, 138
  Strangers On A Train, 137–8
  Vertigo, 134, 141, 144–6, 147, 152
Hobbes, Thomas, 90, 95, 97

Ishiguro, Kazuo, *Never Let Me Go*, 193
  and bioethics, 202, 207
  and biopolitics, 200–1, 202–3, 204, 206, 207, 208–9, 212, 213–14

and contamination, 198–9, 206, 210, 213
and creativity, 212–14
and delusion, 210–11
and economy, 209
and linguisticism, 203
and memes/mimetic, 208, 210–11
and the mirror stage, 199–200
and natural order, 193
and posthumanism, 201, 206, 208–9

James, Henry, 21, 114, 119–20, 126, 129, 144, 159
and America as contamination, 119–20, 124, 125
and experimentation, 122–3
and 'house of fiction' metaphor, 132, 157
and identity as aesthetic, 120
and literature as subversive, 121–2
and perception and action, 129, 130, 146
and science-art opposition, 142
The Ambassadors, 113, 130, 131–2: and economics, 114–15, 118, 121; and globalism, 118; and perception, 115, 119, 125, 126, 130, 131; and place, 124; and Puritanism, 119, 121, 123–5
'The Art of Fiction', 121
The Portrait of a Lady, 113, 122, 131–2, 141: and deception, 147, 152; and imagination, 132–3, 151, 152, 153–4; and knowledge, 139–40, 146–7; and literature, 149–50; and materiality, 126, 153–5; and perception/action, 132–3, 136, 139, 146, 149, 150, 153, 155–6, 157; and politics as aesthetics, 156–7, 193; and suspense, 134, 135
The Princess Casamassima, 132
The Turn of the Screw, 148: and the animal/beast, 141; and contamination, 142; and knowledge, 140, 141, 143, 147; and perception, 143, 148
What Maisie Knew and knowledge, 140–1
James, Simon J., 72

Kandel, Eric, 77–3
Kant, Immanuel, 23
and animal/human divide, 97, 99
and autonomy of mind, 2, 25, 26–7, 31, 32, 33, 34, 37, 97, 98
and contamination, 25, 26, 27–8, 35, 40
and Copernican revolution, 31–3
and the divine, 42
and embodied or material world, 25, 26, 27–8, 33, 40, 90, 94
and epistemological, 27
and freedom, 109, 111
and purification, 31–2
and synthetic judgments, 52, 53–4
and transcendental, 57, 94–5
Keane, Marian E., 145–6, 147
Kristeva, Julia, 178–9

Lacan, Jacques, 29, 30, 171, 208
and Freudian drives, 29
and linguistic/symbolic, 208
and mirror stage, 199–200, 205, 212
and mirror stage and the animal, 99, 200
and Sinthome, 145
Lanier, Jaron, 131
Latour, Bruno
and invisible, 60–1
and measurable, 59
and modern/purification, 59–60, 62, 69, 70, 80, 97, 209
and natural and social, 3, 20, 46–7, 88, 107
Lehrer, John, 58
Lemm, Vanessa, 164
Levenson, Michael, 70
Lévi-Strauss, Claude, 178
Lippit, Mizuta
on cinema, 56
on X-rays, 55
Löwith, Karl, 63, 64, 67
Luhmann, Niklas, 11
and autopoiesis, 65, 67, 68
and functionality, 64–5, 68
and systems theory, 64
and systems theory and the invisible, 65
Lynch, David, *Blue Velvet*, 139

MacIntyre, Alasdair, 10
Maggi, A., 181, 183
Malabou, Catherine, 1, 24, 26, 37, 45
and autonomy in Freud, 26, 34
on cerebral plasticity, 28, 43, 45
on collapse of internal/external to self, 40

Malabou, Catherine (*cont.*)
    and contamination, 108
    on psychic indestructibility, 28–30, 42
materiality, 4, 5
Melville, Herman, 93, 118, 130
    and the gothic, 101–2
    and nature/society divide, 97, 118
    and suspense, 113
    Bartleby, the Scrivener: and economics, 113, 114–15, 116, 117; and invisibility, 116–17; and the law, 113; and light, 124; and mental illness, 116–17; and purification, 117–18; and science, 116
    Billy Budd, Sailor: and the French Revolution, 95; and natural order, 95
    Moby Dick: and contamination, 98; and embodiment, 101; and fluidity, 119, 121; and free markets, 102; and the invisible, 61, 100; and knowledge, 102–3; and madness, 98, 99, 100, 101, 103, 104; and natural order, 21, 78, 96, 100, 103, 194; and neuroscience, 99; and political theology, 100–1; and science, 68, 96, 102, 114
Mendes-Flohr, Paul, 18
mind-body, 5, 50–9, 63–4, 87–9, 94, 97–8, 197, 201–8
modernity, 2, 20, 21, 25, 26, 30, 67
Morton, Timothy, 16, 19, 53
Mulvey, Laura, 145–6, 147
Musil, Robert, 2

Nayar, Pramod K., 194
neuroscience, 24, 26–8, 46, 56–8, 94

Pasolini, Pier Paolo, 9
    and art as discovery of difference, 169–70
    and boundaries of self, 170–1
    and co-presence, 161
    and death, 160
    and embodiment, 159–60, 164, 170
    and frontal shots, 160, 162–3
    and gaze, 169–70
    and homogeneity of self, 166–7
    and mental image, 136, 159
    and scandal, 21, 112, 145, 157, 161, 163, 164, 169–70, 172
    and semiotics, 164
    and sexual politics, 166, 171, 172
    Accattone, 164, 167: and the sacred/vulgar, 167–8
    Affabulazione, 166
    Edipe Re, 164
    Mamma Roma, 164, 167: and bourgeois, 168, 174; and Oedipal subtext, 167, 173
    Petrolio, 174
    Salò, 173
    'Supplica a mia madre', 166: and power/desire, 174; and subjectivity, 170; and the theological, 175
    Teorema, 161–2, 174: and bourgeois order, 161
    Traumdeutung, 166
    Trilogy of Life, 172–3
physics, 53–4, 132
Pippin, Robert B., 1, 118
    on Henry James, 123, 143
Plath, Sylvia, 'Daddy', 56–7
Plato, 121–2
Posnock, R., 157
Posthuman, 36, 189

Quesnay, François, 46, 88, 91–2

Realism, 4, 53–4
Rose, Nikolas, 209
Roth, Philip, 13

sacred-profane, 5, 69, 94, 101
    and Benjamin on allegory, 109, 186–7
    and Benjamin on Christianity, 110–12
    and cinema, 167
    and compartmentalisation in Pasolini, 169–71
    and freedom/nature divide, 109
    and non-empirical world, 61
    and Pasolinian sexual politics, 182
    and Spinozan human life, 41
Santner, Eric L., 37–8
Savoy, Eric, 144–5
Schmitt, Carl, 95
    on the secular and sovereignty, 100
    and 'secularisation theory', 61–7, 69
    and secularisation as translation, 67
    on theology and the political, 61–3
    on theology and tracing, 65
Scholem, Gershom, 9, 168
Scorsese, Martin, *Cape Fear* and the psychotic, 161–3

secularisation, 55, 61–9
Sharp, Hasana, 8
Shuttleworth, Sally, 64
Spinoza, Baruch, 8, 71
   and conception of self, 40
   and Copernican revolution, 32
   and Darwin, 32–3
   and Freud, 25, 30, 37–46
   and God, 41
   and mind/body contamination, 20, 23, 24–5, 28, 30, 33, 37
   and neuroscience, 24, 28
   Ethics and nature, 34, 40

Tauber, Alfred, 7

Van Dongen, Jeroen, 53
Vatter, Miguel, 30, 41, 112, 191, 201, 209

Warner, Marina, 72
Weber, Max, 64, 69

Wells, H. G.
   and modern, 85
   The Invisible Man: and the French Revolution, 79, 84; and paradox of illumination, 80; and power, 84; and science, 80, 81
   The Time Machine: and the measurable, 74; and modernity, 74; and progress, 71; and totalitarianism, 75
Wilson, Edmund, 140
Wolfe, Cary, 65, 202–7
Wood, Robin, 137

Žižek, Slavoj, 20, 23–4
   on Freud, 26
   on Kant, 26
   on libido, 24
   on Catherine Malabou, 26
   on materialism, 24, 25
   on neuroscience, 25–6
Zon, Bennett, 54